THE
RINGER JACK

A NOVEL

MARY SEATON

SWEETSPIRE **LITERATURE**
—— MANAGEMENT ——

Chapter 1

Jack boarded the train in Brisbane bound for Mount Isa. He'd been travelling for three days, and this was his third and last train. The last leg of his journey would be by car. He put his luggage up on the rack and sat by a window.

Jack was tired out, so he closed his eyes and left his mind to its wanderings. It seemed like a lifetime ago since he left the long hut, left his home. As usual his musings flew straight to the arms of his lady love. The girl he'd met years before and fallen head over heels in love with. How he had loved her; had loved and lost her. If only, he told himself, if only he hadn't been such a stupid kid.

Jack opened his eyes, the train had given a lurch and now rolled slowly, smoothly down the track. It always reminded him of that fateful day he had said goodbye to his sweetheart and gone off to war. But first he had gone to Melbourne.

This was the part in his musings that caused him the most heart for he had hurt his beautiful woman as well. He had hurt and hinted her, and he'd let them both down. As long as he lived, he ver understand his stupidity. And Jack was unable to forgive r any of it.

w it was largely what he had done in Melbourne that had cost woman he could ever love. If only he hadn't met the woman waiting at the station for her train to come in. She'd told him she had waited for her fiancé to come back but he'd been killed up in Queensland.

Jack had listened to her sad story and had held her while she cried, he had sobbed himself, he'd been so lonely. Jack was due in the recruiting office the next morning, so he'd asked her if she'd have a drink with him. Jack had never drank liquor before. One thing led to another, and the woman had asked him to her home. He had gone, had made the decision to go home with her. Why had he?

Jack had often questioned how he could have done such a thing. He'd asked himself if maybe he had never actually loved the woman he'd left behind. Deep in his heart he knew he did. Knew he'd never love another.

Jack liked to think he'd not known what would happen at the strange woman's place, told himself he hadn't known. But this was about the millionth time he'd relived his decision and he knew in his heart he'd thrown in for the lot. He had eagerly got between the sheets and tried his best to please her. What an idiot he told himself again. He felt hot tears stinging his eyes, a searing pain in his chest and knew he was destined to do this forever. This was his doing.

Jack couldn't help the shame that washed over him at the thought of it. At this junction in his thinking, he usually introduced Dan into the story. It lessened his guilt and frustration to think that he'd have lost his love anyway. And Jack took it all, it was his penance.

What made it all so much worse was that he loved Dan. He'd been kind of a father figure to him, had looked out for him. Had even helped him to see the deception in the story that he'd gotten the strange woman pregnant.

After she had left him, he'd spent the rest of his life being unable to promise himself to anyone. Not even the woman he'd supposed'ly loved during the war years and had been relieved to get home and fi her in love with another. No one measured up to Mary.

He watched the countryside go by and wondered how he cope with life on a huge cattle station in the top end. He'd never with cattle before, and he hoped he'd like that to. But Jack was aware he had nothing to look forward to. Nothing to lose an to gain. He'd been condemned to live a life without hope.

Jack closed his eyes again and thought now of Wally. He wished Wally was here, but Wally was limited in what he could now do though he had wanted to come with him. He remembered the compound and the long hut. He'd tried to settle there after the war but found the place too confining. He did wonder if this feeling of being trapped was the reason he looked for the great expanse of the never never. That and the fact that there were so few people up here. Hoped he'd find comfort in the isolation and the anonymity.

He'd stayed for a few years in the long hut with his family but found himself unable to accept Dans marriage to Mary. Unable to bear it when they touched or kissed or even went off by themselves. Jack had ended his days of the war in the commando unit of the second eighth battalion. He was a little afraid of what he was capable of.

So, he had packed his bags and like the coward he was these days, had left a note and snuck away. He told himself they wouldn't miss him, but he knew better. It had just been less painful for him to do it this way. To get away quietly, to hide and lick his wounds. He'd write when he got settled, he thought.

He'd left the compound before to go and work in various places, but he'd always said goodbye. He'd always been back in a few months to. This time was different he could feel it, in his heart he could feel it. He would not, could not, return home. It wasn't fair on anyone.

He'd heard the story of the baby Mary had lost and it had grieved him and still did. He wasn't sure why. He'd also heard how everyone had thought the baby to be his. Maybe that was why, because in a way it was his and hers. It had connected them to each other, at least in his mind, at least for a short while.

How he wished it had been his, his and Marys'. Jack tried to shake off the musings and the pain which always accompanied them.

The train pulled into a station and Jack watched the hustle and bustle of people getting on and getting off. A big man came and sat opposite him and smiled shyly. 'G'day mate' he said to Jack, 'how far are you going?' He held his hand out to Jack.

Jack smiled and shook hands with the man. 'Jacks my name, Jack Brown. I'm going to Mount Isa and then on out to a station about a few hundred miles farther up towards Doomadgee up on the Barkley Table lands there. Mable Downs, I've been hired on there as a ringer.'

The big man smiled at Jack now and said 'you don't recognise me, Jack. I fought alongside you in New Guinea. My name's Albert. Albert Jones.'

Jack sat forward in his chair squinting at the man Albert. 'Well, I'll be blowed mate, good to see you again. Last I heard of you, you were missing in action mate. You made it out then.'

Albert laughed. 'I got wounded and ended up in a field hospital about fifty or so miles outside Port Moresby. One of the nurses there took such good care of me that I found I couldn't bear to be without her. We got married right away back in Port Moresby and then had to part for the rest of the dam war.'

'Well congratulations Albert, I'm glad.'

'Yeah, well Jack have you ever done this sort of work before?'

'No Alby but I think I can pick it up.'

'No doubt you can pick it up Jack, and easily to if I remember correctly. But this is not Victoria nor the banks of the lovely Murrumbidgee. It is very hard thankless work and out in the heat and the dust and flies. Yeah, come to think on it Jack, you'll be just fine.' Both men laughed.

Albert fell silent and a great sadness passed across is dark, handsome face. Jack stayed silent; he knew that look well enough. Finally, Albert looked up, 'Sue, her name was. The Japs went through the hospital there on their way out of New Guinea and killed everyone there. Why Jack? The war was over.' Albert sniffed and looked out the window at the outskirts of town. The hopelessness on his face struck a chord with Jack.

Jack cleared his throat, 'sorry mate, I got a real good feel for that sort of heartache. So, where you off to my friend?'

'Looking for work Jack. Is someone meeting you at the Mount?'

'Yeah, the manager no less. He had to come down to get a tooth pulled out apparently. Ask him if there's anything going up there Alby.'

Alby smiled 'I will Jack, I will. I worked up on Mable Downs once before and it was one of the places I was going to hit up.'

The two men talked on into the night for a while and Albert produced a small bottle of whiskey. 'It helps me to cope Jack'.

Jack smiled and nodded. When the whiskey was gone and the conversation lulled a little the two men, calmed by the liquor, fell asleep.

Jack came to with a start, Alby was gone. It was just breaking day and Jack estimated they'd still be a couple of hours from the Mount. Jack sat alone for a while with his thoughts and wished he could get his hands on a coffee.

'Good morning, mate' Jack turned around and there was Alby with two mugs of steaming coffee.

'Jesus, mate' said Jack a smile crossing his face. 'You are the answer to my prayers I think.'

Jack took the cup and gulped at the hot liquid while Alby produced a brown paper bag from his coat pocket. He handed it to Jack and put his hand in his pocket and produced another one. 'Breakfast' he said simply.

A wide grin now lit up Jacks face and he breathed, 'I smell bacon Alby. I'll be blowed mate.'

'Eat up Jack could be a while now before we get something else.'

The two men ate in silence. Jack found that he was mighty glad he'd ran into Alby, and he suspected the feeling was mutual. That Alby was nursing a broken heart the same as him was only part of it.

Alby eased the loneliness; he understood the nightmares and the desperation you could wake up in. Yes, Jack was glad he was with him, he'd felt the old melancholy coming over him which at times nearly drove him mad. Dan had been there for that and had been a big help even though Dan hadn't been to war. That was the measure of the man and Jack knew that.

The two men talked until they had finished their coffee and food. Jack got up to go and relieve himself, Alby dozed off again. In the small rest room Jack took his soap and razor and toothbrush from a small bag. When he was done, he went back to the carriage where he'd left Alby. They had the carriage to themselves now. Jack was surprised to see Alby going through his bag.

He put his hand gently on the big man's shoulder. 'What is it you want mate? You only have to ask my friend.'

Alby turned and looked at Jack. The look on the big man's face all but broke Jack's heart. He knew exactly what went on here.

'Don't you have your service revolver on you Jack?'

'I'm sorry mate I don't trust myself with one of those.' He smiled softly at the big man. He went on 'Come on now man I was getting used to having you around. I could use your help. We need each other Alby, when we get where we are going, we'll just throw ourselves into the work and make plans another day hay. We'll get on with it and make a life for ourselves. We will Alby. If we don't both get work on the Downs, we'll just head off somewhere else, we'll stick together mate. Like we always did remember?'

Alby hung his head. In a voice little above a whisper he said 'I am sorry Jack. I shouldn't have done this to you. I'm ashamed....'

Jacked clapped the big man on the shoulder 'hush Alby there's nothing to apologise for. I bloody know how you feel. That's why I don't carry it because one of my mates found me doing similar. No harm done mate. You know, as if the war wasn't bad enough, we had to come home to cold beds. Yeah, I know Alby, trust me I know mate. By Jesus I do.'

Alby smiled weakly at Jack, 'sometimes it just washes over me. The loneliness the nightmares the sweats. Jesus Jack. I give you my word I'll try and handle it like a...... like a '

'A man Alby? I also know what you went through over there, you buried your sweetheart over there man. You've got nothing to prove mate, not to me. So, lets agree to get each other's backs hay? Just like old times hay Alby?'

Jack held his hand out to Alby who took it and looked at Jack as the tears rolled down his cheeks. Jack took the big man in his arms the way Dan did with him when he was like this. It had made a big difference in Jacks progress. Another person's arms holding you.

The two men alighted from the train and went in search of their ride. They found him in the carpark beside a land rover, also a big man, of about fifty years. The man introduced himself as Wayne Strawbridge. He shook hands with Jack and turned to Albert.

'G'day Alby. Haven't seen you for a while. Are you looking for work to are ya?'

Alby grinned, back to his usual self now and nodded. 'Yeah, I am. You got anything?'

'Just ringing like Jack here only for the dry mate if that'll do. Might be able to fix you boys up with something a bit more permanent down the track you know. A lot of people head south for the wet, so we'll see hay.'

The two men picked up their duffle bags, swags and kits and threw them up in the back. Alby smiled at Jack 'you can take the first turn in the front. We can swap maybe later mate.'

Jack said 'thanks Alby. Bloody glad you are coming mate, yes sir.'

Wayne watched the exchange and knew what went on. He'd been a vet from the first world war. He said this now and the two men turned and looked at him with renewed interest.

'Well thank Christ for that mate' smiled Jack sincerely.

'Yes of course' said Wayne 'you blokes would be still a bit raw. Well, we can look after each other hay?' He'd noticed how the two men cared for each other. 'Good idea thanks Alby, I can have a word with Jack here along the way about the job.'

Alby smiled knowingly, 'will we be doing any bull catching?'

'You know it Alby' Wayne laughed.

Jack smiled at Alby and hopped in the front with Wayne. He was glad how things had worked out, mighty glad.

Jack listened enthralled as Wayne talked about life up here in the top end, and as he listened, he realised that he had made the right decision in taking the job. He hoped so, hoped he would measure up alright.

Wayne was talking now about the job. 'It's nice to have Alby back, he doesn't fare so well when he's away from it.'

'Yeah, this bull catching he mentioned, he seemed to light up at that.'

'Yeah, he's one of the best I've ever known Jack. He's as strong as an ox and is surprisingly fast on his feet. I remember when he first got here, and he took his first turn at catching the bull. He got hold of its tail alright but before he could flip it, he lost his grip on it. Well, the bull turned on him and came at him see. So, Alby punched the thing right on the nose like. That old bull shook his head once or twice and took off into the scrub, obviously more intent on getting away. Well Alby there goes after it; he wasn't finished with it. I sang out to him to leave it, but he disappeared after it, he can run like a hairy goat to mate. He came back just about an hour before sundown, and we were organising a search party. He refused to talk about it, just got on with his jobs. He's a bloody good worker, a powerhouse is Alby.'

Wayne looked in the back to check on the man before he went on. 'Anyway, I found out from a local aboriginal man who was out that way hunting some 'roos, that Alby had spent the rest of that day up a tree.' The two men laughed.

Wayne went on 'you never forget your first bull and if that bull should cause you grief it is ingrained into your head for eternity mate.' Wayne nodded at Jack still laughing.

Wayne looked serious now. 'He's very special that first bull that puts you up a tree to sit there like a scalded schoolboy. And you can sit there all bloody day until the bastard gets thirsty and runs off, and no one's coming to save you because they don't wanna tangle with him. He'll head butt the tree every so often to make you shit yourself over and over again. They fuckin know. And then he gets a whiff of water or a female and he's off, forgotten all about you.

Well, that's how poor bloody Alby spent his first day. He never made that mistake again. He learned a lesson that day, that you don't go off into the bloody scrub after a bull that's just had his fuckin tail pulled. And they don't forget either. We saw that bull months afterwards and it just looked at Alby. Stared at him and Alby refused to have anything to do with it. So as far as I know he's still out there. And probably hasn't forgotten Alby.'

Jack was laughing now until his sides hurt. He hadn't laughed like that for a very long time. Not since the day he left Mary behind. How he wished he could have a few moments with her. He always wished that even though it tore him to shreds knowing she'd never be his. He said now, 'I wouldn't mind having a go at that. Catching a bull, even though it sounds insane.'

Wayne laughed then looking at Jack seriously he said now, 'That's good Jack, I think you'd be good at it to. You certainly look like you are powerfully built through your chest and arms. You need to be strong there. I think you'd also be agile and fast on your feet. Alby is. All you need then is a strong back and small brain and you're set. You're right Jack it helps if you are a little insane and let's face it mate….'

The two men chuckled, each easy in the others company. Jack spoke next, 'When do they start catching them.'

'Well, we like to have a herd ready when next some drovers come near. They hate droving them but if the money's right.' Wayne slowed down to let a small herd of cows cross the road. 'Now Alby and you are here we could go out in a few weeks after we get a few jobs finished.'

Jack nodded, He was still getting used to wearing a hat all the time and riding boots. 'Can't wait' he said. Jack did worry about his riding skills especially where bucking horses were concerned. Ordinarily he sat a good saddle, was quite adept at manoeuvring a horse. But bucking horses now, well he was keen to give it a go anyway.

Wayne said 'We spend a lot of our time on the mundane shit. Fences, bores windmills and that kind of thing always need maintenance. The vehicles need to be maintained to especially the rover we use to catch bulls. That cops a bit of a beating at times. But like I said I think you'd be every bit as good as Alby. Once you master your fear. What unit were you in Jack?'

'I finished up in the commandos. I spent two years with them.'

'Shit, you wouldn't be prone to fear much then mate. You boys had it tough. Did you know Alby?'

'Yep, he was already in the commandos when I got there. We got separated and everyone thought he was dead. Then I met him on the train. Didn't recognise him at first, he carries a little more weight now.'

'Well Jack, the boss is talking about getting in professionals to take out the feral bulls. There's big money in it, and if you can maintain your own vehicle, it's a plus. I personally would get a new vehicle for the job. You'd need a truck to but that wouldn't have to be too flash. Just a thought Jack.'

Jack was chewing it over. He had some money, probably enough for a new Land rover. He knew there was merit in what the older man said. He already liked the man and felt he could be trusted. He said now, 'I would need to save a little more. Don't know if Alby would have any or even if he'd be interested but it's something to think about.'

'Don't underestimate Alby, he'd have a few quid saved I reckon. He's good with cattle and the bulls and he's no slouch as a mechanic. We have a mechanic on the station, but he gets snowed under now and again and we have to help him out a bit. Yeah, Alby knows his way around a motor. Bloody good man to have around is Alby.'

Wayne fell silent for some moments and went on in a gentle voice, 'we all seem to do better at these jobs out here mate. I don't think I've ever met an ex-service bloke out here who was a drunk. I got a theory about the adrenalin. I think when we come home and try to settle into life back in town or on the farm, we miss the adrenalin rush. We became adrenalin junkies and going into battle was the biggest adrenalin rush of them all. So out here we get our fill of that, and it seems to keep us alive and living.'

Jack was flabbergasted. He sat in silence wondering if this man could actually be onto something. 'You know mate I think you might be right.' Jack thought about how he had tried to settle back into life on the farm. He wondered now if this feeling of confinement which he found insufferable could be exactly that.

There was a certain restlessness about it.

Wayne was talking again, and Jack listened intently, 'I'm not saying we don't get drunk Jack. Every month you'll find us in town at the pub getting blotto. We wipe ourselves out for a couple of days, sleep with a woman or two and it's all very nice. But we go home on Monday morning and get stuck into it again. It's the only way I found that I can exist and exist quite happily at that. It's nice to get into bed with a woman and hold her for a little while. One of my problems was that my woman found another bloke while I was at war. First world war.'

Jack nodded, he had a lot to think about and he said so now. 'I just hope I'm up to the task' he finished.

'You will be Jack. Out of all the blokes on this station, if I had to pick my crew you and Alby would be first because I know you are both gunna be chasing that bit of danger. Yeah, you'll be okay mate. And I am willing to bet everything I've got that fear won't be one of your problems. Am I right Jack?' Wayne slid his eyes at Jack.

'Well, I've never faced down a mad bull, but I do find myself looking forward to it. Yes, indeed I do.'

'Once you know how to do it and you follow procedure, you'll be fine. Like when you go into battle you just fall back on your training. You'll probably get hurt sometimes not too many of us don't. All you gotta do is think about what you are doing, you and Alby are the frontline. Know the pitfalls and how to avoid them. Once you've done a few you'll get it sorted out.'

'Yeah, well if the boss is going to get someone in to catch these bulls, I'd be in it.' Jack grinned, 'I think Alby would be to.'

'Yeah, you got a good mate there Jack.' Wayne smiled, 'and yeah I think he'd bloody love it.' He grinned at Jack, 'adrenalin junkies. A lot of poor bastards try to knock it out with alcohol.'

Wayne shook his head sadly. Jack sat thinking about how he could have ended up. He'd thought about it, had thought about using alcohol, to escape it. To escape the horror of the nightmares that plagued him.

Wayne was silent for a few miles and then 'I like my job Jack, but I would invest money into you and Alby. If you pan out to be the kind of man, I think you are. I'd devote some days to helping you to. You'll need a truck driver to come along behind you and pick up the bulls see, and someone to help him. Best way to move them Jack is to truck them. Anyway, you could use my men for a while just until you get on your feet.'

Jack swallowed a lump in this throat. Yes, he was glad he'd pushed himself to get this job, he didn't think he'd look back. Well only at Mary, always at Mary. He'd write home when he got settled, he'd send a letter to Dan and Mary. Their kids, a son and a daughter were twelve and six years old. One of Dans boys was in university and the youngest was a farmer. He smiled at Wayne now, 'adrenalin junkies.'

Wayne laughed. 'Your woman Jack?'

'Married to my best friend Wayne.'

'Shit!'

'They did get a notification that I was missing believed dead. And they love each other. They have two kids now. No mate I'll never get over her, I wouldn't even try.'

'It's a long lonely bloody life without the comforts a woman can bring. I don't have a girlfriend, but I do keep going back to see a woman who pleases me a great deal.' Wayne sighed and fell silent.

Jack fell silent to; he hadn't had any comfort in a very long time, and it did seem to be a long, lonely life. Trouble is Jack didn't know if he could. Last time he'd tried that he had been a dismal failure and upset everybody. The young lady had called his manhood into question and ended up sobbing because he didn't find her attractive enough.

Jack had tried to explain and made things even worse. He'd got out of her bed with a red face, struggled into his clothes and left. Women found him attractive he knew that. He'd gained a lot of muscle over the years and in all the right places. But could he deliver, that was the sixty-four-dollar question? And if not, the aftermath was too horrendous to contemplate.

Jack hadn't tried it again though. Even the woman he was supposed to be getting engaged to had failed to bring any feelings forth in him. Yet he had only to look at Mary and his feelings went wild. Why, he asked himself again?

Wayne went on talking about the life up here of a top end ringer or bull catcher. Jack listened and found the talk a comfort. He was looking forward to this new life but hoped everyone was even half as nice as Wayne and Alby.

Danger didn't worry Jack; he'd had a gun to his head. After that you didn't tend to worry a lot.

Jack had decided in his mind to throw himself into the work. He definitely would consider what Wayne was saying about catching feral bulls. He said now, 'I appreciate what you say about this bull catching. It's something I would consider but I know I have to learn the art first. The art of bull catching if I can use that term.'

The two men laughed at the idea. Wayne said 'Pretty ugly looking art mate. The thing about station life is the men's quarters are probably not what you are used to.'

'I was on the road during the great depression mate, I know how to live bloody rough. We met up with Dan who took us all on. I was just a boy. He took care of us and pulled us all through. Though we lost a couple of children on the road. And then we met Mary.' Jacks voice broke and he drew a deep breath.

'Is that her Jack? That your girl?'

Jack nodded, 'and Dan was my best pal. I loved him, we all did. He is a good man, strong and fair minded. He treats his people with love and respect, and they treat him the same. Of course, there were those who crossed him, and they soon came to regret their folly, and left town.

We'd have followed him off the edge of the world. Dan's wife died of cancer. Mary met us when we were starving to death and helped us. She had a farm and gave us four acres and taught us to grow our own food.'

Jack fell silent and Wayne left him to regain his feelings. Then after a while, 'sounds like one very special woman Jack. And she married Dan?'

'Yeah, I can't blame her Wayne, I was a stupid kid, and everyone loved Dan.'

Wayne nodded his understanding. Didn't make the loss one bit less or easier to bear.

Wayne swerved to miss a kangaroo and checked the mirror; Alby was still asleep propped up on a swag. He smiled. 'Well like I was saying Jack, the food the cook serves up is second to none.'

Jack smiled, took his hat off and dozed for a bit. He found Wayne had a soothing way, much the same as Dan.

At Camooweal they turned right off the highway and headed off up through the Barkly Tableland towards Doomadgee. They had fifty or so miles to go and they'd be at their new home. Wayne stopped for fuel and Jack got out to stretch his legs. He asked Alby it he wanted to ride up front, but Alby declined with a smile.

Wayne said to the big man now, 'How have you been fairing young Alby? You been a good boy have ya?'

Alby smiled down at Wayne and nodded 'of course Wayne. I've been working over near Brisbane on the highways there. Not a bad lurk but too close to the city for me, I can't tolerate it no more. The traffic, the noise the people. I like it up here better Wayne.'

Wayne stood looking up at the man, he was astounded. That was about the most words he'd got out of the big man ever and there was a smile to go with it. He clapped the man on the shoulder now, 'just lucky for us Alby, lucky for us for sure mate. Good to see you again man. Any hoot, let's get going I wanna be home for tea.' He winked at Alby, 'you do remember how good Hilda's teas are Alby?'

'It's why I'm here man, why I'm here.'

Wayne smiled and got in the driver's seat. These two blokes were good for one another he thought now, Alby was a different bloke. Wayne knew all about the horrors of war and knew also the struggle of trying to get on with life. He knew of the flash backs and night sweats, the terror in the night. And if you lost your sweetheart into the bargain, it was a struggle to stay alive. To get up each day and find a reason to go on. Find a reason not to lift a gun to your head.

Wayne could see these two blokes were suffering and he was glad they'd ended up here. He'd damn well do his best, him and Bill.

Chapter 2

When they arrived at the station Wayne pulled up at the men's quarters. Some men came out of the mess and went to Alby and shook hands with him. They seemed glad to see him and Alby introduced them to Jack. They shook hands with Jack enthusiastically.

'This is most of the crew that were here last year Jack, these blokes are ringers. This is eddy. Eddy is a stockman and tracker. Handy for finding where the bulls are at' grinned Alby. 'This here's Garry the mechanic handy for putting your vehicle back together.' Alby shot a glance at Wayne, 'I heard most of that conversation mate.' Looking at Jack he pointed to his ear and nodded, 'ears like a hawk.' He turned to a very young man and said 'Now this here is Pete, he's a bloody good stockman. And this here's Bill, he used to be a drover. The rest you'll meet at teatime.' Alby nodded to Jack, 'this is Jack, used to be in the army with me. We were in New Guinea.'

The men all fronted up to shake Jacks hand. 'Thanks for your service young un' Bill said and nodded his respect. 'You bloke's been to hell that's for sure.'

Wayne said g'day and that he had to go. He turned to Jack and Alby, 'take one of these rooms along there. And we start at six in the morning so be at breakfast at about Half past four, five o'clock. Nice start for you Jack bloody fencing. Know anything about it?"

'A little' said Jack smiling. 'Don't mind it at all Wayne.'

'Well okay' said Wayne looking pleased. 'And then Wednesday I'll get you to go out with Bill here and do the bores. You'll need your swag for that one, takes two or three days to get around them and that's if you don't have to do any repairs. But anyway, we can sort that out tomorrow.' He went to get in the rover, 'Try and be a bit bloody helpful to the new bloke will yiz? Show him around a bit' he turned to look at Jack 'not much to see but might be handy to know where everything is.'

Alby picked up his gear, so Jack did to. 'Follow me, Jack.'

Alby walked into the end room, it was a big room and was partitioned off into two smaller ones. Each had a bed and mattress and a cupboard with two drawers. A mirror hung on the wall above the cupboard of each cubicle. There was also a chair next to the cupboard which would double as a desk.

'A shaving mirror' Alby informed Jack. 'Have you got gloves Jack?'

Jack nodded. The room was adequate and quite roomy, it had been painted fairly recently in a light blue. There was a window over Jacks bed with a fly screen on it. It was a better deal than most of the places he'd camped in with the army. Jack was no stranger to sleeping rough and with others nearby. He unpacked and lay down on the bed.

Alby nodded, 'you'll need them tomorrow for fencing. Brings the blisters out if you aint used to it.'

The next thing Jack knew was Alby shaking him awake. 'Grub time. Come on mate let's go eat, you haven't eaten since breakfast.'

'My stomach was just telling me that.'

When Jack walked into the big mess room, he was nothing short of amazed. There was a counter affair with pots and pans and bowls of all sorts of food. There were three choices, roast beef and vegetables, stewed steak, and grilled chops. There was gravy and a bowl of mashed potato. There were also two deserts, trifle or steamed pudding and custard.

Jack was suddenly hungry it had been a long time since the bacon and egg sandwich. Was that only this morning? He got a plate and joined the end of the line. The other blokes took a serving of each on the oversized plates they ate from. Jack filled his plate the same.

To the side there was hot coffee and tea with sugar and milk nearby. There were also glasses with a water bag of cold water next to them hanging on a hook. Jack sat with the men at a long table next to Alby and met another very young man called Russel, another stockman. Afterwards, he helped himself to a good helping of steamed pudding and custard. Wayne came in for his dinner when they were nearly finished.

When they had finished eating, they all took their plates and cleared them of scraps and left them in a sink. A lady of around forty years introduced herself to Jack as Hilda the cook.

'Listen lovey' she said with a bit of a drawl, 'see that fridge over there. Go in there in the morning and you'll find a packed lunch. And welcome to our humble home lovey.' She smiled at Jack who shook her hand, 'That's my hubby over there, he's the Rous-a-bout here. Nevil.'

'Tea was lovely thank you' said Jack and smiled back. 'I was absolutely amazed.'

'Oh, go on with you, pet and ta a lot.' She flapped her hand at him.

'And quite aside from the food, it's nice to find such a pretty woman up here. Makes the place feel more of a home and the food is second to none. And I've eaten all over the world.'

Hilda's face took on a playful look and Jack wondered if he'd gone too far. 'Army food' she said?

Jack let out a below of a laugh and nodded. 'You have caught me out young lady.'

Hilda laughed with him. 'And to have such a handsome and gallant gentleman in our midst hay?' She laughed with Jack, her eyes openly telling him she meant every word.

Alby walked up and Hilda turned her attention to him. 'It's lovely to have you back darling, they told me you were back. Don't run off this time hay.'

Alby smiled at her, 'it's good to be back Hilda, I missed the place and missed you all to. I've been looking forward to that meal for a long time.' Alby smiled his best at her and turned to Jack. 'I'm Gunna hit the hay mate I'm a bit bushed.'

'Yep, me to. Early start tomorrow. Well goodnight, Hilda, and thanks for a lovely meal.'

Hilda watched him go. She noted his slender tall form and his wide shoulders; the lithe hips that swayed when he walked, the nicely cut brown hair and wondered at who in their right mind would break his heart. And broken hearted he was if she was any guess. She turned back to the kitchen, she had work to do.

Jack lay in his bed about twenty feet and a partition away from Alby. He heard Alby start gently snoring and smiled in the darkness. He knew a peace he hadn't known since he went off to war. As usual Jack's thoughts turned to Mary. 'Oh Mary. Mary' he whispered to the night. He smiled as her face materialised in his mind. And in the dreamy space between wakefulness and sleep, he took her in his arms and danced with her. She put her arms around him and kissed him gently on the lips. It never went any farther than that, he wouldn't allow it. Jack smiled in his sleep.

He slept soundly and never woke up. His job the next day didn't seem like work, not like the night before work usually felt. He'd enjoy it, he knew it. He looked forward to it.

Jack woke the next morning to another shaking from Alby, 'Sorry Alby, I was dancing with a beautiful woman' he smiled at the big man. He stood up and Alby stepped back.

Alby was taller than Jack by a couple of inches and was somewhat bigger and stronger. He smiled at Jack as he went back to his cubicle to shave. 'Mary, was it?' He caught the look on Jacks face before he regained his composure. 'Sorry Jack, that your sweetheart man?'

'That would be her Alby. Yes.'

As the two men walked side by side to the mess hall Jack said, 'are the breakfasts here as good as the teas Alby?'

'They are Jack, and the lunches are damn good to.'

Jack wasn't disappointed. He lined up to get his bacon and eggs and sausage with some tomato, a couple of pancakes and some toast.

He said good morning to the men and was introduced to the last of them. A big fellow called Jim, though he wasn't as big as Jack and Alby. 'He is a maintenance man and doubles as a stockman when we are busy,' said Bill. 'And this is the Rous-a-bout Nevil. He doubles as a cook when we go out in the camps. There's a camp coming up in about four weeks. Hope you blokes are on board for that.'

'What's the camp' asked Alby?

Bill grinned widely at the big ringer he so liked and said 'bull catching Alby. You'd hate that right?'

Alby pulled a face. Then, 'I can't bloody wait.'

'Hay, d' you remember that first bull you tangled with Alby' asked Bill?

'Aw shut up Bill.' All the men laughed good naturedly.

'I'm keen to have a go at that myself' put in Jack.

'Shit yeah' said Pete, 'you'd be good twisting their tails. Just don't let go though, hay?'

'Aw fuck you blokes I gotta piss. See you out there Jack.' Alby walked off to the sound of laughter. He'd missed this place, he felt like he'd come home.

Jack suddenly remembered. 'Hay Alby did you get your lunch?'

'No mate can you grab me one. Any sort of sandwich. Preferably beef hay.' Jack followed the others to the fridge. He got two lunches that had 'beef' written on them and wrapped in brown paper. Jack cast his eye over them yep, they all said beef, he smiled inwardly. There were calico bags to put them in, someone told Jack to look after his calico bag as they were brought back washed and used again.

Must be three sandwiches he thought and there was fruit to take on a sideboard, so he grabbed two apples. Jack got outside and looked towards the east. The sky was lighter, the dawn came. That time of day he had trouble with. Mary usually crept into his thoughts in the dawn. After he'd held her all night in his heart, in the wee hours he had to let her go.

He stopped as he realised, he was quite happy on this morning. He'd even had a few laughs and he enjoyed the company. Most of the blokes were a bit rough round the edges and they were a motley crew, but their hearts seemed to be in the right place. Jack wasn't sure if he was any judge of that. And they all liked Alby. Jack dared to hope that he could forget Mary, even just a little. Maybe he'd even be able to let her go a little easier in the wee hours.

Alby and Jack climbed into the back of Wayne's land rover, and they were off.

About twenty miles from the homestead, they stopped at a half-finished fence. Jack worked all day and found he loved it. He dug post holes and lugged posts. It felt good to do honest work, hard work.

At lunch time the blokes all sat round under a tree and made a billy of tea. The mugs were passed round, and Jack enjoyed the hot black tea immensely. And best of all were the laughs he got; the laughter that made you feel good. That dulled the pain, lifted the spirits, and eased the anxiety. The laughter and the bush.

He did everything that was asked of him and Wayne who had watched him was well pleased. He'd hate to lose the man to bull catching but he somehow knew he would, and with him, would go Alby. He was pleased to see how the two men Jack and Alby had each other's backs. All day they helped one another and watched out for each other. And the two of them were willing to help anyone who needed it.

Yeah, he thought they'd be alright now they had each other. And that the two men had been to hell and back was evident to a bloke like Wayne who'd been by there himself.

At the end of the day Wayne was more than happy with the amount of work they'd done. He called a halt to the day and the men packed up. Jack was tired when they finally drove back into the compound to the smell of tea cooking. He felt good though.

Jack got out of the back of the land rover with his calico bag and Alby's. Wayne smiled at the man he now admired, 'so you ready for tomorrow, Jack? Remember to take your swag and whatever else you'll need. And grab some overalls from the laundry over there. They are up in the top cupboard on the right, just in case you have any big repair jobs. In the morning, Hilda and Nevil will have a bundle of supplies for you to take. Bill will take care of the tool kit and tents. I'd like you to learn the run Jack, I don't like to send Bill out on his own no more. Well, I don't like to send anyone out on their own really, it's almost a thousand miles all up.'

Jack found the old excitement was back in his belly and he looked forward to tomorrow. He dared to hope that he looked forward to his life here. He felt guilty about up and leaving the long hut the way he had but he knew he had to get away. He knew he'd never do any good there, knew he had to get away from the situation. Free himself from the all-consuming heartache. He knew also that Dan would understand and that meant everything to Jack. He had to put an end to the suffering he'd put him through.

The men hurried off to do their odd personal jobs, having showers and getting cleaned up for tea. Jack hurried off to the shower block eager to get rid of some dust and dirt and sweat. He shaved and combed his hair, he'd had a haircut just prior to coming up here. There was a tiny spark in his dark blue eyes that had been missing for so long.

The journey from Balranald to here had been a long and arduous one. He was glad he'd taken it and he was no stranger to travelling. Before he went to dinner, he sorted his swag out in readiness for the next day. He looked forward to seeing the station during the next few days on the bore run. The bores would all need to be in good working order for the long dry season which was almost upon them. They'd have to be checked very carefully and Jack had been told he'd probably be away three days at least.

Jack came back to the mess for dinner with Alby, the more time he spent with the big ringer the more he liked him. And Alby was deceptive, though he gave the impression of being none too bright he was actually very intelligent. He also had a caring way about him, and Jack wished there was more he could do for the man. Alby's pain was etched in his forehead.

Alby was of a quiet nature, but everyone liked him. Jack wondered if he and Alby would ever get over the women they'd lost. Hopefully even just enough to go on and find someone to love, to share their life with. Wayne had given him some hope.

The men sat around with full plates and empty bellies, everybody's favourite part of the day. The talk got around to the war on account of an old digger who'd died last night in the hospital. Heart failure they said respectfully. The room was silent as they ate.

'Who was he' asked Jack politely?

'His name was Dennis Markham.' Said Wayne eyeing Jack.

Jack lowered his head; he felt the tears stinging the back of his eyelids and a lump in his throat he was trying desperately to swallow. You could hear a pin drop and Jack was painfully aware of it.

Wayne noticed and said softly, 'did you know him son?' He felt his heart still as he waited for the answer, as they all waited in silence for Jack to speak. They all knew where Dennis had become so ill and had all pulled for him to survive. But Dennis had been too far gone and had never really recovered. The doctor hadn't expected him to last as long as he had. He left behind a widow and two children.

Jack nodded and after a silence he cleared his throat and, keeping his eyes on his plate, said 'yeah, I did. Met him in Rabaul, I thought he'd made a full recovery. I bloody checked.'

'Shit Jack,' cried a horrified Alby. 'You were in that fuckin pow camp there? You were in that place that killed Dennis? Not even half the blokes got out of there alive.'

Jack felt Bills hand come down on his shoulder as the older man whispered, 'Jesus, mate.'

The silence went on as the information dawned on the men at the table. As everyone realised where this man had met Dennis.

'Ya poor bastard,' said Wayne. He found for once in his life he was speechless. How he wished he had the words, for Jack. But he didn't.

Jack said, 'I'm sorry.' He studied the food on his plate for a while and got quickly to his feet and rushed out the door. His stomach heaved and heaved for some minutes before it settled back down, and he staggered away and fell in the dirt and cried. Alby came out and took Jack in his arms and held him. The tears rained down Alby's face.

The men stood at the door their kind hearts breaking in their tough exteriors at the sight of the two men crying like babies. There must have been something pretty special between Jack and their friend Dennis. And every man there knew they didn't come much stronger or tougher than these two blokes down there in the dirt, reduced to this.

Wayne and Bill stepped forward and added their arms to the mix. Both these men knew the score. They knew what this was all about and Wayne, who had found his voice talked soothingly to them. He talked of how it was over for all of them. Talked about how the aftermath would get better. 'Yes, it's bloody hard but it will get better. With time.'

At last, he was able to separate Jack and Alby and the men climbed up out of the dirt. Bill kept his arm around Alby and the big man leaned heavily on him.

'We'll all go to the funeral, and we'll pay our last respects. It's next Wednesday so anyone who wants to come, can.' Wayne looked around now at the men, 'and anyone who doesn't will still get the day off.'

Chapter 3

Jack had a hearty breakfast though the events of the night before had set him back some. He'd nursed Dennis in that pow camp, had even taken a beating or two for him. Alby sat next to him and just a tad closer than usual. 'You okay to go on the run Jack?' he asked quietly, 'I could do it mate.'

Jack nodded and smiled at the big man who had held him when he badly needed it and said 'yeah mate I'm fine, but thanks anyway Alby. I bloody appreciate it. And I appreciate what you did for me last night to.' He looked about, 'and you to Bill and you Wayne.'

'You would do the same for me Jack, in fact you have.' Alby smiled. 'You saved my life Jack.'

Jack protested he had done no such thing but the men at that table had already heard it. They looked at Jack through different eyes. Jack was a hero for sure. Their very own hero, on Mable Downs. These guys, these top end ringers, walked a little straighter, a little taller. Hell yeah, these two men had risen from the dirt like. … Like that great bird from the coals.

And Alby, who had been there to, and knew what was needed, and then hadn't hesitated to do it. How many men would get down in the dirt and cuddle his mate like that? Yeah, Alby knew what's what and how did he know? Well, he'd been there to, hadn't he? He was a hero to, and they hadn't even realised it.

And their boss and Bill to. Top end ringers or not they'd all felt their bottom lip tremble.

After assuring Alby again that he was fine, and he'd see him in a few days Jack climbed into the Toyota next to Bill. Hilda slipped out to the car, bypassed Jack, and went round the other side of the car where she handed Bill a package, 'your lunches' she said. There was something a little different, a little softer about her voice.

Bill looked up from the wheel and smiled as he thanked her. Jack knew with absolute certainty that he had just witnessed a moment. Hilda turned and went back inside, and Bill watched her go a little bit longer than was seemly. Jack smiled to himself.

The men all came out to watch them go as they set off on the bore run. Jack was more comfortable in his hat, but his boots would need a bit longer. He was excited and couldn't wait to get going. After the longest goodbyes they were off.

Bill planted his foot and the showing off was begun. They left the yard in a cloud of dust to the cheers and laughter of everyone there. Jack put his arm out the window and banged on the roof, he was exhilarated. Wayne laughed and called out some insults. 'Yeeha' cried Jack.

Their swags were in the back and their provisions and a tent. Wayne made them take a tent in case of bad weather though they almost never put it up. Most of the blokes preferred to sleep under the stars. Their food for the three days was in an esky and there were also drums of water and fuel. There was a huge tucker box and some pots etc.

'How long have you worked here for Bill' asked Jack as they got out along the track?

'I came here from the Territory about four years ago Jack. I was only gunna stay a season and retire but I like it here. So, are you thinking about giving the bull catching a go?'

'Yeah, I'll give it a go. I haven't had much to do with cattle or even sheep. We had a few back on the farm. But we mostly grew wheat.'

'Was that your family's farm Jack?'

Jack nodded and smiled. 'Yeah' he said. 'We had a farm down on the bank of the Murrumbidgee. We also did market gardening, and we strove to be self- sufficient, and we mostly always were. Whatever we didn't need we took to market.'

Jack left out the rest, most people went through some tough times during the great depression. To Jacks mind, they hadn't yet got all the way out of it. And if he was honest with himself, it was Dan who'd taught him to think, Dan and his radio. Dan dissected everything he heard on it.

'I see Jack, well you'll find this up here a bit bloody different mate. I worked on a farm down there once, got married to a girl down there. Down near Deniliquin there, farm girl she was. Brought her back up here. I didn't like it much down there always had a feeling I was locked in. She didn't like it up here and we only lasted about six years. I came home from droving one day and she'd cleared off. Don't know if I'm divorced or not, probably am. I have never found another I could take to. I have had women over the years, but they leave me. So here I am.'

Dipping into someone else's Missus thought Jack smiling inwardly. It was none of his business and people had to find some comfort wherever they could. Bill fell silent for a while and so did Jack.

Bill broke the silence, 'anyway I hope you do alright with the bull catching. You'll soon find out if you are any good. I'm too old for it so I just drive the truck. Getting them into the truck can be a bit hairy to. Won't be doing that for much longer I wouldn't think. Probably got another ten years or so hay.' Bill smiled.

After about an hour they pulled into their first bore. By sundown they hadn't made it halfway round the station. Jack was amazed at the size of this place. After they'd had their tea, they climbed into their swags. They'd checked four bores, one needed minor repairs and Bill wanted to get five done tomorrow if possible.

Jack was almost straight to sleep when his head hit the pillow, he was too tired even to think about Mary for very long. Jack lay in his swag, the stars bright above a soft breeze on his face and the sounds of the bush. It was perfect. A dingo howled its eerie note to the moon some distance away. Jack rolled over on his side smiling, he was at peace. At peace at last in this wildest of places. The realities of nature here could be harsh but they were honest.

He seemed to have no sooner closed his eyes and Bill was nudging him awake with his boot. 'Come on young un' the older man said softly.

Jack sat up and watched as Bill stared at the ground and began to look about. He turned to Jack, 'we had visitors in the night as we slept.

Local tribe, hunting party probably. I never heard a thing, but they were mostly interested in you. Tracks all around your swag look.'

Jack jumped up 'shit' he said. There were a lot of tracks, mostly bare foot, some right near his head. A shiver went through him. He looked at Bill who smiled and nodded at him.

Bill drew a breath, 'they could have slit our throats and been away and we would never have known who did it.' He looked back at the ground rubbing his chin, 'mind you, we wouldn't have wondered for long. But most of them aren't violent like that. Come and get a coffee lad and I'll put brekky on hay?'

Jack got his swag rolled up and in the back of the Rover. With that done he walked over and sat at the fire to drink his coffee. 'You wanna hand with that' he asked Bill?

'Well now son, can you cook?'

'I dunno. I think so.'

'Well, it aint as easy as it looks, I can tell you that much. I'll do it mate we only got food for three days. After that we're hungry till we're home.'

'Maybe we should have brought Hilda with us.' Jack smiled at the fire before raising his eyes to Bill.

Bill flicked his eyes at Jack, a hint of a smile in them. 'Hmmm' he said and concentrated on turning the sausages and bacon.

'Why'd you leave droving Bill, had enough?'

'Well, I thought I'd try it out here you know just to see. Anyway at least ringing you are home mostly. I had a woman when I came here see, but she buggered off to. Dunno what I'm doing wrong young Jack. I mean I'm a damn good cook Jack, I'm a catch. I'm not even fat and I got all my hair mate.' He brushed his hand over the top of his head a big grin on his face.

Jack laughed, 'well don't look at me, I'm fuckin hopeless.'

Bill laughed heartily. Then seriously, 'Hilda's man can't please her. Well, he can't do anything really. Let's just leave it at that hay. He turns a blind eye.'

Jack nodded; he was happy to leave it at that. He started eating his breakfast, then 'you're right you know Bill, you're a damn good cook' said Jack as he ate. 'I might marry you and turn a blind eye also.'

Bill looked aghast at Jack; he'd stopped chewing. Jack threw his head back and laughed as he had never done before. Bill gave a snort of a laugh and went on eating. 'Well, you can do the bloody dishes smart arse.' Jack laughed again; he loved it.

They got the Ute packed up and climbed in and got started, the sun was almost fully up now, and it promised to be a beautiful day. Bill started the motor; he couldn't put his finger on what he liked so much about young Jack. There was something about him. Some sort of familiarity. Still, it would come to him, he slipped the Toyota into gear. He never forgot a face nor the man behind it. Not for long.

Wayne put the radio receiver down with a bang. Margaret had been on the damn thing again wanting to know when they'd be in town again and had told him that she needed to see him. When she needed to see him, it was usually to pay the bills. She wouldn't come right out and say it on the radio because someone would hear. She was getting up him more and more lately about what an insult it was for him to treat her as a kept woman.

Wayne heard the phone ring and knew she wasn't finished so he rushed outside and over to the mess for breakfast. Last time she had moaned about that he had said he wouldn't keep her anymore then and that she should start keeping herself. She had kicked him out of her bed for three months.

Wayne was tired, he wished he had the gumption to walk out on that woman and never go back. But he admitted to himself now, she was convenient. But, he mused, she was costly. Wayne had heard what some of the other managers were being paid. He also wished he had the gumption to ask his boss for a raise and then leave if he didn't get it.

He'd managed to save a nice little nest egg so he wouldn't starve. Margaret would leave him of course but he wondered if that would be a bad thing, she was a habit. But he'd have to get work somewhere. One day, he promised himself for the umpteenth time, one of these bloody days. One of these days he'd leave the bloody lot behind and make his way elsewhere.

He walked into the mess and got a plate of breakfast. He looked at his plate on his way to the table and smiled inwardly. None of it had taken the edge off his appetite. Wayne hated that he was getting a fat belly, he needed to work.

Maybe he should look for a job.

He sat opposite Alby and noticed as he talked to him what a nice and intelligent bloke he was. Yes, Wayne would be sad when he and Jack left. He hoped for their sake that Jack would be every bit as good as Alby at catching feral bulls. Wayne stopped his chewing; an idea had struck him. Could he, he wondered? Should he? Shit he told himself, he needed to think about this. He was fifty- four, maybe a bit long in the tooth.

At the end of day two Bill cooked tea while Jack set up camp. He got the tucker box and esky out and then did the swags. Bill slept on one side of the fire and Jack on the other. Jack loved sleeping under the stars, he saw now what everyone was on about, it was different than in the army. It was all about freedom; a free carefree life and Jack loved it. And he found he was tired out and fell asleep contented. Full belly, the night sounds of the bush, perfect. Jack didn't think it could get any better. Except if Mary was in his swag.

Bill had suggested Jack put up one of the tents as there were clouds on the horizon. He'd been shown how to tie the tent down in case there was a storm coming which were often accompanied by high winds. 'Just one'll do' Bill had said, 'just in case we need to keep dry.'

The two men sat at the fire eating a thick juicy steak and vegetables that Bill had cooked, and they'd have some of Hilda's fruit cake for after. Bill said quietly, 'we got the five bores done today, Jack. All being well we should get back home about sundown tomorrow. If we need to do any big repairs, we'll be eating sandwiches tomorrow night. Unless we're close to home then we'll slip home for tea and come back out.' Bill grinned, looked at Jack and wiped the smile from his face.

Jack nodded but didn't stop eating. He reckoned it was the best steak he'd ever eaten, and he said so now. Bill smiled, 'it helps that we're hungry and happy.

You love it don't you Jack' he nodded as he looked around at the surroundings. 'Out here I mean. I bloody do to.'

Jack smiled, 'I'm glad I came up here now. I know exactly what you mean about feeling hemmed in down south.' Jack looked around at the same bush. 'Wonder if we'll get any visitors tonight.'

'Probably not,' said Bill. 'They're not much interested in us mate.'

Jack did feel better hearing that. 'You know I prefer being out here to the camp. You know the men's quarters.'

'Well, you should take well to the life of a bull catcher. You know some of the stations are using bull catchers to get rid of their feral bulls. Then they take them and sell them. That's where most of the bulls at rodeos come from. They also sell them to stations who need an extra bull or two. Some blokes have a small property where they fatten them up, ring them and sell them for meat. Big money Jack. And more and more stations are doing it. This here station is going to change over in a year or two. Nice little opportunity Jack to the right bloke. Wonder if that's why Wayne is taking such an interest in you and Alby. Alby has proved himself as a catcher or roper and you could do the driving. Then all you need is a truck driver and a sidekick for him.'

Jack felt his pulse quicken every time he heard that. Bill saw it on his face and smiled. Jack couldn't wait to try himself at this bull catching.

As if he'd read the younger man's thoughts Bill said, 'we'll be going out to the camp in about three weeks. We go into town in two weeks' time, and we usually go out after that. These trips to town are usually about three days. We do a lot of drinking and laying with women then we're back at it. We can be out there in these camps for a couple of months. I do drive the truck mostly but then I do also take a turn at cooking. Hilda never comes she don't like it much.'

'That's just two months work Bill, I'll need a bit more than that if I'm to consider doing it for a living.'

'Yeah, well most of the blokes who do it have three stations to do at least. And I heard they make thousands at it. And that's after the thousands they spend. Bob Conrad does it over near Katherine, he bought a new Toyota, and he reckons it's saved him a load of cash. It's a rough life on your vehicle and so he's not having to stop for repairs all the time and pay his blokes while he's doing them.' Bill threw away the dregs of his cup and got up to start the dishes.

Jack got up to, he was feeling the excitement in his belly. He just had to figure out where he'd find two more blokes who'd want to do it.

Bill and Jack arrived back at the station a little after dark on the third night. Bill went straight to the kitchen where he found Hilda cleaning up. She turned and grinned at him, and Bill felt a shiver down his spine. God she's lovely he thought wishing he could pick her up and take her to bed. But they had to be very discreet. Bill was having more and more trouble with that.

'So, your back pet, did you have a good run?'

'Yeah Hilda, good run. Jack's pretty good at anything mechanical. Any chance of getting some grub?'

'Sure, thing Bill, I'll make you a plate each'.

Just as Jack and Bill sat at the table Wayne strode in. The two men told him of the jobs they'd had to do, and Wayne made a note of it.

'How are you doing Wayne' asked Bill?

'I'm doing okay man thanks for asking. I have scheduled our next weekend to town for the fourth which is weekend after next. When we come back from that we'll make ready to go camping boys. The bull catching season will be underway. And may the best bull win hay.' The men laughed and Wayne got up to go just as Alby walked in.

'How's it going' he asked?

Some of the other men came in and as Wayne left the mess hall, he knew deep in his heart he'd be making some changes. He had to. He'd got it out of Alby what had happened to his missus and Wayne was horrified. These two men Alby and Jack, so strong and calm, breezed into the place like a breath of fresh air. And with them they brought change. He could feel it in his bones, and it gave him a feeling of excitement in his belly. Him and all his fine talk about adrenalin. He'd noticed the change in Bill to.

Back in his office Wayne sat down and picked up the telephone. He had some calls to make, had to put the feelers about. The idea that Wayne had gotten into his head had him excited. More excited than he had ever been, and he liked it.

He rang three numbers and by the end of it he was almost breathless. He'd need to talk to Jack and Alby, but he also wanted to wait until he saw if they were as good as he thought. Wait and see if they had a love for bull catching.

Wayne also knew he'd have to speak to Margo.

Chapter 4

Jack found himself standing at the railway station in Melbourne and a woman was standing down the platform from him. Suddenly there came to him the sound of machine gun fire and mortar shells. Jack tried to yell to the woman to get down. She turned and stared at him, and he screamed and tried to run to her. His legs were paralysed, and he couldn't move. He screamed again, 'Mary…. Mary.' But she just stood and looked at him. The platform heaved and thudded under his feet.

He held his arms out to her, but she didn't run to him, he couldn't see her face now. She disappeared from his view, Japanese soldiers had run to her and knocked her down, one of them stood over her and shot her. His Mary was dead. They laughed and looked at Jack, but they didn't seem to see him. It was as if he didn't exist.

The chaos went on all around him. Nurses and doctors trying to do their jobs were fired on and killed. They were shot in the back as they worked, or in the head and they slid lifeless to the floor. Their sightless eyes turned to the sky. The sky! The station began to spin.

His attention was drawn once more to Mary who was trying to get up. 'No! No!' he screamed over and over but she made it to her feet. A child lay on a stretcher nearby and Jack watched horror stricken as one of the soldiers took aim at her again.

Mary threw herself across the child and took two more bullets in the back. One that was meant for her and one that was meant for the child. 'No! No! please no! God…Oh God.' Jack was sobbing now but still couldn't move. But the soldiers had seen him, they had him. They had his hands and would tie him up. He struggled in vain to get free. He thrashed and fought and yelled at them, but they had him. He couldn't go through that again, couldn't go back to that place with them.

What were they saying? Why did they care about him? Their voices droned on, and the mortar shells faded. It all faded away but for that voice. A voice of comfort and love.

'Jack mate, Jack. Come on Jack it's alright I've got you. I'm here mate I'm here. I got you Jack it's alright buddy.'

It was Alby. Alby! 'Alby get down mate get down.'

'Alright Jack we are down they won't find us here Jack. I give you my word mate. Come on Jack it's over mate, it's over. It's all over now Jack.' The voice was soothing, so soothing he had to believe it. Wanted so much to believe it.

Jack stopped fighting and held on to his captor. No, it was Alby. Yes Alby. Jack tightened his grip on Alby. He started to cry, and Alby rocked him as if he was a baby until he stopped.

Alby no. What if Alby finds out? No, it's awful. Poor Alby.

The voice came to him faintly, 'if Alby finds out what Jack? Finds out what Jack?'

'Alby no. I'm sorry mate, I'm sorry.'

Alby let go of Jack while he lit the lantern beside the bed. He sat back on the edge of the bed and peered at Jack. Noted the white face, the sweating, the wild eyes, and something else. He couldn't put his finger on it, but this was no ordinary dream, not an ordinary flash back. This was worse, so much worse.

Alby's breath caught in his throat.

He got a waterbag and gave it to Jack and Jack drank eagerly from it. Alby took it and put it on the floor. 'Tell me what you seen Jack. Can you tell me that Jack? You said something about a nurse. Jack! Did you see what happened Jack? Did you? Did you see my Sue?' Alby wished he would stop asking, he couldn't bear it. But Jack had seen something, he knew it.

Jack gave a great sob and said 'I dunno Alby. I thought it was Mary, but I didn't see her face. You know?' Jack searched his mind to try and make sense of it.

Alby sat quietly looking at Jack, studying Jacks face. 'But did you see nurses Jack?'

'I think they were nurses and doctors to in white coats. And the soldiers shot them all. Shot them as they worked, and they didn't see it coming.' A lie formulated in Jack's head now, his mates face was breaking his heart. 'She never knew what hit her mate. No one did, and it was all over, over in seconds.'

Alby sat there staring at him. His voice held a tremor as he said 'thanks mate. That is something to know. Something better than I was imagining.' He reached out and touched Jack's hand 'are you alright for a minute, I need a piss.'

'Yeah, mate I'll be right. I'm sorry Alby.'

'No need to apologise Jack. Now I'll be as quick as I can. When the melancholy washes over you it's gunna hit you like a freight train mate. Just hang on I'll be back.'

Alby hurried out the door taking a great gulp of fresh air as he did. He stood holding onto the corner of the building, shaking from head to foot. He made it to the toilet and vomited.

Jack sat in the bed and waited. And when the melancholy came it did hit him like a ton of bricks. He hung on to the side of the bed and tried and tried to drag his head out of it. But it had a grip on him, the fear had his belly in a knot.

Jack felt himself fill up with hopelessness and he wished he had his service revolver. There was a razor blade on his dresser. He swung a leg out of bed and then the other. He just had to make it to the dresser.

But suddenly Jack came to himself and in his mind's eye he saw Alby. Alby was hunched over his dead and bloody body crying softly. Jack fell back on the bed. And to his wonder he smiled to himself. Jack hadn't realised it, but he'd found an inner peace, sort of a coping mechanism. Alby was a big part of that.

Alby came back and was pleased yet shocked to see Jack looked fine. Suspicion clouded his face and Jack smiled, 'no I'm alright mate, I am. You know what I think Alby?' Alby gave a shake of his head, so

Jack went on. 'I think we are going to be alright you and me. I'm sorry I woke you. Get some sleep mate. Don't worry about me.'

Alby smiled at Jack now, 'okay it's only midnight so we can get a few more hours. Are sure you are okay Jack?' Alby got to his feet.

'I'm sure thanks Alby.'

'Well then you won't mind if I take these.' Alby picked up his razor blade and his razor and went to bed, 'Goodnight Jack' he smiled.

'Okay Alby, be seeing you' Jack smiled back. Jack felt bad about lying to Alby but what he'd seen was horrendous. How could he tell his mate that? And it probably wasn't real anyway.

All the men were at breakfast, Jack noticed that Jim never took part in the conversation. He kept himself to himself. The blokes always included him, but he always remained silent and would only usually grunt a reply. Jack put the term surly to him.

On this morning, Wayne came in with a very worried look on his face. He stood at the end of the table and cleared his throat. The men all turned to listen; they knew Wayne was about to make a speech. They thought it might be about the trip to town soon, but they'd never seen Wayne's face like that.

Wayne took a deep breath, he hated this. He took a deep breath 'It grieves me to say this, men but there is one among us who may be a little light fingered. Now I checked the fuel shed this morning to see how much I needed to order. There are two four-gallon drums of petrol missing, one of diesel and a pint of oil. Now you all know if you need fuel, you only have to tell me. But you also know you cannot go and help yourself. So of course, I am going to ask the question, who took it?'

No one answered. The kitchen was quiet. Bill spoke up he just seemed annoyed, 'What do you mean coming in here Wayne interrogating us when we're trying to eat? We're....'

Wayne cut in 'no, no no, now hang on, I have to try and get.......'

Again, Bill's voice was louder when he cut in, 'No mate you can't come in here and accuse all of us of pilfering fuckin petrol, and so on. We're entitled to eat in peace.'

'Yeah, well what you're not entitled to do is help yourself to the fuckin fuel. Now I'm going to ask is anybody taking it or is there anyone who might know who is? Or did the heat of the day evaporate it and suck the bloody drums up with it.'

Bill flew into the ring. 'Well, what we don't have here are any fuckin dobbers.' Bill dropped his knife and fork with a clatter. 'Who are you looking at here Wayne?"

'You. And anyone else who has a vehicle they might be putting it in.'

To Jacks horror Jim spoke up 'well I saw him hangin round down at the fuel shed.' Jim was thumbing towards Jack. 'Why don't you ask him? Search his room.'

Alby sucked in air and got up from the table. 'You fuckin did it didn't ya? Did you plant it in his room while he was out ya mongrel?'

'No' Jim's retort was a vehement denial.

Alby was on his feet now to, 'Jack's been at the tool shed since four o'clock. I'm gunna have a look and by Jesus if I find any four-gallon drums in Jacks room I'll fuckin throttle you ya bastard.'

'Now wait a bloody minute' bellowed Wayne. Wayne looked like somebody who'd dropped a match in dry grass in a strong North wind and was now trying to control the bushfire with a can of petrol.

Alby turned to Jack, 'I know you didn't take it mate. You come with me, and we'll have a little look see in your room hay.' He swung round towards Jim now, 'and of course my bloody room. God help you old son if there's anything untoward in there.'

Jack rose to his feet and the room fell silent. Jack hadn't taken his eyes from Jim. 'No need to look Alby the drums are in my room aren't they Jim? Why? What the hell did I ever do to you?'

Jim shrugged and refused to talk. Jack grabbed him by the scruff of the neck and hoisted him to his feet. 'Come on bugger ya, you come with me and help me haul it back where it belongs.'

Jim allowed himself to be pulled towards Jacks room. Alby got there first and they searched the room. There were no drums of fuel or anything else that shouldn't have been there.

Pete the young stockman watched on with a grin. Wayne scratched his head this had well and truly got away from him. Pete spoke up now. 'Let's all go and search Jim's room. See what we find there, hay?'

'Now this is getting silly' started Wayne.

'Why? You want your drums of petrol so we're looking for them' Bill snapped.

He just wanted his breakfast and a leisurely coffee. He wasn't good without those under his belt.

At Jim's room they found the drums of petrol. Wayne looked from the drums to Jim and back. Jim had shock registering on his face. 'What the fuck. I never....'

'Yes, you did,' cried Pete. Everyone turned to look at Pete. 'Me and Eddie watched him take it. He put the diesel and oil in his car and stuck two drums in Jacks room.' Pete giggled now, 'so we took em and put em in his room.'

Wayne exploded, 'why don't you bastards just grow up. Jim, put that fucking fuel back in the shed and get your things and clear out. I'd like you to be gone within the hour. You Pete for your mischief I'm gunna dock you two days' pay. Don't even think about whinging any of ya or you can go with him' Wayne thumbed towards Jim. Wayne wasn't good without a coffee either.

'It's a bit of fuckin fuel' whined Jim.

'Yeah, but you tried to get Jack in the shit for it. Why I don't know but get your things and go somewhere else and make trouble. Now get to fuckin work the lot of ya.'

Bill roared just as loudly, 'Well I'm going back to my breakfast. Which I was enjoying before I was rudely interrupted.'

Jack was speechless and when he found his voice he demanded, 'why Jim?'

Jim didn't answer and went to pack his stuff. Wayne watched him go and shrugged. 'What the fuck for? Well come on you blokes get fed and get to work unless you wanna catch a ride out with him.'

Wayne walked away, he hated these little dramas and he'd had enough of Jim and all his little dramas. He was a senseless man who did senseless things.

Wayne also knew if it had been Jack who stole the petrol, he wouldn't have sacked him. Jack represented something to Wayne. He didn't know what it was yet, but he did know he had to find out.

He walked over to Jack, 'don't take it personally Jack I think he picked on you because you are the newest here. He probably figured no one knew that much about you so he could deflect onto you. Anyway, I been wanting to catch him for a while. When he comes by, I'm gunna have a look in his Ute, he'll have fuel in the back of that thing no doubt. He'd be taking it to town and selling it if I know anything.'

Jim came by in his Ute and Wayne stepped out in front of him. Jim stopped and yelled 'what now. Get out of the way Wayne or I'll run over you.'

Wayne walked up to the window of the Ute and reaching his hand in turned off the motor. 'Just get out for a minute Jim.'

Jim opened the door, 'why?'

Wayne untied a couple of ropes and pulled the tarp back. There were six four- gallon drums. 'That's what I thought' murmured Wayne. He took the drums out of the back of the Ute and told Jim to get back in.

Alby watched with disgust; Jack had no expression on his face. Jack wasn't the sort of bloke to judge how others behaved. He'd done some fairly iffy things in his time.

Jim spat at Jack as he walked past, and it was too much for Alby. He aimed a punch at Jim which Jim side stepped easily. Jack grabbed Alby but he knew the man's ire was up. 'Alright Alby' said Jack softly, 'it was me he tried to wrong I'll take him on.'

Jim sneered at Jack. 'I would dearly love to see you try and beat me in a fair fight. Think you're some kind of big hero don't ya? Well let's see if you got anything but talk ya bastard.' Jim was taking his shirt off.

Jack took his shirt off and threw it to Alby 'hang on to that.'

'Yeah, you can bring it to him in the hospital.' Jim spat in the dirt towards Jack's feet.

'Gunna talk all day' asked Jack in his usual quiet voice? The blokes standing around wanted blood. Anybody's really! They shouted their encouragement.

Waynes's voice drowned out everything as he shouted, 'Hay now come on you blokes this is just fuckin stupid' all heads turned to Wayne. Wayne went on a bit quieter now that he had everyone's attention. 'The first bloke to swing a punch loses a day's pay.'

Pete sang out 'just bloody add it to mine. Come on Jack teach the mongrel a lesson hay?'

Jim rushed at Jack and swung a haymaker. Jack dodged it, jabbed at Jim, and got him in the temple. Jim tried a couple of jabs and Jack dodged them. For the next few minutes Jack just dodged everything. He got in a couple of jabs which caught Jim on his jaw. Jim shook his head and rushed at him again and Jack threw a hard right jab to the forehead and knocked Jim clean out.

He turned away and went to finish his breakfast. Halfway through his bacon and eggs he heard Jim leave the station. He breathed a sigh of relief. Jack had sought only peace when he came here. Today his peace had been broken in an altogether startling fashion. Pete came in and sat beside him. 'Good on ya Jack.'

'I don't like what I've done.'

Alby sat on the other side of him, and Bill and Wayne sat opposite. They understood what it meant to a man to have his peace shattered like that.

Wayne knew Jack had no choice but to fight back. And anyway, he'd be flat out docking Jim a day's pay now.

The men finished their coffee and left the kitchen. Hilda touched Jacks arm on his way out.

Chapter 5

It was Friday morning, and the men had a few jobs to do and then it was off to town. Spirits were high, excitement ran rife through the lot of them. Jack felt the excitement, he hadn't been into town in just over three weeks, it seemed a long time to him. He loved this station life and never wanted to be anywhere else now but getting into town was gunna be a blast. Everyone was in such high spirits he probably couldn't have helped being uplifted.

So, Jack walked into the mess to find Wayne sitting at the table with a hang dog expression on his face. He got some breakfast and sat across from the older man. 'How's it going Wayne? Can't wait to get my laughing gear round a beer.'

'Me neither' chimed in Pete, 'can't wait to get my hands on a woman either.'

The place was in an uproar, Jack himself let out a loud guffaw. Even Wayne joined in the laughter and insults. Bill was all excited, but Jack thought it was none of his business. Hilda and Nevil weren't going they stayed to look after the place.

It was about three hours to the town, so the crew got going around eleven o'clock. Wayne had booked single rooms at the back of the Drovers Dream pub. Jack had naively asked why all single rooms and the men laughed loudly. So, they all piled into the two four-wheel drives and set out for town.

Bill had answered Jack's question very quietly 'well there's some who might be lucky, and they will need a room to themselves. And then there's some who are just gunna get drunk and stay drunk and no one wants to sleep anywhere near them.' Everyone had laughed.

Wayne drove one vehicle and Garry the mechanic, a very quiet man, drove the other. Bill got in the front with Wayne and Eddy rode shotgun with Garry. The rest piled into the back; Jack climbed up behind Alby. It was almost second nature now for these two men to follow one another. Pete and Russel got in the other vehicle. Jack thought Russel didn't look much over twelve, but the boy claimed he was fourteen. He was an orphan they said, the blokes looked out for him.

When they were all in and sitting down the two vehicles pulled out. Hilda waved goodbye from the veranda at the mess. Nevil waited at the gate to shut it behind them. The two Hilda and Nevil never went to town. Jack had learned that they were saving to get their own hotel. Jack couldn't see how going to town would interfere much with your savings. But then Jack hadn't been to town with this lot before.

The trip was an eye opener for Jack. He thought he'd seen it all being eight years in the army, and six of them were in war time. He'd seen men wipe themselves out before with an altogether desperate need.

He walked into the pub and fronted up to the bar with them. Drinks were ordered and downed. This went on for a while. These men weren't what you'd call seasoned drinkers, but they did their best to sink as many as they could.

By teatime Jack had had enough and went off with Alby to the shops. Wayne had gone to see Margaret. Jack wondered about Wayne he looked altogether nervous. He hoped it wasn't anything serious, Jack knew all about inner turmoil.

Jack called into a couple of shops he had things he wanted to get. He needed better thicker socks, his bloody feet hurt in these boots. But everyone wore the high heeled riding boots so he would to. Eventually he would need to get on a horse, so he'd best get used to them. Horses always reminded him of Lilly, he had loved that horse. Dear, sweet, gentle natured Lilly. How it tore at his heart to think of home and Lilly.

He also called into a bookstore come news agency. He got books, he had started reading at night to quiet his mind a little. Alby waited patiently for Jack to finish his errands.

Jack was decidedly tipsy and suggested he and Albert should eat, so they had tea at a café. Jack ordered for them both, thick juicy steaks. After their meal they sat back for a while to drink the cup of tea Jack had asked for. A curiosity was growing fast in Jack and so he broached the subject of bull catching with Alby.

'So, you are pretty keen on this bull catching Alby?' Jack watched as the old familiar excitement flooded across Alby's face. Jack found he envied the man having something which caused that much of a stir in him.

'Yep, looking forward to it Jack.' Alby's face lit up as it always did as he began to talk about this most favourite subject now.

'What is it you like so much about it, Alby?' Jack sat back and watched his friend closely. This man had become very quickly someone that Jack trusted completely. He trusted the man's instincts.

'I dunno Jack. I think it's the challenge. It's definitely the excitement but it's one hell of a challenge to. And when you face that bull, you know you'll only come through alright if you maintain your concentration. He's got you on size and strength and he's fast and quick on his feet and the bastard will dance with you alright. He's got the balance, he's a beautiful animal and a hell of a fighter with stamina in spades. So, you gotta outthink him, and the rest of the world fades right away Jack. It's just you and the bull you know?'

Jack nodded but remained silent watching Alby transform.

Alby sat forward in his chair, putting his elbows on the table he went on. 'You're fighting a fight you both understand. The rules are crystal clear and understood by both of you, one of you walks away the other doesn't and everything goes.

And for those few minutes it's just you and the bull. And if you give him half a chance, he's gunna kill you. He's never wanted to be your buddy, doesn't need you, and he sure as hell don't wanna bow down to you either. And he knows he just needs you to lose your focus for an instant and he'll snap you like a twig.

It's a powerful thing Jack, nothing like it. The thrill of it trumps everything I've ever known.'

Jack found he wanted more, wanted to try it for himself. Suddenly he remembered something Alby had said when they arrived at the station, 'you said you overheard a conversation between me and Wayne on the way home Alby. May I ask....?'

'What that was? Yes mate of course you can. Now if we are gunna go bull catching together the one thing we need to take with us is complete trust in each other, and an eye for what the other is gunna do next. I think we can take that with us Jack my friend. So, my answer is yes Jack I think we should do it.

Wayne was right I do have a fair bit of money because I don't spend it. No one to spend it on. Wayne would have a bit to. You did get that didn't you Jack, that he wants in? He'll bring Bill with him. There's your wing man and your truck driver.'

Jack stared at Alby in amazement and opened his mouth to speak. He closed it again and nodded a smile appearing on his handsome features.

Alby went on softly now, 'Why do you think Wayne is looking so worried?'

Jack shook his head and kept it shut. That was something he'd learnt in the army, keeping that shut.

Alby said 'He wants in but the first few years the money might not be too great. Margaret will turf him out and get somebody else. I'd say he's probably told her by now and he's back at the pub getting blotto.'

The two men chuckled, and Jack stood up. 'Well, we'd better go see, and try and be there for him hay.'

Out in the street the two men turned and headed for the pub. Jack said 'so what would we need mate? I think a four-wheel drive and truck. So, what else Alby?'

'Yeah well, we'd need the chaser, and a wing vehicle though you could probably do that with horses. Truck would have to be big enough to put six bulls in at least but wouldn't have to be too flash, long as it was good mechanically.

Again, Wayne was right I know my way around trucks. First two years in the army I fixed them. We'd need the gear to be able to throw up quick fencing, ropes and a pole and loop to fit a rope over the bull's head. But you'll learn all this stuff when we go bull catching in a couple of weeks. And Wayne will be able to teach you everything you'll need to know. What you like at driving Jack?'

'I can drive alright Alby' Jack said softly. He was thoughtful on the way back to the pub. They walked unhurried, each man lost in his own thoughts, his own dreams. Each man so comfortable with the other they had no need to talk.

They had in fact, fought side by side for years in the hardest of battalions, in the hardest of conditions. They'd had to rely on one another with their lives and by the sound of it they would again. Alby had just succeeded in whetting Jack's appetite.

They walked into the pub and looked at the mess the blokes had made of themselves. Wayne was sitting away from them tossing down large whiskeys.

Jack guessed it had gone just the way Alby had said it would. He turned to Alby now and said, 'I might go and have a drink with the boss. You coming Alby?

Alby nodded 'I gotta piss though first mate I'll be there shortly.' He walked over to the 'Mens' door.

Jack looked up and down the bar and noticed that Bill had a woman on his arm that bore no resemblance to Hilda. Except that he judged her to be in her early forties and a bit of a looker. Drunk, but a bit of a looker. He smiled and clapped the man on the shoulder as he went passed.

'Hay Jack' Bill was slurring his words as he put his hand on Jack's arm.

'What's going on Bill, you okay old man?'

'Yeah mate' Bill almost fell off his stool and walked away a bit with Jack. 'You found yourself some company Bill?' Jack stopped; he liked Bill.

'It would seem Jack' Bill was nodding a silly grin on his face. 'Though I don't think I'll do any better than Nevil tonight' he giggled. 'You gunna have a word with Wayne?'

Jack nodded and helped Bill back on his stool.

'Good man Jack, good man. You are a good man, Jack; I have no doubt of it.'

Jack laughed and said, 'likewise my old mate, like wise.' Jack smiled at the man. Patted him on the shoulder and turned to walk away.

He had taken a few steps when he was brought about by a crashing sound and a shrill scream. He swung round to see that Bill had crashed to the floor taking his lady friend with him. She was screeching like a banshee as she got to her feet and started clocking him with the heel of her shoe.

Bill rolled over to prevent her from hitting his face and promptly started snoring. The woman made a beeline for Garry the mechanic, who immediately threw his arm around her grabbed his bottle of Johnnie walker and headed for his room.

Jack shook his head and bent down to check Bill. He found the man to be sleeping peacefully and put him in the coma position. That done he went and sat on a stool next to Wayne.

Wayne put his hand briefly on Jack's shoulder and threw back a glass of whiskey. Jack smiled at the man and said softly. 'Your style of drinking has a purpose to it Wayne. May I help you with that?' Jack ordered a pint glass of beer.

'I would consider it a favour Jack me old son' Wayne was not slurring his words; he was a man trying to get drunk with little success.

Jack put his hand out and grabbed the glass to lift his beer to his mouth when he got a shove in the back. It sent him crashing into the bar and his beer flew clear across the bar which found its mark down the front of an already unhappy barman.

Purely from instinct Jack stood on his stool on one leg and brought his elbow up and knocked the man clean out. The man as it turned out was Jim. Jack got off his stool and checked the man, he was also sleeping peacefully. Jack put him in the coma position also, a handy little trick he thought now. He'd seen an American medic come into a pub and do that once, years ago when Jack and his mates were getting drunk with some American soldiers.

Wayne stared in amazement at Jack. He had an idea those bulls out there would wanna look out for this joker. The man just never lost his cool and he was nothing if not methodical in all he did it seemed. He turned back to the bar and Jack did the same.

'Now where were we Wayne?' Jack picked up the beer the barman had just put in front of him.

Wayne started to laugh and then his face took on a serious look, 'you should probably lock your door tonight, Jack. But by Jesus.' Wayne giggled a little, 'he'd be a fuckin lunatic to try and get into your room, wouldn't he?'

Jack laughed and looked over to see Alby stop in his tracks and survey the mess. 'Jesus Jack, you been busy? Fuck, what did Bill do?'

'No, he fell on the floor to have a bit of a camp mate' replied Jack, 'he's alright Alby. And I have no doubt that Jim will fill me in on why he attacked me as soon as he wakes up. Come and have a drink with us Alby.'

'Is it safe Jack?' Alby approached the pair gingerly stepping over Bill and Jim. The barman put a drink on the bar and Alby took a swig. The three men talked for a while and Jack and Alby didn't push Wayne for anything. They knew he'd talk in his own good time.

A wailing sound came from the other end of the bar, a little like a mating cat. The three men turned and smiled; it was Pete trying to sing to a woman he'd spent the last three hours plying with liquor. Alas the liquor had worked only on him from what they could tell. Eddy who was asleep slumped across a table in the corner came to and yelled something unintelligible at him.

At last Eddy got his eyes open and promptly accused Pete of stealing his woman. He jumped up to fix Pete and, knocking the table flying he followed it to the floor. Finding himself entangled in chairs and table legs and such he gave up and went back to sleep cuddling an empty bottle. 'Fuck the lot o' yiz' was his last word on it.

The three men at the bar laughed loudly. Pete's girl looked up and stared belligerently at them. It did encourage the three of them to be quiet, but alas the man laying behind Jack on the floor was waking now.

Jim got to his feet and looked around him at the carnage. He remembered what had been done to him, well some of it. He assumed the man sitting in front of him had also been responsible for the rest. He turned his beady eyes on Jack.

Jack tried to keep his head down. But Jim, who had thought the woman drinking with Pete had been his for the taking, was in no mood for reason and had fastened on to him. He'd deal with Pete next, maybe even get his woman back if he was impressive enough.

At the last-minute Jack realised what Jim was going to do, and it was too late.

Jim rushed at Jack and brought his head back and aimed a head butt at Jack. He was right on, found his mark and brought his forehead crashing down on the back of Jack's head. Jack had turned his head just in time and Jim had knocked himself clean out again. He went to sleep almost where he had before.

The barman huffed and asked Wayne to get his men out of his bloody bar. Wayne replied casually that it was his bar, and he should clean it out. 'What exactly do you expect me to do' he asked naively? Waving his hand around he said, 'you are the one that kept serving them when they were clearly rotten drunk.'

'Get them to bed and out of my way. It's closing time.'

'Oh, get fucked it's not even ten o'clock ya mug.' Wayne bore the man no malice, but he was drinking. Wayne was drinking with little success.

The barman moved down the bar a little and sang out 'time gentlemen please.' He turned 'it is nearly twelve.'

Wayne right on the ball said, 'fuck yeah mate now you're talking. Time for another drink gentlemen. Fill em up man.'

Jack leaned across the bar and said quietly, 'if we was to get rid of these unsightly bodies would you sell us a few more beers mate,'

The barman thought about it, looked around and nodded. 'Okay but I need to start cleaning up so straighten that table up, right. And throw this mug out' he nodded at Jim. 'This young fuller at the end here can take his bloody woman and his bottle and nick off to.'

With that the woman, who'd been thrown out on other occasions, got up and grabbed the bottle and headed for Pete's room. He got up and followed the bottle. Alby took Jim to the door and shoved him out and locked it. Jack took Bill to his room and rolled him onto his bed and closed the door. He returned and righted the table and chairs.

Wayne dragged Eddy to his room and stuck him on his bed. And as promised when they got back to the bar there were three beers on it. The men settled down to a nice quiet drink.

On his way to bed that night Jack walked out onto the front veranda and checked on Jim. He knelt and checked he was breathing and rolled him on his side. In the coma position. Jim stirred but didn't waken. Jack bore the man no malice, he didn't like him, but he bore him no ill will.

He crept into Bill's room and turned him over. Bill was very drunk. Jack smiled as he walked to Bills door and turned the light off. 'Thanks buddy' he heard in the dark. Jack felt better knowing the man was in command of some of his wits.

Next, he went into Eddy's room, the man was on his side snoring softly. Jack was satisfied and went to get into his own bed. He went out into the yard to the gents first and entered the hotel by the back door. There was a hallway and their rooms all led off that. It was dimly lit, just enough to see where you were stepping. He closed the back door and turned around.

In the darkness a smell assailed him. It was a mixture of alcohol and a very strong and overpowering perfume. The worst he'd ever smelt, and he'd had to venture into brothels all over Europe and the middle east to retrieve his mates.

It was accompanied by stale whiskey. He guessed it was probably Pete's lady friend.

Jack was wrong it was Garry's lady friend. She tried to walk seductively towards him, glancing up coyly at him in the gloom. He was sure she was unable to focus and wondered if he could've been just anybody. Nope.

'Jack' she breathed as she came. Jack had an almost uncontrollable desire to laugh but tried not to. She tripped over her foot and fell into his arms. 'Oh Jack, you do care, you do care for me. You feel it to don't you Jack?' She traced his face with her fingertip, 'Oh I knew it, Jack.'

Jack dragged her to the back door. 'Yes', he breathed, 'I cannot deny it. But you wait in the back yard I don't want Garry to see us. I'd hate to hurt him. Have you seen him fight?' Jack slipped his arms around her and pulled her roughly against him.

She moaned loudly 'take me Jack'.

Jack opened the door and tried to push her through it. God, why me he asked himself now? She had her hands all over him. Jack tried to keep them away from his crutch, but she was quick. For somebody so drunk she was very quick. He almost had her through the door and in the back yard.

'What are you doing Jack?'

'I don't want to ruin your beautiful dress. I'll just go and get a blanket and a pillow. Go on now.' Jack went to turn away and was brought abruptly around to look at her, the gentleman in him coming to the fore. He hissed urgently, 'no…. no don't take that off. Wait until I get back. No…. you leave it on just wait.'

When she was out the door Jack closed the door and locked it and heaved a great sigh. Shit, he thought, the woman would've eaten him alive. He turned just in time to see Garry come out of the darkness and lunge at him. 'You dirty bastard Jack…. I'll fuckin….'

Jack opened the door and Garry stumbled right on through it. 'She's just there Garry. You look after her mate.' Jack slammed the door.

Jack got into his bed his door firmly locked with a chair in front of it as well. He lay in the dark in the safety of his room and started to laugh. He hoped that Garry would have forgotten the whole thing in the morning. Jack wasn't sure if Garry would be serious about her or not. Bloody hard to tell with a bloke like Garry. Surely not he told himself as he turned over.

Wayne heard it all from his bed and smiled. He pulled his blanket up over his head and stayed put. Jack could handle himself he thought.

Jack lay in the dark, he wondered what Dan would make of it. Dan thought himself to be a man of the world, but Jack wasn't sure how many, the like of these girls, were in his past. Jack was just no good at dealing with nice woman let alone drunken ones.

Jack hoped fervently that the lady in question would be forgotten it all by morning. Oh Jesus he thought, but he hoped that Garry would have gone out there and taken one for the team. Jack smiled in the darkness; he should have thrown a blanket out there.

After a time, he heard them stagger past his room and go into Garry's room. Jack closed his eyes and drifted off to sleep. 'Take me Garry' he heard. Jack smiled in the darkness and went to sleep.

Chapter 6

Jack was amazed that at six am on Monday morning everyone was in the vehicles and ready to head home to work. These men had drank solidly from the time they opened their eyes, stopping only to sleep when they passed out. For three days and three nights.

Jack had to admit to himself he was glad it was over and so was Alby he knew. He'd seen the strain on his face. Wayne looked a little happier to be going and so did Bill. Most of the others just looked pathetic. Jack understood Nevil and Hilda staying at home, it was no place for a woman.

Russel had a mate in the Mount and had gone to stay with them. He was too young to drink anyway. He came back and sat in the back with Jack and Alby, sensing they weren't as sick as the others.

Jack looked at the young man, 'so what did you get up to young Russ' he asked softly?

Russel grinned and lowered his head. 'I have a girlfriend' he said proudly, his chest puffing just a little.

Jack smiled now, 'you don't say mate. I'm glad somebody had a somewhat productive visit to town mate.'

Alby smiled and nodded to the boy. 'You love her son?' Russel looked at Alby a light in his eyes and Alby grinned at Jack. 'Lucky little bastard.'

Russel laughed and said 'her name is Sandra and she's seventeen. Boy, did she show me what's what.' He dropped his head a faraway look on his face.

Jack and Alby sighed inwardly. They remembered that look, it had once been theirs. Alby took a cigarette from his pocket and getting down on the floor out of the wind he lit it. He sucked the soothing smoke back into his lungs, he'd be glad to get home. Alby was considering not taking any more trips into town, Unbeknownst to Alby, Jack was thinking the same thing. They'd babysat the whole weekend!

Jack looked up and sang out to the driver's window. 'Bill…. Bill!' He jumped forward, reached through the driver's window and smacked Bill in the ear.

They had left the road and were now sailing through the scrub. Wayne up the front stopped and felt his innards turn to water as he watched the Land rover bump crazily to a stop in a cloud of dust.

He reversed up and jumped out of the car and ran to the men. Jack had caught a tree branch in the face, he had an ugly welt growing, but he was alright. 'Are you okay' asked Wayne now and the men in the back said they were.

He breathed a sigh of relief, but his temper flared. 'What the hell Bill, and you Garry? Did yiz both go to bloody sleep? Fuck! So, get in the back maybe that'll keep you awake. Jack, Alby you two get in the front and one of yiz drive for Christ's sake.'

Bill got out and smiled at Jack, 'sorry boss' he said to Wayne and got in the back. He stretched out and fell asleep. Garry did the same. Jack got in the driver's seat and started the motor. They were stuck in some dirt, but he engaged four-wheel low ratio and got up on the highway.

Jack had lost his hat to a tree branch, but Russel ran back and got it. He liked Jack and Alby. He liked Bill to; Bill shouldn't have been put in the driver's seat even he could see that.

He jumped up in the back feeling a little safer with Jack at the wheel. He felt very safe with Jack there was something about the man. He inspired confidence in him, and people relaxed around him. Him and Alby. Russel saw at once how good these two blokes were for each other. The youngster had taken these two blokes on as his role models. He wanted to be like them, calm and cool, they never let much ruffle them. They were solid.

Jack drove through the homestead gate and stopped as Russel got out to shut it. He looked at Alby and smiled, the man had been a little on the quiet side since the episode. The only comment he made concerning Jacks driving mirrored Russel's thoughts. 'Blind Freddy could see Bill wasn't fit to be behind the wheel.'

Jack said now, 'Home Alby. Thank Christ. Still, I did enjoy some of the trip and that's something hay?'

Alby nodded and grinned back. 'Yeah, I guess we got a few laughs, and it does make you appreciate home. By Jesus it does. And that Jack, is something else, I'd say.'

The men got out and went off to get ready to go to the mess for lunch at twelve thirty sharp. It was only eleven thirty, but Wayne told them to get ready and get fed. 'There's work to be done for anybody who thinks to.'

'Me and Jack'll be there Wayne. We'll drag Bill along and Russel will probably come to. See you here at lunch hay?'

Wayne nodded; he kept being knocked over by the difference in this man Alby since Jack had come to stay. Wayne smiled and nodded and walked away. The thought that struck him now, were the changes the man had brought about in himself. With his ready grin and his kind heart. He inspired people to do their best, be their best.

Wayne wondered now at the man called Dan. The man who had been Jack's role model. And that was after swiping his bloody girlfriend. Hell's Bells! I'd like to meet that man he thought now on a smile. Of course, Wayne realised there were two sides to any story. Even his.

Wayne sighed deeply now; well, he'd done his dash with Margaret. He was getting a bit of a refresher course on how these two men felt. Wayne was amazed to discover he was still missing his first love. His Goddess Rhonda, his first and last love. And that was almost thirty years ago. Jesus did it never end? Well, he'd throw in with Jack and Alby and go catching bulls, he'd be their truck driver or maybe wing man. One thing was sure Bill wasn't getting behind the wheel again any time soon. He smiled to himself again. He'd forgive the man and he knew it. The blokes who'd been up in the back of that vehicle already had.

Wayne went back to the mess the radio was depressingly quiet. To hell with the bitch, he told himself, he was better off, wasn't he? And as soon as he stopped hurting, he'd realise that the woman might have backed him up. But there you were, she hadn't.

Well, he'd get on with his life, if Alby and Jack could then so could he. He smiled at the laughter and teasing coming from the mess.

Wayne got a plate and sat down. He looked about at the men at the table. These would be the only men working today. There was Jack, Alby, Russel and surprisingly Bill. Wayne smiled now and looked at them in turn.

He spoke quietly his eyes on his plate, 'Thanks for showing up lads. There's nothing too pressing on today. Why don't you lot take the rest of the day off. Unlike the others you four will get paid for the half day.'

'Thanks, boss' said Bill looking a bit sheepish. He opened his mouth.

Shaking his head, Wayne said, 'I just fuckin hope you aren't going to apologise again Bill. You do and you can spend the rest of the day going over the Land Rover for damage and you can go wake fuckin Garry up to help you.'

Bill closed his mouth and started eating. Bill knew better than anyone that his drinking was getting out of hand. Unbeknownst to any of them here he had also fought in the first world war. And unbeknownst to Bill, Wayne was very much aware of it.

Wayne smiled at Bill across the table and Bill felt a gratitude for the man and with it a loyalty he hadn't felt in years. Not for anyone. And now Jack as well! He told himself in all seriousness that he needed to straighten himself out. He tucked into his meal, he needed to sleep it off first.

When lunch was done Jack hurried back to his room to unpack, he had bought three new books in town. And he had all afternoon to start reading them. He got his things put away and some things in the wash, which had got a quick wash when he got home, hung on the line. He rolled his swag out on the bed and grabbed a book and lay down with it.

His mind went briefly back to a meeting he'd had with Jim out the back of the pub before they left town. Jack had braced himself for a fight, but Jim had spread his hands and shook his head.

He'd said softly, 'I'm sorry Jack. No hard feelings, I hope. I'd like to part mates and for what it's worth I give you my word I won't bring trouble to you again. You never did me any harm Jack, and even after I attacked you a few times you cared enough to make sure I was alright.' Jim looked down to his side now, 'you know when I was out to it. Thanks.'

Jim took a step forward and offered his hand. Jack stayed alert as he took the man's hand and shook it. He said 'no mate, no hard feelings. Maybe next time we meet we might have a drink together hay.'

Jim stood scrutinising the man for a moment and smiled faintly. 'Yeah Jack, I'd like that. Be seeing ya Jack.'

Jack looked back at his book, he smiled at how life turned out sometimes. You'd lose a few but you'd win a few to. He opened his new book; he loved a new book. Loved it. It wasn't long however before Jack nodded off to the sound of Alby snoring in the next room.

In fact, the whole camp was sleeping peacefully. Even Wayne slept and surprisingly when he danced, he danced with Rhonda. He held her to him letting the joy of it wash over him. And in his dream, he turned to her and asked her why she was here.

She smiled at him, kissed him tenderly on the lips, 'because you asked me silly.'

Wayne roused out of his sleep for an instant, a smile on his face. He made up his mind he'd write to her. Damn it she was his woman; she'd been his before she was anyone else's. He had every damn right to.

At teatime the men were turned out showered and shaved and, in their work, clobber, all clean and ready for tomorrow. They sat and talked as if the weekend had never happened. They might have all dreamed it, and none of the talk was about any of it.

Jack smiled to himself and soon found himself in a conversation with Bill, he liked talking to Bill. Liked the stamp of the man. Jack had watched the man closely and realised with a jolt the man had military in his background, maybe had even seen combat. His actions, habits, the way he flinched a little at a loud sound. It was in his personal stature and just the way he carried himself and conducted himself.

Jack, looking across the table at him realised now with a start that, given his age, he was probably in the big one. And then there was the way Wayne favoured him and never stayed mad at him for long. Like today. Jack wouldn't mention it.

Alby was tired still and hardly talked at all. Jack wanted to get back to his book, he'd light his lantern for a while. Jack had also bought a notebook, envelopes, and pencil. He'd write home soon; he had a few stamps, and he could send mail out every fortnight when the cart came. Funny he thought now, how he'd always thought of the Murrumbidgee as home. Mary's place. He sighed; home was where the heart is he guessed. He got up from the table his food had turned to sawdust suddenly anyway.

'Here hang on a minute Jack, would you?' Wayne cleared his throat and Jack sat down realising the man had something to say to them all. Wayne smiled around the table. 'Tomorrow lads, I suggest we get old Betsy out and see how she goes and knock the bloody dust off her. We'll need to spend some time on her.'

It was bedlam. 'Yeah bull catching time again!' Was the theme. Some of the boys were on their feet throwing punches at the air. Alby stamped his feet and gave out a great 'Yeeha.'

Jack had no need to ask who Betsy was, and Jack had no way of knowing how his eyes shone. At last, he thought, a step closer to bull time. He was probably the most enthusiastic man of them all though the quietest. A fact not lost on Wayne. A quiet achiever he mused, bloody good.

He stood up now, empty plate in hand and said, 'Until tomorrow gentlemen.' He left with a satisfied smile on his face. As he walked away, he turned back and made another announcement. 'I have a letter to write which is way overdue.' He smiled across at Jack and turned away from the table.

Jack had seen the twinkle in his eye and wondered as to its origins. He stared at the table a smile in his heart, if he didn't know better.....

Jack got up and took his plate and mug out and said goodnight to all. All but Alby, he was right behind Jack. Didn't look so tired now.

A roar went up at nine o'clock the next morning when Betsy finally fired up.

Jack had never seen or heard anything like it. It had been made like a Sherman tank and twice as loud. There were gadgets all over it and a bull bar with no equal anywhere, he was sure.

She had iron plates and bars all up and down. No roof, no windscreen, and no doors. Wayne drove it out of the shed into the sun light grinning from ear to ear. It was an old, long wheelbase rover but no longer bore much of a resemblance to one.

He climbed out and grinned widely at Jack 'git in' he said indicating the seat he'd just vacated with his thumb. Jack was taken aback and stood for a moment as Wayne went round the other side and got in the roper's seat. 'Well come on man, let's go hay.'

Jack got in the seat his stomach alive with butterflies. He sat behind the wheel, and they all disappeared. Jack knew a calm just like the moments before battle and Wayne saw it. So did Bill standing beside him while Alby thanked God inside his head for the light in Jack's eyes.

Jack knew land rovers and turning the key he hit the starter button and had it started up again in less than a minute. He gave the accelerator a few pumps and with eyes shining bright and a smile of anticipation Jack slipped her into gear. He cruised to the corner in the road leading either out the gate or round the station yard. Around the corner he straightened her up and tramped his foot. They could hear the roar from the blokes over the sound of the thing.

The open gate was calling to Jack, and he knew it called just as loudly to the man beside him. Jack was off, both men grinning from ear to ear. Through the gate they sailed, Jack couldn't believe the speed of the big heavy vehicle. Safe as houses he thought, she's steady and, she's sure. What a piece of work!

About a few hundred yards from the gate Wayne sang out 'go on son head bush. Come on lad.' Wayne was impressed, and he told himself so. 'Come on Jack give her some fritz; see how many trees you can miss. She'll take down anything gets in your way. Just hang on mate.'

Jack was used to driving like a maniac through jungle and desert and had never lost a vehicle yet. He didn't slow at all as he left the road, they bounced over the shoulder and onto the open countryside raising dust as they went, and he planted his foot.

About a quarter mile in, a feral bull came out of nowhere as if sent by God himself. 'Chase him Jack' Wayne was yelling excitedly. 'Come on son chase the blighter down. Keep up with him Jack, keep him close as you can as long as you can.'

Jack knew he could do it; he'd had plenty of practice, a good eye, and a natural feel for the vehicle and what she could do. He was flying and the bull was right in front hurtling through the scrub. Jack kept him to the right. In no time he had the front right fender sitting right on the beast's rump.

Every time the beast tried to duck away Jack adjusted speed and direction and had him again on the right fender in a few seconds. On through the scrub they weaved, the bull and Jack and Wayne.

Wayne, sitting beside him also knew he was as safe as houses, but he hung on for dear life, knuckles white. There were no doors on the vehicle and Wayne didn't fancy getting thrown out and take his chances with a very angry bull. So, Wayne, though he had complete trust in the man next to him, hung on for dear life.

Jack missed every tree and never let the bull get away more than about a hundred feet. He was exhilarated, it was wild, and it was free. Along with the great excitement and the adrenalin rush, a strange peace settled on Jack. His head was as clear as a bell, his focus unshakeable.

The excitement and the adrenalin rush Jack got had no equal. It frightened him a little, but he loved it. And he found he wasn't a bit frightened of the beast or the rover or himself, had no doubts in himself. In these minutes in this situation, he knew he was equal to the task. He got the feeling he could take this on with an ease, an excitement, and a love that he'd never felt before.

Jack stayed with the bull for a few minutes, and it began to slow up. Wayne shouted 'okay son just pull away now he's had enough for today. Don't want to harm him.'

Jack slowed up and pulled away to the left and brought the rover to a standstill. He sat watching the bull hurry away. Jack sat breathing steadily a smile on his face.

'No real need to say anything Jack' said Wayne as he looked at Jack in awe. 'You are a bloody natural. I've never seen anything like that. Where'd you learn to drive like that.'

Jack watched the bull disappear into the scrub 'New Guinea probably' he said quietly.

Wayne sat watching the bull to now. 'What reflexes Jack and split-second timing. And you really wanted to catch that beast, didn't you? You wanted to get out put a lead on him and take him home.' Wayne was laughing.

Jack knew in his heart Wayne was right and he was actually proud of himself.

He also knew that he would embrace this life, make this his home. These blokes, for better or for worse were his family now. They had taken him in, had accepted him the same way.

As for catching bulls, well he'd had a little taste of chasing them and it was with great anticipation that he looked towards the future. The trepidation he woke with in the mornings would now be changed forever. Mary would forever be the love of his life, but this… ? Well, this would replace what he couldn't have.

And Alby? Well thank God for Alby.

Jack smiled at Wayne, slipped the rover into gear, and turned for home. Home!

Chapter 7

That night Jack picked up his book, but he couldn't read it. He picked up the pencil and wrote 'Dear Dan,' in his notebook. Jack gave that up to and lay down on his bed to go over the day in his mind.

He had some saving to do. He had felt nothing to equal that chase today, nothing at all. He grinned to himself, how he had loved that chase. What, he asked himself now, would it have been like to have gone on and caught the bull? To actually watch Alby, tie that thing to a tree. A few hundred pounds worth of bull. A bull weighing in at a couple of thousand pound. The danger of it, the excitement of it!

It had got around today what a chase he had put up, Bill had come up to him after listening to Wayne, smiled, and said, 'you're a mad bastard Jack.' He'd shaken hands with Jack and said softly, 'you'll do son. You'll do nicely I think.' With that he'd walked away, and Jack saw that he and Wayne looked at one another and grinned.

Jack looked up now into the smiling face of Alby. The big man said proudly, 'you did a bloody good job today mate from all accounts. Wayne don't impress easily. You chase em down and I'll tie em up, if that is to your liking mate. Wayne reckons you're the best he ever seen.'

'Wayne said the same about you Alby.' Jack smiled up at his big friend and said, 'it was like nothing I've ever felt, that today, Alby.

Thanks mate, thanks for being here and bringing me to this. I bloody owe you.' Jack took a deep breath and shaking his head now he went on, 'now I know why you love it Alby. We got some saving to do mate.'

Alby smiled at Jack and lifted his hand in salute, 'good night, Jack. I owe you to mate.'

When Jack met Mary in the space that night, he smiled at her and took her in his arms, held her tight and kissed her most passionately. 'Oh Mary, it was almost as exciting as the day I met you' he whispered. His imaginary conversation in the dark there with his sweetheart, ended on a sob and a sigh as was usual.

Jack was suddenly wide awake. A certain glimmer of hope had showed itself to Jack though. A hope that one day he would get over Mary and live as any other normal man. Maybe even find someone he could share his life with. Yes, he told himself, he'd hang on to that. He needed to get stronger.

While some of the blokes got to work on Betsy the next day Jack and Bill with Russel and Eddy went out to look about the station for any signs of where the feral bulls might be. They took two vehicles and went different ways to try and cover half of the station.

Bill took Eddy and Jack took Russel. Jack liked the young bloke and found him to be sensible and very interested in bulls. Much like everyone was, and now Jack had been bitten by the bug.

He had found himself thinking more and more about the idea of bull catching lately. Jack thought that doing this for a living would be a wonderful thing. To work with his friends and they could be their own boss so to speak. Not that Wayne wasn't a good boss, he was one of the best. But Jack had had some corkers. The army had cured him of wanting to be controlled or even accepting it.

It was close to lunch time when Jack and Russel sighted the herd of feral bulls grazing peacefully in a gully near a creek. Jack felt a compulsion to chase them and an excitement in his belly and wondered if you ever got over it. If you ever got used to this. He didn't think so. Not going by the excitement which had gone through the place like a tornado.

The herd was about twenty strong a nice little pay dirt if he was working for himself. Almost ten thousand pounds for sure thought Jack. The excitement just grew bigger and stronger. The money added a dynamic which Jack hadn't yet considered. He had a lot to learn.

He'd done his job, so he made a note of where they were and headed back towards the homestead. Jack skirted the herd not wanting to hurry them away. There was plenty of feed here and water to so, left alone they'd probably stay here for weeks. It never occurred to Jack to wonder how he knew this already about cattle.

He said this softly now to Russel and the boy grinned at him. Jack was fast becoming his hero. Jack turned to the lad and saw it in his face. He was humbled by it; he was about this age when he'd been rescued by Dan. And he had hero worshipped that man at once and ever since. He had loved Dan as a brother but also as a father, he had been all things to Jack. After his father died, he'd had no one.

They met back up with Bill and Eddy at the gate to the number four bore and pulled up. Jack got out and walked towards Bill who was putting a new pin in a trough float. He hailed Jack and told him to come look.

'This often happens. We didn't strike one the other day on the run yet it's the biggest problem with these bloody set ups. Old archaic fuckin shit. You don't have this problem with the new ones.' Bill drew a deep breath and went on, 'but your water will run out without it.'

Bill showed Jack how to spot it and fix it. 'Thanks Bill' Jack said. 'Did you find anything?'

Bill shook his head 'and you?'

'Yeah, nice little herd must be about twenty bulls. Out by the creek crossing near our first night's camp. They're in a gully there out of the weather. Plenty of shade.'

Bill looked at Eddy who grinned back at him and said softly, 'yeah well that's why I had the tracker with me see. So, I could come in with nothing.' The men all laughed good naturedly. It was the very thing Jack liked about these men they may take offence at some things that were said sometimes but their mate ship was first and foremost.

He liked their ability to laugh not only at each other but also at themselves.

And yet when you needed it, they could be sympathetic or they could be critical, but they were what you needed when you needed it.

'We didn't disturb them' put in Russel excitedly. 'Jack says there's plenty of feed and water there so hopefully they'll not stray too far away.'

Russel's hero worship for his idol was obvious to Bill who smiled kindly at him. 'And Jack is quite right young Russ.'

'Well, we might have some lunch,' said Jack. 'You two want to join us? I can get a fire going and put the billy on if ya like.'

'Okay' said Bill, 'that looks like a nice spot' he said indicating the patch of shade under a big old tree with branches hanging almost to the ground. 'I'll just go get the jeep and bring her up and we'll get a bight to eat hay?'

He looked at Eddy who grinned as only Eddy could. Eddy amazed Bill, the amount of tucker the little bloke could put away. Bill walked off towards the jeep with his bag of tools in his hand and Eddy beside him.

Sitting under the big tree, two big beefy sandwiches under his belt and a mug of black, sweet tea in his hand Jack marvelled at the peace he felt. Pretty much every day he was at peace. He was at home. His peace grew with each passing day as did the love that grew in his heart for this place. For this place and the people in it.

He was even getting along better with Mary. He loved her all night, his heart beating nice and steady. Then he released her just a little easier in the wee hours. He had things to look forward to now.

A cool breeze blew across Jack's face cooling the sweat and bringing with it the gentle smell of the Australian bush, the hint of eucalypt a most comforting thing. Birds sang in the tree top and somewhere farther off a crow cawed his lazy, mournful note to the day. Yeah, Mary would love this. He had just remembered Mary without pain.

Jack stood up at last and made to clear away the mess and gather up the mugs and the calico bags. He just realised his boots had stopped hurting his feet. He vowed he'd wear these things all the time now, he'd wear them every day. He never wanted to go through that again.

❋

Back at the homestead it was a hive of activity. Garry and Wayne worked on Betsy, they had tools and grease pots and oil everywhere. As soon as he got back Bill was set on to do some welding.

Eddy was sent to start checking equipment. The ropes and poles, and then to sort the rope into neat piles. Eddy knew how to line it up so they could start applying it to the vehicles in the right order. Everything in its place. Couldn't have Alby trying to tie a bull to a tree without a decent rope.

Jack spied Alby working on a big mammoth of a truck. It was an incredible thing. It was reinforced on all sides with steel, and it had a massive steel chute which lowered down to the ground to allow them to lift the bull up in the truck. Once the bull was in the chute it was raised again and closed behind the bull. A revolving door for bulls no less.

The bull's head was then secured with rope, to the bars over the top in much the same way as it would be secured to a tree. The bull was encouraged to get in the chute by a rope passed through the truck, one end around the bull the other secured to a horse on the other side. The horse then gently pulled on the bull's horns, and he walked, somewhat reluctantly up on to the truck. Care was always taken not to hurt the huge beasts or to stress them out unduly.

Jack had thought he'd seen heavy duty trucks in the army but this thing. Jack looked closer; it was in fact an old army truck. It was no longer kaki but was mostly a black colour. But it was an old six-wheel drive blitz alright. She'd cart the big bulls and go just about anywhere with them.

Jack walked around it; the thing had been almost completely rebuilt, the shell anyway. The back had been lowered and the roof was missing, and it had no doors. Jack felt the excitement in the pit of his belly. Everything about this business was going to be hard. These bulls were a phenomenon to be reckoned with.

'She'll cart six bulls easily' Alby had told him the night before. Now he could see it, Jack knew what these vehicles could do, he'd driven them during the war. This one had the doors and roof missing as did most of them but there was a canopy on a light frame that you could sling over the cabin area. Another canopy on a frame covered the bulls to protect them from the hot sun.

Alby looked up and smiled, 'just the man I wanted to see. Can you give me a hand with this bloody tail shaft Jack. It's a heavy bastard of a thing.' He looked at Jack, 'it's making a bit of noise so it's better to change it out now than halfway through the season. If it goes when there's half a dozen bulls in the truck we have to let em go.'

'Sure' said Jack in his easy-going fashion. Hearing a bang from the direction of the mess hall he looked over to see Nevil was throwing all sorts of camping equipment out onto the veranda. He had tea chests full of pots, pans, and all manner of tin mugs and plates etc.

Jack smiled this was an exciting time. How was he going to wait to get out there in the bush amongst it?

By teatime there was a mess all over the place. But the men were tired, and they were hungry, and they were happy. They sat round all cleaned up as Hilda insisted with empty bellies and full plates. Hilda had been known to throw someone out for showing up at meals dirty and smelly.

Wayne spent his days hovering over the works going on and secretly reckoning up everything that was his and how much of the plant they would need, and what he would be able to get here for little money. If the station was no longer doing their own bull catching how much of this gear would be surplus? Wayne was always looking to save money where they could.

Nevil was gradually going through all his cutlery items in the kitchen and driving the long-suffering Hilda mad. There was a hell of a racket going on in there tonight with Hilda being very vocal. Almost shrill thought Jack now, not like her at all. Jack worried about that situation, he thought it was a powder keg and Nevil had the matches.

Jack turned to look at Bill who sat and listened to it with a face completely devoid of expression which was pretty unusual for him. 'You okay Bill' asked Jack?

Bill shrugged and shook his head slightly. He leaned in and said softly, 'Nevil has regained his sight in both bloody eyes Jack.' Bill nodded at Jack, 'yep 20/20 no less.'

'Shit' said Jack and touched Bill briefly on the shoulder. Someone came and sat at the table, so Jack knew the conversation was over. It wasn't as if everybody didn't know it was just that they pretended to not know. Everyone liked Bill and they also liked Hilda.

He sat and ate his tea in silence. That's four of us thought Jack glumly, me Alby Wayne and now Bill. Hell of a thing.

Jack was cheered a little by the thought of writing to Dan and Mary, but he was also nervous about it. What would he say and how would he start? He also worried if it would bring up more pain, stir up feelings and all. Maybe blow the lid of the proverbial can of worms. Who knew?

Jack shrugged it off, it would come to him. He'd sit down and it would come to him. He would rely on faith alone. Faith and the man at the other end who loved him. Jack knew there wasn't much that Dan would not forgive him for. And Jack knew for sure that the feeling was mutual.

Chapter 8

Jack was tired as he got up from the table to take his plate and cup to the sink. He looked at Hilda and found himself worrying about her. She looked tired, worn out.

'How are you, Hilda?'

'I'm okay Jack thanks. You know you are the only one around here who always asks me that. Thanks Jack, for caring. I am okay.'

She smiled sadly at him and unable to help himself he smiled knowingly back. 'Did you enjoy your bit of peace while we were gone Hilda?'

'No Jack. I did not. It was too quiet and it's not like Nevil and I had a civil word for each other.' Hilda turned away, she'd said too much, and she knew it.

Jack reached out took her hand and turned her to face him. He said softly, 'I'm sorry Hilda I take liberties and I know it but… He doesn't hurt you does he Hilda? I would take exception to that, girl.'

Hilda smiled happily but before she turned away again a tear ran down her cheek. Jack stood behind her, 'Hilda?'

She leaned on the sink 'no Jack. Now please just leave it, I can't talk just now.' She turned to face him and looking him in the eye she said, 'if I need you Jack, I will send for you. I promise.' With that she fell into his arms and hugged him.

She disengaged herself and said softly, 'I'm glad you are here Jack, so glad. Now go and get some sleep.'

Jack smiled as he turned to go, but the smile didn't hide the concern in his dark blue eyes.

❀

When Jack got back to his room that night, he decided that he couldn't face writing a letter to Dan. It was just too daunting, and he didn't have a clue what he would say. But he had to do something it was only right. And maybe then he would be able to get on with this new life. He decided to write a brief note. He would offer a minimal explanation and ask for no understanding and no forgiveness. He did hope deep in his heart that he wouldn't have to.

He sat down and opening the notebook he took up his new fountain pen which Dan had given him as a birthday gift on one of his leaves. He dipped it in the ink and slowly drew the black liquid up into the pen, breathing life into it. He was ready to write, to compose the most important note of his life.

20/4/52

Dear Dan and Mary,

    I am sorry for the way I left you and I hope you can forgive me. I must tell you now that it broke my heart to leave you. All of you, but I was falling apart, but I think you knew Dan.

    I am working as a ringer on a station up here on the Queensland/Northern Territory border. I am situated on a place called Mable Downs in the Barkly Tableland just shy of the Gulf of Carpentaria. You can write to me at; Mable Downs, C/O Post Office Camooweal, QLD. If you can see your way clear. And I will understand Dan if you can't.

    I remember one of our talks Dan, I was feeling pretty low, and you told me to follow my heart. I did that. Thank you, Dan, from the bottom of my heart. I have found peace and contentment up here in this wild and beautiful place. I will make the journey home some day and see you all again.

I will write again soon; we are busy here just now. We are preparing for the bull catching season and I am most excited about it. I feel as though I have had new life breathed into me. I am among friends. Please don't worry about me old man, we will meet again soon. I promise. Dan, please give my love to all and Mary and the kids.

I remain Yours faithfully,
Jack

It was done. Dan blew the ink to dry it, a tear rolled unbidden down his cheek. He got an envelope and addressed it to Mr. and Mrs D. Roberts. He folded the note and slipped it into the envelope sealing it down. His heart was sore, how much more of this could he take he wondered? How bloody long could he keep this up?

He sat back in his chair now drawing air deep into his lungs. 'As long as it takes' he told himself and went to his bed. He didn't feel much like reading or talking to Mary or anything else. He turned his light out and cried himself to sleep.

In the next room Alby's heart broke for his friend. His woman had died loving him. A small mercy but a mercy all the same

When Jack was leaving his room the next morning to go to breakfast, he stuck a stamp on the envelope and slipped the letter into his pocket. He would be gone by the time the mail cart came but Hilda told him to leave it in the outgoing mail on the wall in the kitchen and it would go with the rest. 'In a sealed bag' she had nodded and smiled at Jack.

He sighed and walked out the door and found Alby waiting for him at the corner. He was slouching against the building smoking and straightened up and walked quietly with Jack to the mess.

Jack walked beside the big man and said simply, 'thanks Alby.'

Alby's big hand came down on Jack's shoulder, but he didn't speak. He smiled at Jack and stayed beside him. He threw his cigarette on the ground and stepped on it as they went.

At the mess hall Jack wanted to get the letter out of his pocket and out of his possession as soon as he could. He walked to the kitchen taking it from his pocket. He passed Wayne, letter in hand at the door. Wayne was coming out and smiled knowingly at Jack. Jack said, 'good morning, Wayne' and entered the kitchen. Wayne responded in like and carried on out. He seemed to be in a very good mood.

He heard Wayne talk to Alby at the self-serve counter in the mess. He also heard Hilda laugh at something at the back door. Jack stepped up to the pigeonhole for outgoing mail. The letter on the top, in Wayne's handwriting was addressed to a Rhonda Beasley. Well, well thought Jack a smile playing around his lips. Seems he didn't know better.

Out in the dining hall he grabbed a plate of food and sat down at the table between Alby and Bill. He'd got his usual, some bacon two eggs a fried tomato and two sausages. He had two slices of toast to go with it. He found he got very hungry up here.

'The air' Nevil had told him in a very knowledgeable tone. Nevil was a very serious type and Jack wondered how he had got together with the very vivacious Hilda. Jack looked at Bill who seemed to be intent only on his food.

'You blokes all know what you're doing today' asked Wayne? Everyone nodded as Wayne spoke now to Jack, 'you mind helping Alby today, Jack? Gets pretty bloody heavy some of that work.'

'Be glad to Wayne.'

'Good man. How are you faring with those bloody ropes Eddy? I dunno how you do it.' He picked his coffee up and took a long swig. 'Make a note of any ropes that need replacing.'

Eddy nodded, managed not to roll his eyes, and said, 'no worries.'

'Well pay particular attention to any ropes involved in Alby tying bulls up, right? We can't have Alby trying to tie a bull to a tree with a three-foot rope.' Wayne grinned at the young stockman now. 'I know you know what you're doing, but they are most important. They are vital Eddy. The ropes for the catcher vehicle are most vital.' Eddy grinned and nodded. Wayne looked at Bill and Garry now, 'and we must get

Lizzy started as soon as we can lads. I'd like to be out there in a week. And we lads, are draggin our feet.'

Jack listened intently to Wayne. He seemed all business as usual but there was something making him edgy. Jack thought he might know what that could be. If Wayne had done what Jack thought he had done, then he had Jacks undying respect, even admiration. Yes indeed. And Jack acknowledged that Wayne would have reason to be a bit on edge.

Over the next few days, the mess and the chaos took on some semblance of order. A very specific order in fact. Jack was amazed and at Wayne's instructions he was left to move about the yard helping wherever he could and hopefully learn something. Jack asked questions, all the men were instructed to fill him in and get him up to speed.

The truck was like a new one and Jack told Alby he had done a job second to none. 'Not even engineers Alby.' Alby grinned delighted at the praise from the man he admired so much. Jack was amazed at Alby's ability. He never would have guessed, Wayne was right.

Wayne and Garry had Betsy already to go and as Jack stood admiring the work, they had done Garry went off to get Lizzy. 'The wing vehicle' said Wayne with a smile.

Jack heard it before he saw it. It sounded a little like Betsy but a little higher on the revs. When it flew around the corner into view Jack stepped back. It was an old, short wheelbase, Willys jeep, a grand old lady from the pages of history.

She still had all her doors and the roof, but all reinforced with light steel. It was sporting a bull bar every bit as good as Betsy and big thick tyres. And for effect Garry pulled her up right beside Betsy. Garry had a flare for the dramatic thought Jack with a wide grin.

He opened the door and smiled widely at Jack. 'This is Lizzy', he said proudly. 'Wayne always drives her. She will help you to control those dopey bloody bulls, Jack.'

Jack felt a lump in his throat. He walked up to her and rested his hand on the bonnet. He had driven one of these through the deserts of Tobruk. Garry found he understood what was in the man's heart. He also found that it meant a great deal to him that Jack was so moved. Lizzy had always been Garry's favourite of the vehicles with her flared mud guards and wide tyres. She had speed and manoeuvrability, but she also had grunt. She had everything.

Wayne stood back watching Jack's reaction over the top of his glasses while pretending to clean a fuel pump bowl. A plan had struck Wayne. Why didn't he offer the owner to clear these feral bulls from his land and pay him for the privilege. Then he would offer to buy the truck whose name was Beasty, and Betsy, and Lizzy. Wayne knew how well these vehicles were maintained, and he knew they'd be around for years yet. Especially with Alby, Jack and Bill and himself, looking after them.

Wayne got back to work his mind ticking over. He had a pretty fair idea of the tools they'd need, there would be a few they'd need to get. They'd need some more vehicles, four-wheel drives, and trailers. They'd need a plant. And maybe, thought Wayne, a place just outside of town where they'd have room to move and store their equipment.

This very night Wayne planned to sit down and get some figures ready to show Jack. He'd make another phone call to.

Wayne had been impressed with Jacks efforts finding bulls so quick the other day. He thought Jack was a natural at this life and found it was easy for him to pick it up. And now Garry had taken to the man. Wayne was well pleased. Jack had also shown himself to be no slouch around motors.

Wayne walked over to Jack now, 'what do you think Jack?'

'Needs a little work. My main concern is that the rings are on the way out.' Jack looked it over smiling and stepped back to admire her. Garry nodded to Wayne behind his back.

'Way ahead of you Jack' grinned Garry holding a set of rings. 'These came in on the last cart.'

'Well, is that the lunch bell I hear boys' said Wayne now dropping a ring spanner onto a tarp on the ground.

Jack turned and noticed everyone walking towards the mess. There was a mighty good smell coming from there. The noise in the kitchen had all calmed now and Jack assumed the new order brought about by Nevil had been heard and understood by all concerned.

All overalls had been removed and left back at the work sites. No dirty, smelly men in Hilda's eatery. Jack admired Hilda, the amount of respect she and her food could command from these rough tough raggedy men.

Wayne asked Jack and Alby to stay after breakfast today, that he wanted a word with them. Jack was a bit nervous about it, but he had an idea what this might be about. He just knew he'd be disappointed if he didn't.

After breakfast Wayne told the blokes that he wanted a word with the two of them. Every one of them smiled and nodded and left the room. Bill even closed the door behind him. It amazed Jack sometimes at the closeness and the regard these men had for him and each other. He could see it was Wayne's ways that did it, he never kept anything from them, and they respected him for it. And they were consequently more open with him.

Jack got the impression everyone knew what the talk was about and that it was more or less the details they were going to hash out. These blokes weren't the least bit interested in detail unless it was under a truck maybe or round a bull's neck.

The three men sat at the table with fresh coffee. Wayne cleared his throat and pushed some papers around on the table and Alby stared hard at the ceiling, his eyes fixed on a spot there. Alby did that when he was nervous Jack had noticed. He'd find something to focus on and then give it all his attention. It was as if he expected the object on which he was focused would materialise into a UFO or some such, and then aliens would rush out and set about him.

Wayne started. 'I think you might know what this is about Jack. It's this bull catching thing'

Alby sprang forward in his chair his elbows on the table. He was all ears, the UFO forgotten. Jack on a lesser scale had done the same and Wayne on the other side of the table noticed.

He smiled now and went on to tell Jack and Alby about his idea from the day before. Jack listened he was impressed. Wayne outlined the equipment side of it, the offers to the owner and the possibility of buying most of the plant from the owner. 'He's not a bad bloke, John, but he'll want his money. He has had enough of worrying about these feral bulls I know that, and he's talked about farming the job out to professionals. He reckons he could get by with half the staff if he didn't have them to worry about. Think he might have to, right.' Wayne finished on a laugh.

He sat looking at Jack. Jack thought for a while. 'So how is this John going to feel about losing you Wayne?'

Of all the questions Wayne had thought might come, had prepared for, this was not one of them. He was taken aback by it and sat in silence as it dawned on him. The significance of such a question dawned on him. He dropped his eyes and nodded his head. 'I will need to exercise great diplomacy here young Jack. Will need to proceed with caution, yes indeed. How right you are.'

Alby had not missed a thing and he spoke quietly. 'Maybe we'll need to get him to focus on the fee Wayne. Make him a good offer on the rights to collect his feral bulls. Then maybe we can argue that point again, later on down the track hay.'

Wayne was floored once again that morning. He nodded at Alby, 'good point Alby' he said softly.

Jack chimed in now, 'had you thought Wayne, about remaining on as manager for a couple more years you know in name only. You could be out helping with this business venture, but you could be here to. You know, sit on the fence for a bit. John will catch on eventually how much time you spend out there with us and will be expecting it.' Jack gave a pause.

Wayne thought about it. 'Yeah, well that was in my original plan Jack. I suppose I could ensure you have access to bulls here for a few years that way. Okay we'll aim at that.'

'Will we have to look for somewhere to live and store the plant, Wayne? I mean we will sooner or later but how soon' asked Alby?

'Well,' said Wayne thoughtfully, 'we should possibly aim at taking this on maybe next season and all stay put until then. I just wanted to get your opinion before I mention any of this to John. We can start saving and collecting. In answer to your question Alby, I have a mate who has a big property, approximately one and a half million acres which does border the outskirts of town for a bit. He'll sell us a small portion or lease it to us. About five thousand acres would do, that would give us a little pasture to keep the bulls on till we're ready to sell them. But we are gunna be busy we need to put up sheds and build fences. Then we'll need all manner of tools to fix these heavy bloody vehicles, most of the tools me and Garry use are mine.' Wayne stopped to draw breath.

Jack went on. 'I can get a loan Wayne, if you let me know how much, so we can get started on the work. Now if you could secure the land for us that'd be good, and then we gotta sort out who's coming with us.'

Wayne got to his feet, 'let me see what I can work out and we'll meet again in a couple of days. You boys have raised some very good points.'

'Alright' said Jack, 'we'll get back to work.' He and Alby rose from the table.

Men were sent out every day now, two men in a vehicle each. They had to keep their eyes on the movements of the bulls. Wayne suggested that they start with the bulls closest to home which was the herd of about twenty that Jack had spotted.

Eddy and Pete were now using their spare time to check and load up all the fencing gear. Wayne told Jack that the fencing they were working on when he'd arrived was a yard to hold these bulls short term. He said it was about ten square miles.

Wayne had ordered a road train for a few weeks hence. There would be a couple of road trains but then they would try to utilise any droving teams which would be about by then in force. He kept Jack informed; he wanted Jack to head this new company. Wayne was tired and despite all his talk to the contrary, was well off financially.

Wayne was tired today, so he knocked off for a while before lunch to go sit in his office. He would get some paperwork done and make a few calls. They had a phone at the station now. Because of their excellent airstrip it was a preferred landing for the flying doctor. Sometimes mail came in by plane. So, they were a large medical supply unit and needed the phone.

Wayne had just sat down when the phone rang. He picked it up thinking he really should have a woman here to answer that thing full time. He'd had a bell installed so that Hilda could answer it when they were all away. So, Hilda knew if she heard the bell, that she needed to answer it.

'Hello' he said.

'Hello Wayne, I've been trying to ring you.'

'Okay Margo what do you want?'

'Is that any way to talk to me Wayne?'

'Well, I'd really rather not talk at all Margo. You and I are history so why don't you just get off my bloody back?'

'I was just wondering if you had changed your….?'

'No!'

'You're just a fool Wayne….'

'Bye Margo' Wayne put the phone down.

Wayne put his head in his hands, how had he tolerated that bitch all this time? He got up, no peace here now he thought so putting his hat on he left the office. He went in search of Jack.

He found Jack up to his arm pits in grease down in the garage. 'Jack' he said.

Jack stood up and grabbed a rag to wipe his hands on. 'What can I do for you Wayne?'

'I rang my mate Walter last night just to sound him out. I asked him about leasing a few thousand acres with a view to buy and he was on board with it. I told him about you, and he said he'd like to meet you whenever we have some time. He's alright Jack, he'll keep it to himself. You know…. Leave me out of it like and deal with you.'

Wayne looked about for a while then went on, 'a buddy of mine is selling a big shed he used to do his welding business in. I told him we'd come and grab it after bull catching season.' Wayne gave a giggle now, 'he reckons "of course after bull season. Everything revolves around bull season with you blokes." But he was happy with that. He says since we are pulling it down and shifting it, we can have it for fifty pounds.'

'That's great Wayne, this thing is really gunna happen mate.'

'Anyway, must be lunch time again.'

Jack got out of his overalls and the two men walked to the mess. 'Got a phone call from Margaret Jack. You know for the life of me I don't know why I didn't get out of that before. A bloody man's a mug.'

'I think we just do what we need to do to get by sometimes Wayne. She must have been some comfort to keep going back hay.'

Wayne looked at Jack and smiled and nodded. 'I reckon that's about the size of it mate.'

Once everyone was seated Wayne stood up and announced that he hoped to be moving out in around four days. 'We'll start in the Northwest No.4 paddock. We'll start on that nice size of herd Jack and Russ found. So, I would like you Eddy and you Bill to get out there to the bore and rig up some fencing. I would also like you to take Jack. Take your swags. Take the truck and the front ender and knock the path clear to the camp site. When you are done leave the front ender out there and come back to help with the rest of it. Take axes and shovels and a couple of bloody rifles.'

There was a silence in the room as the men digested the news. It was happening, really happening. Jack felt a peace come over him that was accompanied by a surge of excitement. This was what you never learned at school. Not that Jack learned much of anything at school.

Alby looked at Jack and smiled. Bill looked down; he was feeling it more this year. The excitement, it was huge this season. He was enthused beyond anything he'd ever felt.

Wayne told the men to throw the tents on the truck along with the cooking gear for Nevil and anything else he had to go. The first aid cabinet the tables and chairs. You need to load the showers and toilets and camp stretchers and any personal shit. You can bring the swags with you in the trailers as well as your kits. 'And not to forget Nevil's kitchen. All waiting at the side of the building here' he finished.

When Wayne got into bed that night, he thought about how good it was to have such things to look forward to as bull catching and a brand-new enterprise. To have mates around him that he got to work with.

He thought how nice it was to have someone to talk to and he thought about Rhonda. Yes, he'd think about her, whenever he damn well pleased. Wayne thought that night to give thanks for Jack. Jack and Alby. And of course, his old mate Bill.

Wayne turned over and pulled his covers up. He didn't really think he'd stay on here another three years. He'd push these changes through if it killed him.

To his surprise Wayne realised that he no longer felt old. He wasn't sure what he did feel but he felt younger and more alive than he had for many years. He was happy, he found to be out of the clutches of the lovely Margo. He had grown tired of all her drama.

He worried sometimes at how fragile Alby and Jack still were. He hoped he could be of some use to them in their healing. Bill's drinking worried him to.

Wayne hoped that the threesome Bill was in would stay under control until bull season was over. For Wayne knew the lid would blow off that situation sooner or later.

Chapter 9

It was Dd day. Do or die day as Wayne was wont to say. The men were hooking up the trailers and throwing swags in them. There were, mostly tools and fuel and spare tyres etc. The fridge and freezer were also on this load. They would run a huge generator while out here to keep the food from spoiling. This way they weren't always needing to kill and butcher. They usually stayed away about four to six weeks, maybe a little more depending on how well things did or didn't go.

They pulled out leaving Hilda and Pete behind. They left a four-wheel drive just in case they needed it and a couple of motor bikes. Wayne had a radio with him, and they would keep in touch that way. He had instructed Hilda to be on the radio every morning at six and every night at six also.

Wayne had also promised to be available at lunch time. Apart from that she could drive out there or send one of the lads. They had left behind the best of the vehicles for her to drive. All the blokes got in and shut their doors. Those who had doors.

Jack drove the chaser and Wayne drove the wing vehicle. Bill and Garry each drove a land rover pulling a big heavy trailer. Alby rode with Jack in the chaser, and they headed up the convoy. They had the station truck with half a dozen horses in it, just in case. This brought up the rear, Eddy drove it and Nevil rode with him.

Hilda waved and wiped her eyes; she didn't want to go but she'd miss them.

She'd miss Bill to; oh, she missed him. She missed Bills slow hands and tender.... 'Oh, damn' she told herself. She'd just about had enough of the bloody pair of them. But Hilda wasn't sure how much Bill wanted her. She'd leave Nevil and go off with Bill tomorrow but.... She sighed and walked along in their wake for a bit. Walked forlornly in their dust.

Suddenly she stopped and let the tears fall from her eyes. Bill watched it with saddened heart. He'd have to come to some sort of decision concerning that bloody woman. He was bloody miserable without her, and he knew for whom she cried. Knew very well, and it wasn't for the bloody goose back there in the truck.

Bill had some talking to do, some sweet talking and he wasn't good at it. In fact, he was very bad at it, if he wasn't he'd probably know whether he was divorced or not. What sort of a man doesn't know that he asked himself now? He dragged his eyes away from the rear-view mirror, a man on the run from life he told himself. Yeah, it was time he found the guts to talk.

Jack, up the front saw it and so did Wayne. They all liked Hilda she was a god send to all of them. Nevil didn't see it for all his 20/20 vision. He had broken up the arrangement between Bill and Hilda because he suspected she was getting to like him a little too much. Nevil didn't want to be alone it was as simple as that. Unwittingly he may have sealed his fate. Most everyone knew that what Bill and Hilda had was special.

Jack felt it and he knew the big man beside him did to. They all liked Hilda way more than they liked Nevil. The general consensus was that she was too good for him by far. Jack tried to keep his heart out of it, but it was a bit hard. He knew what it was like and so did Alby. Jack suspected Alby had just wiped his eyes.

As they got along the road out to the camp Jack had to keep telling himself to go slowly. The urge to take off was strong and he was certain everyone else felt it. Wayne, coming up behind Jack marvelled at the thrill in his belly. The boys had done a good job bull dozing a road through to the camp.

About half a mile from camp the procession passed by the herd of feral bulls that Jack had spotted. Wayne stopped to get a good look at them. He counted seventeen bulls, if they were working for themselves, they could expect to make around eight thousand pounds just here. He'd have to get moving and talk to the boss. Wayne knew he could get a few more stations interested in giving him a contract to, but he'd have to move on it before someone beat him to the punch.

He said this to Jack and Bill and Alby as they sat at the campfire eating their tea. Jack was amazed. Wayne was talking again, 'so from the whole station we'd have to make about twenty thousand pounds. That's one station. I think I can get another two or three as well.'

'Let's see how we go converting these feral bulls into sales hay,' said Jack.

'We'll be right mate' Wayne smiled at the man, 'you get your shot tomorrow.'

Alby leaned forward and patted Jack on the shoulder, 'you catch em and I'll tie em up mate hay.' Alby grinned at Jack and suddenly Jack worried about the man getting close enough to one of these demonic beasts to put a rope on it. Fear struck Jack and he had no idea where it had come from.

Wayne saw the look and knew he had to say something. 'You don't gotta worry about Alby here Jack, he knows what he's doing alright.'

But Jack did worry. When he climbed into his swag he worried, in the pit of his stomach a bad feeling gnawed at him. He couldn't figure it. He worried about Alby, poor broken bloody Alby facing down a wild, two thousand pound beast. Hell of a way to get over a woman.

He worried about Wayne in his wing vehicle sporting his broken heart. His anxiety about the letter that Jack was certain he'd written. Jack hoped against hope that he'd get what he wanted. He worried about Bill and his broken relationship if you could call it a relationship. Jack was certain he loved Hilda.

Jack also worried about Hilda back at the station and he knew she was sporting a broken heart. What a bloody world thought Jack now. Was it the war? And the war had solved exactly bloody nothing. Jack couldn't find Mary there in the darkness. All he could feel was the churning in the pit of his stomach. The feeling of dread that was growing in him by the minute.

Jack lay, trying to relax in his swag while listening to the bush and feeling the comfort of the soft breeze blowing. It was so peaceful that when it happened Jack couldn't quite comprehend what went on.

Everyone else did and they were up out of their swags and running about shouting. The night was split wide open by a noise that was like nothing Jack had ever heard. A horrific thundering, and bellowing. An unholy noise accompanied by an unholy stink.

The camp was in an uproar as the men tried to hunt the rogue bull that had just torn through the camp and was now turning to make another pass. It stood pouring the dirt and bellowed his murderous intention. Dogs barked, men screamed, and the bull lowered his head for another charge. It was a horrendous scene.

Jack ran to the chase vehicle where he knew there was a rifle. He grabbed it pointed it at the bull which was now chasing Wayne. It got its horn under Wayne's backside and hoisted him up in the air. Jack let off a shot the bull turned towards him and without hesitation, came straight for him. Jack stood his ground and took aim, he had only a few split seconds.

'Shoot' screamed Wayne holding his arse, the seat of his pants all but. Jack held steady and let off a shot. The bull dropped in its tracks. Jack had seen Russel go down and ran to the still form on the ground. 'Russel, Russel' he yelled lifting the boy into his arms.

The boy was to have gone back to the station house the next day. Why? Why?

Jack's mind was trying desperately to grasp the situation but all it came up with was, why?

Bill ran over with a tilly light, and they inspected the boy. Jack couldn't believe it as he stared into the sightless eyes of the youngster, he'd become so fond of.

He looked at Bill and Bill gave his head a shake his eyes full of pity as he looked into the pleading in Jack's eyes. Jack dropped his head, 'no' he cried, and Alby put his arms around Jack and rocked him and the boy gently from side to side.

'Bloody hell' said Wayne, his face ashen he still held his backside. Garry had jumped in and slit the bulls throat allowing it to bleed where it lay. They'd have to butcher it in the morning. You just couldn't waste meat like that.

Garry and Nevil got lights and started the butchering process on the bull, they'd need to gut it now. It helped to have something to concentrate on. No one could look at Russel. They got the bull strung up in the tree with the help of a winch. Russel wasn't the first to be killed by the bulls, but as far as they knew he was the first who had been minding his own business at the time.

Wayne got down on his knees beside Alby and tried to gently extract the youngster from Jacks arms. 'Come on son' he said gently to Jack. 'Come on mate let me help you, Jack.' Wayne put his arm around Alby and said to the big man, 'Alby let me help you.'

Alby's eyes had a glazed look about them and he closed them and shook his head. Wayne knew it was still raw what they had seen in the war, the things that had happened to them. He'd had more time to get over it but these two were still fragile, still broken.

Jack wept and Alby cried softly. Bill told Wayne to get ready to grab Jack's hands and he then gently pulled the boy from Jacks grasp. 'I'm sorry old mate' he said to the two men. 'I'm sorry.'

Bill carried the youngster away and laid him on a plank of wood in a lean to under a tree. Bill knew he'd taken a horn through the heart. He'd tie a couple of dogs to the tree to keep away predators, this was a harsh world with some harsh realities. Wayne got up and went to get one of the land rovers and cleaned it out in readiness to put the body in the back and take him to town. Bull season was on hold.

It was a week before the men got back out to the camp, they'd gone to Russell's funeral in the Mount. Alby had stood beside Russel's girlfriend in awkward silence. She had slipped her arm through his and Alby felt obliged to stay put. The girl had stuck by his side the whole time they were in town. She cried in his arms and stayed at his side.

Alby was glad to be leaving, Sandra had got too familiar with him. She threw her arms around him and kissed him goodbye making him promise faithfully he would come and see her whenever he was in town.

Alby looked at Jack and disengaged himself from the girls' arms. Jack knew Alby was getting confused between being bothered by the attention and liking the attention. Jack watched as Alby dropped his head and kissed the girls' upturned lips. He walked away and jumped up in the back of the rover.

Jack dropped his hand on Alby's shoulder, in an ideal world Alby might have found happiness in the girls' arms but this was no ideal world. And Alby was just confused. And they'd just buried Russel. Jack lowered his head the hot tears ran down his face onto the floor of the Ute.

Alby was having trouble keeping his feelings under control. He found the girl most appealing, and she was of a pleasing character. Alby knew he was a little old for her, but he also knew he'd come and see her when next he came into town.

Jack had seen it all and had found something else to worry about. Alby was gone on the girl that was clear. How gone she was on him was what worried Jack. Jack said a silent prayer that Alby wouldn't get hurt again. He knew it was up to the Gods and the girl Sandra was still a few months away from eighteen.

But Jack looked on the bright side, it may be possible for Alby to find love again. Alby got down on the floor and lit a cigarette.

But they had a job to do, and Jack knew Alby was professional enough to get on with it.

It was decided that the men would stay at the station tonight and head out to camp in the morning. Hilda had come straight home with Wayne and went to get their dinner. She avoided even looking at Nevil.

Upon their arrival at the station Bill went off to the mess. Nevil had gone to the first bore with Wayne. Bill strode into the kitchen and grabbing Hilda, turned her to face him. 'We need to talk woman' he said and kissed her.

'I hope so Bill. You just left me.' Hilda drew her hand back and slapped him on the shoulder.

Bill stepped back and gazed at her. 'Well, what was I supposed to do?'

'Tell, bloody Nevil where to get off. Anyway, you can go to hell Bill I'm leaving. As soon as the bloody bull catching is over, I'm off. So good riddance.' Hilda tried to push Bill away, but he held on to her.

'Hilda I'm sorry alright? Leave Nevil by all means but don't leave me. I've done nothing Hilda.'

'That's right Bill you've done nothing and now it's too late. Get out of my kitchen Bill.' Hilda picked up a heavy ladle and swung it at Bill. Bill ducked it and took it from her.

'You don't mean any of it, Hilda and you know you don't. You are my woman, and he can go to hell. Soon as the bull season is over, I'm coming for you, you just wait and see Hilda.'

'Well, isn't this fuckin cosy.'

Bill and Hilda both stared at Nevil who was standing in the doorway. 'Oh, fuck off Nevil ya bastard.' Bill was losing his patience.

'What is all this Hilda' Nevil was glaring at the woman? 'You are nothing but a slut Hil....'

Bill lost his temper and swung a punch at Nevil that knocked him to the floor. Bill, in his late fifties still packed a punch. As he fell Nevil took a rack of dishes with him. Hilda added her screeches to the racket, all directed at the two men.

Jack sallied through the doorway and tripped over Nevil. The two men were attempting to rise with dignity, Nevil with blood down his face, when Wayne and Alby appeared.

'What the hell is all this' demanded Wayne? As if he had to ask. He for one was glad it was all out in the open. But he couldn't afford to lose both cooks at this stage. He waited for an answer.

Nevil turned on him, 'I should think its fuckin obvious.'

Nevil picked up a tea towel and wiped his face. Wayne and Alby stood where they'd stopped, and Jack got back on his feet. He shot a glance at Alby who was watching him closely. 'You hurt' he asked Jack now?

'No mate I tripped over fuckin Nevil. Sorry Hilda' Jack apologised for his language, smiling a little to try and calm the situation. Jack knew in his heart of hearts that the woman didn't need this. Bloody Bill! Just like him to charge forth like a bull in a blasted China shop.

Hilda threw the towel she'd snatched from Nevil in the sink and as she left the room she said, 'you can all get your own fuckin dinner.' She marched to the door saying loudly, 'you might want to take the roast out in half an hour and carve the bloody thing up. Or you could let it burn. You could do nothing and just let the damn thing burn.' She turned in the doorway, 'and if you're not sure how to do that just ask Bill.'

Wayne followed her out to the dining area 'now Hilda...' he dodged Garry who stood with his mouth hanging open, then he dodged Eddy who looked the same. The men knew of the great love that had sprung up between Bill and the cook and none of them actually liked Nevil.

Wayne was walking sideways beside Hilda to the back door now, 'Hilda please will you talk to me. I need you now Hilda I can't manage if you walk out on us.' There it was said.

Hilda stopped and turned-on Wayne her voice shaking with emotion 'Oh shut the hell up Wayne. You all drove out that bloody gate and all you had to do was come back. All you had to do was bring him back. My Russel, you took him and didn't bring him back. I hate the lot of you.' Hilda burst into tears in Wayne's arms.

Wayne cursed himself for the fool he was. He had noticed how the woman mothered the boy; she was even teaching him to dance. He held Hilda tight in his arms and put his mouth to her ear, his voice just above a whisper. 'Forgive me woman, I know I failed you. In a most horrendous way, I have failed you. I loved him to Hilda. Please find it in your heart to forgive me woman.' Wayne's voice shook with emotion to.

Wayne let out a great sob and Hilda clung to him. He sidled around the corner with her and stood holding the woman as she wept. Wayne wept for her more than anything.

He held her at arm's length and told her softly now, 'I have let you down Hilda and I swore I never would. You have been such a good woman, more than any of us deserve. More than Nevil bloody deserved. I will do anything for you woman you know that. I should never have taken him on such a dangerous mission. Please Hilda, don't leave us, don't leave me.'

Wayne stood weeping now in the woman's arms and they comforted each other. Presently Hilda stepped back. Wayne led her into the mess to the table and sat her down waving the men to get out. Even though Wayne knew how much the men loved and respected the woman he needed the room. They got to their feet and filed out; Eddy touched the distraught woman softly on the shoulder as he was leaving.

With the mess hall to themselves he took Hilda's hands and held them. 'Hilda, I need you to forgive me. Please.'

'Oh, you are forgiven Wayne, I know you wouldn't do such a thing through carelessness.'

'No Hilda it was careless, I relented to his begging me to take him....'

'I know and to be truthful I was glad for him when you did,' Hilda was moved by the pain in Waynes's face, and she put her hand to it.

'You are forgiven. There is nothing to forgive Wayne.' She drew a deep breath and went to get up, but Wayne held onto her hands.

'Hilda, can I help with any of this here? If it comes down to it, I will give you what you ask to stay, and I will send him packing.'

'You'll send who packing?'

'Whoever you say woman. Were the choice mine to make I would send Nevil packing and keep Bill. I'm just saying now.'

Hilda drew a deep breath 'I am tired Wayne, so tired.'

Wayne felt embarrassed that he hadn't noticed how tired she looked. He stood up and helped her to her feet also. Pulling her into his arms once more he said now, 'can I count on you Hilda? Will you stay with me even though none of us deserves you. You are right woman we sailed through that gate like boys on a bloody summer camp. And we brought you back the body of your son. I'm sorry Hilda. So sorry.'

Hilda smiled sadly and put her hand to his face, 'we all sent him to his death Wayne. But let's face it, it was the bull who took him. Now the next time you sail through that bloody gate I want you to be more careful. I want you all to come back. I'm just a foolish old woman and I loved a young boy as my own. It's not your fault Wayne. You have my word I will stay to the end of bull season. I am leaving Nevil, I expected too much from him. And Bill, well I don't know but I wouldn't want you to send him packing Wayne. He is a good man, and you know that.'

'Alright Hilda, you have my word. Is there anything else?'

'Yes, Wayne you need to be careful out there. The lot of you.'

'Alright Hilda. And Hilda, would you consider staying on? After, the season Hilda?'

'Not really Wayne.'

'But why Hilda? Do you want more money?'

Hilda smiled at the man she had come to like and respect. 'Of course, that may be a factor, Wayne. I don't get much. Fifteen pound a week is a bit miserable.'

'Done Hilda, how about twenty pound a week.'

'Well yes Wayne a twenty pound a week rise would do nicely.'

'Hilda!' Wayne was fighting a losing battle and he knew it. He knew he'd give her what she wanted. He had to. 'Alright Hilda.'

Hilda looked at him, 'I will need to get a room to Wayne. I can't stay where I am.'

'Why can't you? Well alright Hilda I have an idea.'

The men were hiding in the kitchen waiting with bated breath as they listened to the negotiating. Listened to Hilda putting the screws into Wayne. Jack smiled and turned about; Bill had gone.

Hilda walked back into the kitchen and began picking up the mess. Nevil stood awkwardly for a while watching her. 'So, is that it Hilly? You not gunna talk to me?'

'Go away Nevil, I want nothing farther to do with you.'

'I suppose you want Bill?'

'At this very moment all I want is to not be able to see you or hear you. Do you think you can manage that Nevil?'

Nevil walked away, he just hoped she'd calm down. Wayne beckoned to him to come and see him, and Nevil knew he'd need to pack his things. Well to hell with the lot of them. It's not like he hadn't seen this day coming.

Chapter 10

The men arrived back at the camp the next day, loaded up with supplies from Hilda and minus Nevil, he'd left for Mount Isa the night before, Wayne had sent him packing. Bill would temporarily do the cooking as penance for bringing this all to a head before they were ready. And he was the only decent cook amongst them, he'd done his share back in his droving days.

Hilda was at the station by herself for a few days until help arrived. An employment agency was sending two males up and they would arrive the next week on the mail truck. Wayne would leave one of these, a young bloke with little experience at the station with Hilda. The older was an old hand at station duties and had been a cook, he would come out to the camp and relieve Bill.

Wayne had Hilda move into the house. She would occupy a room there now for as long as she wished. Her room was off the side veranda at the front of the house. She could come and go as she pleased without running into Wayne and she had her own bathroom.

There was a secluded section of garden right outside her French doors. On the veranda she had a chair to sit in and Hilda loved it, she had her early coffee there. Wayne himself had loved this area but he would leave it to her. As he saw it, it was a small price to pay.

Hilda sat now in the room Russel had occupied, her heart was in tatters. The room was bare, so bare. The only two things he had displayed on his dressing table were two photos. One was of a strange woman, probably his mother she thought. The other was of her, Hilda had given it to him when he'd asked for it.

She had a small box which she sadly packed the young boy's life into. She took the photo of the other woman out of the frame and looked at the back. There was a name, Elsie Brown. She took the box to her room and snuck into the office as if she was afraid, she would get caught any moment. She made a phone call to the Mount Isa Police station.

'Hello, this is Sergeant Billy Judd speaking how can I help you?'

'Hello Billy, it's Hilda Slater here. I hope you can help me.'

'Well, I can try Hilda. It's nice to hear from you again. How have you been?'

'Oh Bill, have you got a half an hour? I have a story I'm afraid and I could do with some advice.'

'Well, Hilda as it happens, I have a mug of coffee in my hot little hand, and I will put my feet up on the desk and you can bend my ear for as long as you need to. So, tell me, what's been happening Hilda?'

Out at the camp the men were getting ready for the next day. Ropes being fitted, vehicles being fuelled and tested. A certain excitement was building even though the men were heavy hearted. They couldn't help it; it was like a calling to them. Early in the morning they would be chasing bulls. Most of the men were finishing off the yards to hold them in.

Bill got around like a thunder cloud for the first part of the day. Wayne caught up with him at the camp kitchen. 'Bill, I'm sorry how things worked out alright. As soon as this other bloke gets here, you'll be back out with us. It's good that things are out in the open now and Hilda is happy where she is. Or so she told me on the phone this morning. You know at some stage I am gunna want to know what your intentions are towards her. I mean if they are not good, well…. I would like you to do the right thing. That's all just do the right thing.'

'Have you quite finished Dorothy bloody Dix?'

'Bill! This is Hilda we're talking about man.'

Bill put his head down, 'I know, I know. I got things to do.' He walked away a few steps and turned around, 'I dunno Wayne I think I do love her, well I do know that I do. I'm not much good at this sort of thing you know. But what can I give her?' He shrugged helplessly.

Wayne shook his head a look of frustration on his face, 'for Christ's sake Bill. The bloody woman is in love with you. Find out what she wants. At least do that Bill, just find out.'

Wayne turned to go but as he did, he said, 'I asked her to decide who she wanted and let's just say she did not choose Nevil.'

'But did she choose me?'

'You know what Bill? You need to fuckin grow up. And while you're at it grow a set.'

Wayne walked away. The weight on his shoulders just seemed to get heavier with each passing bloody day. A footfall right behind him made him spin around. It was Bill. 'What?'

'Yes, Wayne, I love her. But I don't even know if I'm free.'

'Find out.'

'How?'

Wayne sighed; his face softened. 'Come and see me when we get back. I'm pretty sure you would be mate. And Bill, think on it, man. That's all I ask. I shouldn't stick my nose in but damn it all, I love you both. Now clear off back to work.'

Bill cleared his throat. 'I'll be there Wayne…... when we get back… I'll be there.'

The campfire burned bright that night, the men had built it up and kept it burning all night. Though no one even remembered hearing of a bull tearing up anyone's camp before and killing someone into the bargain. Even so the men felt better with a big fire. Also, that night and for many nights there after the men slept closer together and nearer to the vehicles. Jack had the rifle by his side, and he made no apology for it. Secretly they all approved because Jack had been a sniper during the war. Alby slept closer to Jack, he told himself he was being protective of his mate, but he felt safer.

Jack lay quietly in his swag in the space between wake and sleep, the place where he chose his dream. He had Mary back though something strange was happening. Jack had an attack of the guilts and it disturbed him. Though it hurt he began to realise, after all these years that his dreams were an exercise in futility. He sighed and pulled Mary closer to him, he couldn't let her go. Could he?

❀

At last, it was here. It was the day they would go catch some bulls. Alby and Jack had gone out the evening before and spied the bulls in a gully about a mile away. Now Alby and Jack got into the land rover and Jack started her up. Jack and Alby let out a yell and laughed at each other. Wayne let a yell rip from the other vehicle as he started the motor.

Eddy and Pete had saddled horses, they'd slow them up a little bit, but somebody had to know where the bulls were tied and guide the truck in. The truck would follow on with Garry driving. But after the first bull he'd need the horses to be his go between. It was with some thought that they had given this task to the tacker amongst them.

The men Jack Alby Wayne and Pete would catch and tie the bull and move on to the next while the truck came along behind and picked them up. Pete would primarily help with getting these monsters in the truck.

The men found the bulls and Jack singled out one bull which was away from the others and went after it. Alby hung on and was amazed at the ease with which Jack stayed on its rump, the man seemed to stay relaxed in his seat.

Wayne on the other side came along on the right of the bull and kept him as straight as he could. It helped Jack to get the bull lined up and keep it lined up nice and straight.

The vehicle had a mechanical arm fitted so all Jack needed to do was flick the switch when he had the animals neck lined up with it. Jack concentrated on that bull and soon had it lined up. It was a lot more physical than you'd think and Jack knew he'd have to get used to it.

It was just a couple of minutes before he flicked the switch, the animal was secured. Jack gently applied the brake and brought the bull to a stop near a fairly sturdy looking tree. It surprised Jack the amount of bucking and bellowing, it was a little frightening.

Alby jumped out and on his third attempt he had the bull's horns tied up. He took the other end of the rope and secured it to the tree. Now Jack had to release the animal from the arm. Alby got back out of the way. Jack flicked the switch, and the animal began to buck around pulling against his restraints and bellowing his indignation at the vehicle.

'Back up' yelled Alby as he jumped in. Jack backed up just as the bull tried to gore him. The horn missed by a few feet and Jack stopped the rover and sat looking at the bull. The five minutes it had taken to secure the bull seemed like at least a half an hour.

'Wow' he said and looked at Alby. They were both grinning from ear to ear. 'Now I see what all the fuss is about Alby' he breathed. His innards were alive.…. He was alive. Wayne was right about the adrenalin rush, by God he was.

Alby laughed and punched the air. A very loud 'yahoo' from Wayne in the other vehicle set everyone off laughing. Eddy spurred his horse on to go and talk to Garry in the truck. He'd help him get the bull loaded onto it.

Pete stayed to help; he'd use his horse to guide the bull into the chute. He was amazed at Jack's driving, at the skill of the man; he'd heard but seeing it.

Smiling to himself he urged his horse into a canter, getting the bull on the truck was mostly a two-man job.

By the end of day one they had caught and secured seven bulls. After they caught five, they took them back to release them into the yard. Wayne told Bill they'd all have lunch while they were there. Bill didn't look so pleased. 'Well, you can eat the lunches you've got and I'm not waiting on you' was his reply.

Wayne stared wide eyed at the man, 'when did you ever?'

The men let the bulls go in the yard, a semi was coming in two weeks to pick up what they had and take them to market. At this rate they'd have close on a hundred bulls.

Wayne knew the bulls would start hiding and they'd soon be harder to find. It was on day four and they were catching their fifth bull. Alby got out to secure it to the tree, it was a struggle from the start. The bull was not puffed out at all and was putting up a hell of a fight.

Alby tried twice to get the rope over its horns, but the bull was able to twist its head. Alby got the rope over the horns and tied it fast but before he got it tied to a tree the bull turned his head and stuck his horn into Alby's arm as he turned away. With a bit more of a struggle, Alby got his horns tied to a tree.

Alby knew he was hurt fairly badly, and he was bleeding a lot, but he gritted his teeth and finished getting the bull secured. He stepped back and turned to Jack, there was blood all over his shirt front. Jack released the creature and backed up. Alby jumped in and smiled at Jack.

'Just a flesh wound Jack, nothing to worry about.'

'Bull shit Alby we've gotta stop the bleeding.' Jack had seen men bleed out from so called just a flesh wounds. And then there was the danger of infection.

He said this now to his mate finishing with, 'and how are you supposed to tie these buggers to the tree if you only got one arm. Come on Alby let's see.'

In the other vehicle Wayne watched as Jack jumped out of the rover and ran round to Alby. He knew the big man must be injured and he floored the jeep to get to him. Coming round behind Jack he watched as Jack expertly tied a bandage on the bloody arm. He had applied a torniquet to the arm and after a few minutes the bleeding began to slow. Each time Jack released it the arm bled less until Jack was hardly applying any pressure. 'Jesus Alby are you alright mate' asked Wayne?

Alby turned and smiled at Wayne, 'course I am. Safe as houses Wayne, I seen this man save lives in the army. He's already got it to slow up look. Down to a trickle already. You shoulda been a Doctor, Jack' Alby's face turned serious and nodding he went on to Wayne, 'he was our medic was Jack. We all knew we just had to make it back to Jack and those who he couldn't save were comforted to die in his arms.' Alby's voice broke as he ended.

Jack stood with his hand on the big man's arm, a smile made its way across his face. He raised his head and lifted his eyes to Alby, 'not today buddy, you are not dying today. Thank God.' He turned to Wayne now 'I need to stich this together so it will heal faster.'

'Okay' said Wayne now, 'I'm gunna call a halt to today. No more catching today. We can spend the rest of this day looking for where these bloody bulls are hiding. Come on let's get Alby back to camp.'

Wayne sent Eddy back to let Garry know they were going in and that Alby had been gored. Jack took it slowly back to camp and so by the time they got there everyone was waiting. Relief washed over them all as they saw that Alby was sitting upright in his seat and appeared to be talking to Jack. And Jack was laughing.

Bill put his arm around Alby and helped him to his swag. Alby smiled at Jack; they had made it up ready for him. Alby lowered himself onto it and lay back, the pain was really bad now. His arm was throbbing like a bastard, the bull's horn had got him just below the elbow.

'Just wait here Alby' said Jack as he went off to get disinfectant, a knife and a needle and thread. He hated to do it, to hurt his mate this way but he had to. The sooner the wound closed over the safer Alby would be from infection.

On his way back past Bill the man held out a flask of whiskey to him, 'tell him to drink the lot Jack, it will help. Well, you know that hay.' He smiled softly at the man in front of him. Jack was a good man to have around he was calm and clever and never seemed to lose his cool. And now he was a medic and from all accounts he'd done a bloody good job. From all accounts Alby was lucky that Jack knew just what to do. 'Thanks. I appreciate this, Bill.'

Bill went to turn around to get Alby some food. 'You're very welcome young Tom.' Bill sucked in air, so that was it! He swung back to peer at Jack. So that was who Jack reminded him of. 'I do apologise Jack, but I have just realised who you remind me of.' Bill looked closer at Jack now, 'my old drive boss Tom he was a good man, none better. Yeah, that's who you remind me of.'

Jack smiled at Bill, the man was all heart and he hoped that he and Hilda would work it out. He slapped Bill on the shoulder, 'glad to hear it. I just gotta go and fix Alby's arm. Bill, could you bring me some boiled water please. And thanks again hay' he said lifting the flask.

Bill went to the kitchen area to get Jack what he wanted. He was flabbergasted, more so that it had taken him so long to click. The two men were so similar in every way. Bloody good men. And so was Alby and of course Wayne. Bill counted himself lucky, very lucky indeed.

Bill picked up the kettle yes, he would throw in with these blokes, he had the excitement stirring in his belly. Alby's arm was only a bit of a hiccup. Tomorrow he'd be back out there if Bill knew anything. They all would be, it's what they did. 'Course he'd be stuck in camp doing the blasted cooking, him and his big mouth and his hot head.

❈

The mail cart was due to arrive, and he'd have the two new blokes with him. Hilda decided she'd take them out to the camp, and she'd take the mail as well.

This morning she'd spoken to Wayne, and he had asked her to bring a few things out with her, which she had ready to go. It was then she learned about what had happened to Alby. Hilda knew that blokes got hurt all the time, but this had just added to her sense of foreboding. She'd be glad when this season was over.

She was tying the mailbag when she heard the truck. As the truck pulled up at the front of the mess hall, she came out to meet it. She had an order on the truck, so she'd have to put that away. She stepped out on to the veranda and stopped dead in her tracks. There was no mistaking who the woman getting out of the truck was. Hilda knew a moment's panic and then the woman looked up and smiled sadly at her.

Hilda walked up to her smiled and said softly 'Elsie?'

The woman nodded her head, Hilda realised that she was a very pretty woman. 'I bet you could go on a cuppa. Do you want one Berty?'

'No thanks love I'm running a bit late.' Berty smiled and said, 'do you know these blokes, Hilda?'

Hilda shook her head, and Berty went on 'well this here's Geoff and the young un's Mike. I'll leave you to it lad's'. The lads unloaded the stores from the truck.

Berty looked at Hilda now, 'I'll be back tomorrow, and I'll pick Elsie here up then. Can you put her up for the night Hilda?'

'Of course.'

Hilda smiled at the three that were left 'well I guess you could use a cuppa.'

When they were sat alone at the table Hilda spoke, 'so you are Russel's mother?'

To Hilda's surprise the woman shook her head, 'no, my sister was his mother, I'm his aunty. My sister was a single mother and she died during the birth. My father unbeknownst to me gave the baby over for adoption. Said they both had died. I learned of this years later and I went to see him in the orphanage and was able to tell him that his mother had loved him. I also told him that I loved him and gave him the photo. The policeman who came to see me told me the story of you and the others out here so on an impulse I got myself here. I wanted to visit his grave and meet you all, his family. I got a letter recently and he was going on about a man called Jack. I would like to meet him.'

Hilda smiled 'yes Jack had taken quite a shine to him, and Russel idolised Jack and Alby.'

'He spoke a lot about you in his letters to Hilda. He said he thought of you as mum.'

'Well, we are going out there a bit later so if you want to come you can meet them. All the blokes looked out for him, and they all attended his funeral.'

'Lovely' said Elsie, 'I can't thank you enough Hilda.'

'Well, I loved him to' Hilda said lowering her head.

Hilda and her visitor reached the camp a bit before teatime and the men were preparing for the night and the next day. Hilda went straight to Alby who was still wearing a bandage. She had brought with her more bandages and painkillers and a sterilizing agent. Alby grinned at her when she started fussing and accepted the wedge of cake, she handed him. It was his favourite and when she kissed him goodbye he grinned and said 'thanks Hilda.'

The men looked at the strange woman and Hilda announced who she was.

Most of the men there cringed but Elsie put them at ease with her quick smile.

'I came out with Hilda to meet you all because Russel spoke so highly of you. He loved it here and I just wanted to see it. I hope you don't mind the invasion.'

'No of course not' said Wayne taking her proffered hand, he smiled and went on. 'We all liked young Russel he was a good kid.'

When Elsie shook hands with Jack she said softly, 'his last letter was all about you Jack. He'd intended to be just like you.'

Jack was taken aback, his eyes misted, and his throat wouldn't let him talk at once. He swallowed and began, 'I liked Russel, and I was sorry what happened to him. We miss him miss him a lot.' Jack shook hands with Elsie and smiled kindly. Elsie saw what Russel had seen.

Wayne hesitantly told Elsie how the incident had killed her nephew and she could feel the great sorrow in the man and in all the others here as well, who stood with their heads down. She said now 'I am glad that he was in a caring environment where he felt happy. And thank you for letting me know it was quick and he hadn't suffered.' It meant a lot to the people there to hear her say that.

Hilda had given Wayne the mail for the men and Wayne was flicking through it when he stopped and stared at an envelope. Coming to himself he took it and folding it over stuck it in his pocket and went on flicking through the mail.

Wayne was glad when the girls left with Mike for the homestead. He had a letter he was itching to read, a letter that was causing him a deal of anxiety. It was from Rhonda and the return address on the back was Mount Isa. He didn't know whether the prompt reply was a good thing or a bad thing. In fact, Wayne was beginning to wonder what had gotten into him to even write to her.

Jack had noticed the boss's anxious behaviour and guessed it had something to do with the letter in his shirt pocket which he kept touching. His heart went out to the man, and he hoped it was good news. They could do with some he thought now. There had been no mail for him, but Pete had gotten a letter from his father.

Alby had gotten a letter but had shared with no one. Jack wondered if it was from Sandra. Alby would tell him in good time he thought now and with his back against a tree, he settled on the ground to eat his meal. Dan was a lot farther away, so Jack thought it a bit soon to start hoping for a letter. Bill was a bloody good cook, he thought and hoped vaguely that Geoff would be just as good. Jack hoped also that Hilda would stay.

Geoff got busy immediately helping Bill and finding his way around the camp kitchen. Mike had left for the homestead with Hilda and everyone there was glad she was no longer alone there.

The next day Alby was back with Jack tying bulls to trees though by lunch time Eddy was doing most of the tying. Jack checked his arm at lunch and could find no reason to stop the big man from doing what he was doing. Jack told Alby that the wound looked no worse but then it didn't look any better either. His advice to Alby was to take it real easy, half a day was long enough. 'If it's sore' he told Alby, 'you are probably overdoing it.'

Each day after that, Jack changed the bandages and checked the wound when Alby was finished his half day. Jack had spent hours that night at the campfire fashioning a leather strap which he strapped on Alby's arm to protect it. Alby was delighted at the freedom it gave him to spend longer each day doing his job. 'It's bloody great Jack, my arm's not sore at all' he informed Jack with a wide grin.

When Jack took the bandage off, he was pleased to see it was getting better. And when he took out the stitches two weeks later the arm had healed completely. 'I still want you to wear this Alby for at least another two weeks.'

Wayne and Bill and the others were amazed, and all took turns trying it on. It was basically a leather strap that reached from the wrist to the elbow. Wayne said, 'I reckon if you made another one, we could have the ropers always wear them on the job. It would be good to cut down on these injuries Jack. Even a bit.'

Wayne sounded excited and Bill was enthusiastic. Bill said now, 'it is probably the most prevalent injury on the job Jack. This could save time and money for sure. Where did you learn to do leather work like this?'

'Picked it up mending saddles and harnesses that sort of thing on the farm. Then I did a bit of leather work in the army for a little while.'

Nodding, Bill smiled at Jack and thumbing at himself he said softly 'Light Horse Infantry Jack.'

'Hells bells' said Jack his voice dripping with admiration now, 'you blokes are legendary. Bloody legends mate the lot of you.' Jack held out his hand and Bill shook it. Alby grinning widely offered his hand and Bill shook it grinning back at him. Such praise from these two, he got a lump in his throat.

Jack noticed Wayne staring at the man with his mouth hanging opened. He hadn't known that. Jack flicked his eyes around and saw that everyone there was amazed. They had another hero in their midst and these blokes were all, without exception, heroes. The name 'Light Horsemen' was synonymous with bravery. They surrounded an embarrassed Bill wanting to shake his hand.

Bill fished into his top pocket and pulled forth a very scrawny and dirty looking emu feather. All the blokes wanted to touch it and Bill held it out. Jack could see he'd started to feel awkward.

Alby and Jack were out cruising looking for bulls on the third day after mail and Alby took a deep breath. 'That letter I got Jack; it was from Sandy. Jack, I like the girl, but I can't mate. I can't I just bloody can't, she's just a kid. She says she wants me to take her out next time I come into town. I need to write to her don't I Jack? I need to do the decent thing.'

'Why Alby? I thought you were stuck on her.'

'No Jack, just flattered, I think. A girl like that stroking my ego huh. But maybe one day Jack… maybe.'

Jack smiled at the big man and was secretly glad that Alby wasn't blinded by the attentions of a very attractive young girl. Alby had his feet planted firmly in reality but still… he had seen the possibilities.

Back at the camp Jack watched from under his brim as Alby strolled casually to the fire and burned the letter. Jack prayed the man wasn't to hurt, as hurt he had to be. Poor bloody Alby.

When Alby lay down in his swag beside Jack he rolled on his side and pulled his blanket up. It wasn't cold but he needed the security of it.

'You okay Alby' Jack asked very softly?

'Yeah Jack, I was foolish to dream.'

'Maybe' replied Jack. Then after a while 'maybe another time, another place. Probably best to wait until she's a tad older anyway mate. Then see what happens hay?'

'Yeah mate. But for now, I need to hang onto my Sue a little longer.'

Jack felt like he wanted to cry. Wayne, on the other side of Jack heard it, he had a quandary of his own going on. if only he could remain that objective he sighed and let the blackness of sleep engulf him. The sometimes-merciful blackness.

A couple of days later Wayne sat beside Jack on a bore run to check the number two bore. Alone with Jack he started to speak. 'I wrote to my ex- girlfriend Jack and the other day I got a reply.' He fell silent.

'Was it good news Wayne? A nice letter?'

'Yes Jack. She informs me that she lost her husband around ten years ago. And she said she was delighted to hear from me and that she looked forward to hearing from me again. She said she was sorry for what she had done and that she had made the worst mistake of her life. She said she'd love to hear from me again. I just dunno Jack, but I will write to her again.'

'Well Wayne it's encouraging. How long ago how long?'

'She left me nigh on thirty years ago Jack.'

'So, I would say you ought to hear her out Wayne. Hear what she has to say. People change mate, for better or worse they change.'

Wayne nodded and smiled. 'I want to send Bill back to the station for the mail this week Jack. He needs to see Hilda. I'd like you to go with him Jack. You are discreet and he listens to you.'

Jack chuckled, 'and I know how to lay low and mind my own business, Wayne. Do we actually need to do any work at number two Wayne?'

Wayne laughed now, 'of course not Jack. We'll get there boil the billy and have a nice cup of tea. We'll eat our lunch which Bill and Geoff made for us and enjoy the peace of the bush. And we'll have a

quick scout around for bulls on our way back. What do you think of
Geoff's cooking Jack?'

'It's good Wayne. Not as good as Hilda's though. When we branch
out, is she coming with us or is Geoff?'

'Well now that rather depends on her and Bill. I personally hope
it's Hilda. She's a good woman Jack but I'd like Bill to sort himself out.
I guess it's not easy for the poor bastard after so many let downs.'

Jack wondered if he was the lucky one here. He somehow doubted
it. He did hope that things would work out for them all and if they
didn't? Well, they had each other, didn't they? And that was an enormous
comfort to Jack.

'You know Jack, I never knew that Bill had been in the Light Horse
Infantry. He must have been a boy.' Wayne shook his head and pulled
into the number two bore.

Jack sat quietly with Wayne as they ate their lunch. Wayne said
quietly, almost matter-of-factly now, 'did you write that letter to Dan?'

Bill smiled softly and nodded 'yes, I did Wayne. I haven't had an
answer it's a bit soon. I'm hoping they can all forgive me for clearing
out without saying goodbye.'

Wayne pushed his hat back on his head. 'Yeah, well sometimes you
gotta save yourself Jack.'

Jack went on 'Dan runs a compound for homeless waifs and strays
of which I was one. About thirty adults and fifteen kids there now, he
takes care of them all. They all love him and would follow him to the
ends of the earth if he wanted. But he's a good man and he asks nothing
of anyone they are unable to give. I know he will forgive me Wayne.
I also know he worries about me.' Jack lowered his head now and said
very softly, 'I do know that he was the better man for Mary. Don't make
it hurt any less though.'

Wayne sat staring at Jack a look of wonder on his face. 'But didn't
you ever feel like killing the bastard Jack? Not even once?'

Jack smiled now 'I can't answer that, Wayne. I owe the man too
much and I did behave like an idiot. I cheated on her with a whore in
Melbourne.' Jack gazed at the fire, 'I love them both, I'm happy for them.'

Wayne looked at his boots 'yeah well that don't make it hurt any
less either Jack. In fact, I'd say that would make it all the worse. I'd like

to meet this bloke.' He paused for a moment; I'd like to meet Mary to he thought. Wayne kept that thought to himself.

Wayne changed the subject. 'How do you feel about the bull catching now Jack? Now that you've been doing it for a while?'

'Yeah, I love it, Wayne. I love the life, not just the actual catching of them, but being out here. I love camping and I love the bush; it has a calming effect I reckon. I can't imagine how good it would be to do this for a living. How about you Wayne?'

'Yeah, I love it to. Margo left me because of it, and I have no real reason to expect that Ron would be any different.' He sighed now and threw the dregs of his tea in the fire. 'Time will tell young Jack. It's a great little sorter outer is time.' He smiled softly and got to his feet.

Jack smiled and got up, 'well that's exactly what I'm hoping Wayne.'

Wayne nodded at Jack his face full of compassion. 'What do you think Alby will do with this girl Jack?'

'Well Alby's got his head screwed on right, but his heart seems to have go involved. So, who knows. I hope they can work it out. Bill and Hilda to.'

---oeveo---

Chapter 11

---ovevo---

T he road train came and collected the bulls that the boys had caught. A makeshift stock race was thrown together for the purpose. There were fifty-five bulls, and they were a horror to get into the semi. Luckily the driver was an old hand and knew what he was doing. Also luckily, the dogs knew what they were doing. Jack had certainly learned the value of a good, well-trained cattle dog.

It was during this time that Jack and Bill went into the homestead to pick up the mail and some supplies. The camp was being packed up to go on to the other side of the station to catch bulls over there, a move of about six hundred miles. So, Wayne told them to do a few jobs around the place and come on over there to the new camp Monday to help set up.

Bill knew what he was being sent home for and it wasn't that he was without gratitude, but last time he'd spoken to Hilda, he'd upset her somewhat. Bill felt like he was on a mission. He decided he wasn't going to push the woman; and he was glad Jack was with him. The old proverb 'lamb to the slaughter' comes to mind. Bill realised with a start he'd said it aloud.

Jack laughed; he couldn't help it. It was the best laugh he'd had in a while. Bill shrugged his shoulders and laughed along with him.

Jack stopped and wiped a tear from his eye. He said now. 'Come on mate it can't be that bad hay?'

Bill fell silent and kept his eyes on the road, 'I really don't know how I feel right now. She didn't even look at me when she brought that woman out with the mail. I'm not gunna force myself on anyone Jack.'

'Of course not, but I do think Wayne is right. She's just hurt. You know Bill with Russel and then Nevil leaving without so much as a goodbye. And now she's not sure of you. It's natural Bill. Just be your charming, gentle self-mate and she'll be putty.' Jack drew a deep breath 'just talk to her Bill. Just aim for that.'

'Thanks Jack.'

Jack smiled 'sure mate. Good cook, full head of hair not an ounce of fat on ya, how can you lose? You got nothing to worry about mate,' The two men laughed good naturedly.

Hilda heard the vehicle coming and wondered who it would be. She tried not to think of Bill she didn't want to be just waiting around for him. She sighed yes, he could please himself. Hilda wished now that she hadn't promised Wayne she'd stay. Maybe she'd tell him on the radio she was leaving and then just clear out.

Hilda was tying the mail bag for the camp; she'd finished boxing up the supplies they wanted out there. A tread at the doorway brought her round to look into Bill's beloved face. He smiled softly at her, and she went weak at the knees. She smiled back at him.

'Good morning young lady' he said and stood there in the doorway. 'Are you still doing the cooking out there, Bill?'

'No, Geoff is, thank Christ. How are things here Hilda, you okay?'

She looked intently at him, and said softly, 'things are fine Bill thanks. You in a hurry to get back or do you want to have some lunch?'

'Jack is with me Hilda we got a few things to do here so we'll be here a couple of days, you know putting new tyres on rims, that sort of thing. Didn't Wayne tell you?'

'No. I'll have some lunch ready in an hour. Could you put that box there back in the cool room for me please Bill, it is perishables?'

'Sure' said Bill and took a step forward to pick up the box. To his dismay his feet kept walking to her. His arms went around her and left him standing there at a loss to explain himself. When her arms went around him, he relaxed into them and dropped his head and kissed her gently. He kissed her long and lovingly and during that time Bill realised he did love her and couldn't be without her. He'd need to talk, and he told her this now.

'What about Bill?'

Bill took her hand and led her to the mess and sat her down at the table. He sat across from her and told her how he had no idea if he was divorced or not. To his surprise Hilda laughed.

'Oh Bill, I don't want to marry you. I just want to be with you. And love each other for as long as we can.'

Bill took her hands in his and smiled, 'you sure?'

Hilda nodded, 'surer than I have ever been about anything.' She took his face in her hands and smiled reassuringly.

Bill went on, 'well, Wayne is going to help me to sort it all out. I need to be free, to love you. I dunno woman Oh, don't bloody laugh. Does this mean we are back on? But just know this, I won't share you. You are mine no one else's, right? Nothing wrong with my fuckin eyes woman.'

'Yes Bill of course, and I won't share you either.'

'Well, you won't have to.' He got up from the table and pulling her into his arms held her to him and kissed her.

Bill looked into her face for a moment then said. 'You know there are moves afoot, I don't know if you've heard anything. Wayne Alby Jack and me are gunna go into the bull catching business and I shall want you to come with me. Is that gunna be a problem Hilda?'

Hilda smiled, 'I heard a whisper, and I wondered if you were going to just leave me behind.'

'No never woman' Bill kissed her. Lifting his head, he looked into her face 'what do you mean you don't want to marry me?'

Hilda smiled 'I mean it's not necessary. As long as I'm with you I don't care.'

'Oh, shit woman. You got me I'm yours. Forever and a day.'

'Well hallelujah' said Jack wearing a big grin from the doorway. 'Any chance of a cuppa Hilda?' He walked in smiling at them.

Hilda smiled she liked Jack, 'of course I just told Bill I'll have your lunch ready shortly. I'll get you two a cup of tea.'

Jack grinned at Bill when Hilda left and said softly 'see Bill, you two were meant for each other.'

'Thanks Jack. And she's gunna come with us when we go.'

Jack clapped the man he had come to admire on the shoulder, 'you gunna have a cuppa with me. I'm famished and looking forward to lunch.'

The two men sat down and talked amicably over their tea until lunch arrived and Hilda sat down and ate with them. She realised that these two men and Wayne were her favourite people in the world. She'd go with them, and she would marry Bill when the time was right. She wasn't yet free herself anyway came to that.

Jack complimented her on the lunch, she'd made them a salad with steak and potatoes. She watched them tuck in and she did realise this would be her job out at the camps. Well, she'd negotiate a price that was for sure. Hilda also realised that Bill though he'd be driving the truck would be putting himself in danger almost daily. She'd need to be with him.

When Bill and Jack caught up with Wayne at the new camp, they handed him the mail bag. Wayne saw at once that Bill wore a happy demeanour. Jack already knew there was no mail for him, so he wandered off to put his swag out. Alby caught up with him and smiling said 'G'day Jack good to have you back.' Alby pointed to a patch of ground next to his swag and Jack threw his down on it.

Jack turned and grinned and said 'bloody nice to be back Alby. How's your arm mate?'

Alby held it out for Jack to look at, 'it's good Jack, no pain and hardly a scar. I reckon I'll wear that arm brace always now Jack.' Alby held out his other arm which had an ugly welt mark on it. 'See Jack another bloody bull. We were trying to get the three bulls we had up in the truck to move em here and he got me. Just as hard as last time Jack but didn't break the skin. It bloody hurt but there you are Jack. I'm gunna wear these all the time now catching bulls.'

'Well, I'm glad it helped Alby.' Jack stepped a little closer to the big man and said softly, 'I think Wayne's got another letter for you mate.

See what she has to say, bearing in mind she hasn't got your letter yet.' Jack patted Alby on the shoulder.

Jack went back to sorting his stuff out and waited for Alby to respond. He knew the big man hadn't moved and he thought he knew what was in the man's heart.

Alby cleared his throat and softly said 'I'll go and get it then Jack.' He sauntered off, his shoulders stooped, his tread heavy. Jack wondered how much he was expected to take.

When Alby read the letter and sat looking at it in silence, Jack asked 'how's it going Alby?'

Alby handed Jack the letter. Jack was astounded at the maturity of the girl who'd written this. It was full of love and concern for Alby. She'd heard he'd gotten hurt. She finished off by telling him she couldn't wait to see him, and she thought she was falling in love with him. She told him she knew he wouldn't go out with her till she was of age and asked him to wait a couple of months until she was eighteen.

Jack lowered the letter and looked at Alby. 'Shit!'

'I sort of feel bad about what I said to her now Jack. I told her I wouldn't go out with her and that she ought to find somebody her own age. But it had to be said.' He sat staring enquiringly at Jack now.

Jack swallowed and when he spoke all he could manage was a shake of his head and, 'I dunno Alby.' He stared at the big man, and he had to smile. Alby relaxed visibly. Jack went on, 'mate, she seems pretty keen on you. And you gotta take a chance some time. Maybe just write to her as a friend for a while. You know…. See what develops if anything, but yeah, she is still a child Alby. You're gunna have to wait but it's not like you're doing anything right now is it mate? Not like we got em lined up round the block or anything.' Jack smiled kindly at Alby and handed him the letter. 'It's up to you mate, if it makes you happy, I'm all for it.'

Alby got to his feet and threw his arms around Jack; and Jack hugged him back. It wasn't very manly but what could he do? Alby spoke a tremor in his voice, 'thanks Jack. You know for not getting mad at me. I'm not good at this.'

'Come on Alby, I smell something good coming from the kitchen.' Jack was rewarded with one of Alby's wide grins that lit up his face and made everything good.

When the camp was set up the men were back out catching bulls. They were all without exception glad to be out doing what they loved to do.

On day three Alby was having trouble with a particularly nasty bull. Alby grabbed its tail and tried to flip it, but the bull twisted and stepping to the side it had Alby pinned against the land rover. Alby heaved with all his mite but the bull a huge heavy thing, weighing probably over two thousand pounds was leaning on him. Crushing him to the side of the vehicle.

Jack jumped out of the rover his heart in his mouth and rushed to get to his mate. He hadn't thought what he might do but he knew he had to do something. The bull had its back hooves spread far apart and swinging there was the answer to his dilemma. He ran round the side and coming up behind the monstrous beast he pulled its tail to the side and booted the bull in the balls.

The action had the desired effect in that the large heavy murderous beast sprang away from Alby, releasing him. Alby gulped the sweet life-giving air into his tortured lungs. But the now bellowing bull had taken exception to the kick and head-butted Jack in the face. Jack went down as the world faded away on him.

It looked to Alby as if Jack's face opened up as he sprang away from the bull. He screamed for Wayne as he jumped in and reached for Jack and pulled him to safety. Clear of the bull which was tethered to the vehicle Alby held Jack in his arms and lay him gently on the ground and leaned over him. He could hardly see Jack for tears, and he knew a terror like nothing before.

Not Jack... not Jack...not Jack was all he could think. 'Not Jack, Wayne' he said now looking beseechingly at the older man for help. 'God no' Alby was shaking his head from side to side, down in the dirt with Jack wishing there was something he could do. 'Help Wayne......help!'

Jack was unconscious, 'holy hell' breathed Wayne as he looked down at Jack. He put his hand over the wound closing it up a little and stemming the flow of blood. 'Jack' he shouted 'Jack'. Jack was unresponsive and Wayne wasn't all that surprised. The bleeding slowed and he and Alby both were relieved. Wayne looked at Alby 'don't worry mate he's tough. He'll be right.'

Alby nodded but continued to worry. Wayne put a padding over the wound and bound it tightly. Bill and Garry arrived.

Jack's wound was so bad that Wayne had Bill take Jack into town to the Hospital. He called on the radio to Hilda to get an ambulance to meet them. Preferably a helicopter. Bill prayed as he drove, for the first time in his life he prayed.

Jack came to but was still dazed. Wayne had strapped a padding to Jacks face to try and stop the bleeding and it looked to be working. The doctor told Jack later he was lucky the man had done that, 'may have saved your life' he'd said, 'pulling the wound shut and padding it like that.'

Jack couldn't speak the pain was so severe. He was choking on his own blood and Bill could only look at him in horror. Because of the choking the men had decided to keep him sitting up. They tied him in his seat. Bill drove like the devil was after him, straight through the fences and anything else that was in his way. Bill was on a very important mission, the most important of his life. He had to save Jack.

An hour later the chopper pilot spotted the rover and Bill waving to them and landed on the road. The medic smiled at Bill and said 'the bleeding has slowed but we'll have to get going. He'll be right mate; we'll get him there okay.' One of the others was getting a drip into his arm.

Jack was vaguely aware of the chopper and had some episodes of flash backs. He tried to speak to Bill but he had nothing.

Bill saw it and leaned over Jack, 'you'll be alright now mate. these blokes will see you right,' Bill ended on a sob. He put his hand out and stroked Jacks hair and even the medics were moved. A tear slid down Jacks cheek and Bill wiped it away. 'Don't fret none mate, I'll be here. We'll all be here just waiting for you to get home okay. You gotta go with these blokes now and they'll fix your face hay.'

All Jack could do was put his hand on Bill's arm and wink his right eye at him. It was enough to comfort Bill as he put his hand over Jack's and squeezed it. He held onto Jacks hand as the two men in attendance lifted Jack onto a stretcher and into the chopper all the while asking Jack questions and telling him he'll be right. They gave Jack a shot of morphine and Bill saw him visibly relax, he even smiled. 'Do you know what day it is Jack?' All sorts of questions like that they asked him.

The doors closed in front of Bill, and he stepped back. He was numb as he let the tears sting his eyes. He watched on as the helicopter took his mate into the sky. He couldn't even wave. He got back in the vehicle and watched the helicopter disappear from sight. Bill felt sick and getting back out he bent forward and brought up his last meal.

By the time Jack was laying in the hospital he'd lost a deal of blood, but the main thing was he'd copped a horn in the face. After another good dose of morphine Jack started making sense. He had a gash from his forehead near his eyebrow down the side of his face stopping just short of his jaw. His ear was torn, and his nose was broken.

It took two operations in Brisbane and a few weeks for Jack to heal enough to get back to work. He'd had seventy-eight sutures in his face and his nose was set. His face had been laid open to the bone and his left cheekbone had been fractured. The surgeon shook his head 'what makes these blokes do it, the money?' He put Jacks face together with precision and care. He took a few hours, but he did his best work.

The nurses changed Jacks bandages every day and told him he didn't look so bad. The swelling would go down and the redness would fade over time they said. But when someone finally handed Jack a mirror he was horrified at his now misshapen face. He stared at it.

What will Mary think he wondered? Then dismally he realised she would never see it. Would never know how much he loved her. The nurses all thought the tear that rolled down his cheek was because of his looks. They smiled at him as they reassured him, he still looked very handsome.

The bull catching had slowed down a great deal without him and bull season marched on. Jack was anxious to get back to it, he'd been stupid he knew, but he'd thought Alby would be killed. Wayne had phoned up and had briefly spoken to him and told him the bull catching was a bloody shambles without him.

'The doctor reckons you should make a full recovery with no lasting ill effects so that's the best news mate. He reckons you won't be quite so pretty, but the surgeon did a good job. They also said that you could have died if we hadn't sent you off like we did.'

'I'm sorry mate' Jack mumbled through the bandaging.

'Don't be mate just concentrate on getting well. Do as you are told and give yourself the best chance to heal and get back here. We all bloody miss you, you bastard. And nobody drives like you do, I think we've caught a dozen bulls these last weeks. I have half a mind to go and do something else until you get back. But you know how it is mate, nobody wants to do that.'

'Well thanks for getting me here mate and thank the others for their help to. I can't wait to get back at it, Wayne.' He heard Wayne chuckle as he said goodbye and hung up the phone.

In another phone call Wayne told Jack that they had pretty much put bull season on hold and were out mending fences most days. 'Especially the ones Bill went straight through to get you to the helicopter Jack.' Wayne laughed and Jacks heart swelled with gratitude. 'Just a few gates mate really.'

So, it was almost a month after the accident before Jack arrived back at the station on the mail cart to a hero's welcome. Jacks face was scarred. His nose was a little crooked and the scar ran from above his left eye to beneath his left ear. Hilda, after scrutinising him carefully declared that it only added to his appeal, and she meant it. And Jack could see she meant it. The doctors had done a wonderful job was her verdict.

Bill had come into the homestead to pick him up and bring him to Wayne. Wayne wanted to see him before he decided if he was going back to work or not. Just before teatime Wayne and the boys returned back to camp to see him.

Wayne stood looking at Jack for some moments the hint of a smile on his face. He handed Jack his mail as he was throwing his swag down on the ground. He told Jack that he could come out and drive, but he wouldn't be getting out of the fuckin vehicle. 'Jesus Jack, I thought you was a goner.' Wayne sniffed, 'now get into your swag and get some rest. And it's good to have you back ya bloody maniac. Ya got out and ran round the rover and kicked a bull in the balls Jack. A very nasty bull at that. You'll go down in the history of the whole bloody district as the mad bastard that kicked a bull fair in them.' Everyone laughed and Jack had to also, though carefully.

Jack looked at Alby who was approaching him now, Alby stood for a moment and rushed into a tirade of apologies. 'I'm sorry mate, you could have got killed because of me. I'm sorry…. I…. I couldn't help you. You saved me Jack…... and '

Jack broke in, 'Alby you saved me to, don't apologise mate. I'm the dopey bastard that kicked him in the nuts. You jumped back in to pull me clear Alby. He'd have stomped me to death if you hadn't. Thanks Alby.'

The men there laughed and joked for a bit, and it felt good to be back. Jack had a laugh and then got down on his swag. He was anxious to get back in the driver's seat. It occurred to him just then that he had come through the six years of the second world war without a single scar on his face.

Jack was the talk of the stations and the towns round about. In the bars, around their campfires and in their saddles. They talked about the big wild bastard, Southerner at that, but a war hero no less, over on Mable Downs who had casually kicked a big two-thousand-pound, feral bull in the bollocks. He was trying to save his mate who was pinned to the rover and the bull was crushing the life out of him. So, the story goes.

Yeah, by Jesus and it was said round about that they were war heroes the pair of them. They'd been mates with Dennis Markham in the war and had survived the same horrendous prison camp. And the story had got out that Bill was a hero also, had to be. He was a light horseman.

Seasoned bull catchers shook their heads at the story and as the years rolled away the story was told over and over. How the man had almost lost his life saving his mates life. And the story went on to tell how this mate had then turned around and risking his life saved Jacks life. Then the light horseman charged in and raced his mate Jack to a helicopter taking out half the fencing on Mable Downs as he went. And Wayne another war hero had saved his life with his first aid and quick thinking.

And Jack had made an arm strap to keep his mate from harm and everyone in the business of bull catching suddenly wanted one. People wrote letters to Wayne the heroic station manager who had saved all the men. These letters were asking for arm bands as arm injuries by horns were the main injury involved in catching feral bulls. Men were spending a lot of time laid up with them.

It hadn't escaped the blokes on Mable Downs that their station was famous. Even before Jack got back from the hospital it was famous, he was famous. Wayne on the other hand had had a please explain from his boss. Wayne had done his chewy and told the boss that that was the nature of the game.

Catching feral bulls, though necessary, was a bloody dangerous business.

Jack was the only one blissfully unaware of his hero status. In Jacks mind he was just a dope who charged into a fight he had no hope of winning. But he told himself, in his defence he had thought Alby would be killed. It turns out, so did Wayne.

Jack had also been pleased with the way the wound had healed up. His face looked much better now that the swelling had gone down. Shaving was a delicate operation, though whiskers didn't seem to grow near to the scar.

He noticed that his swag was all freshly made up and he smiled. Probably Bill he thought. He remembered how upset the man had been. He hadn't stopped for gates and took them all with him. Bits and pieces of gates dragging along on the bull bar for miles.

Jack was eager to get out amongst it again as was everyone else. He'd be a bit more careful, but he knew that in the same circumstances he'd do it again.

Without any hesitation he'd do the same thing.

Alby brought Jack his tea and he brought his own over as well. He sat on the ground and ate with Jack, and they talked idly about nothing much. They were at peace once again in each other's company. Afterwards Jack lay down, he was sore. Alby got up to take the dishes back and he'd help Geoff with the dishes.

Give Jack a little space to read his letter.

There was something hard under Jack's pillow. He reached his hand round and pulled out a flask of whiskey. Jack smiled there in the deepening twilight. Just the thing. 'Thanks Bill' he whispered to himself.

Jack was tired, he picked up the letter Wayne had handed him to read it before it got too dark. It was from Dan. Sipping on the flask, Jack opened it with trembling hands and a dozen thumbs. Eagerly he read:

25/6/1952

Dear Jack,

I was overjoyed to get your letter mate. There is no need to apologise Jack, I'm just glad you have found happiness and peace. I knew in my heart that one day I would lose you and I understand how you had to leave. All is well between us Jack as usual.

They tell me that I can catch a couple of aeroplanes and be in your corner of the world in a couple of days. I am going to make the journey as soon as I can. I need to see you lad and see that you are happy there. Wally wants to come to.

It is almost the end of June, and we have finished seeding and now watching the grass grow. Mary says it's going to be a bumper crop this year, but she says that every year, and every year she is right. Please let us know if you need anything Jack and keep an open mind to coming home someday. When you are ready Jack. My heart won't stand the thought that I won't see you again.

We still spend most of our time at the long hut Jack, some of the people have built themselves a small house and have moved out. But they remain close by, and always will. We are a family. We still have our gardens for food and market, and we always will. We haven't forgotten Jack, the starvation.

Bryce and Kane always ask if there has been any word and were glad when we got your letter, everyone was. Mary wants to buy a small farm for Bryce, he is quite the farmer now so maybe one day. Libby is doing well at school and wants to be a doctor. Bull catching sounds dangerous Jack, please be careful, I lost you once.

Well goodbye for now Jack, Mary sends her love and says she will write next time. I'm sorry you had to go Jack; I miss you. I will let you know when I'm coming up and maybe you could advise me on when it would be best to come. I have no wish to intrude where it will cause you concern.

Please write again soon mate I look forward to your letters always. And remember all is forgiven. I remain,

Yours faithfully,
Dan Roberts

Jack put the letter down and unaware that Alby watched him from a distance he cried. He couldn't stop the tears or the pain in his heart. Alby sat down beside him and waited patiently, dear, sweet Alby. 'I'm sorry mate....' Jack croaked.

Alby put his hand on Jack's arm 'at least you got a letter mate. Is all well at home Jack?'

Jack grinned at Alby through the tears 'yes Alby, all is well. All is forgiven.'

Alby slung his arm around Jack's shoulders and hugged him to him. He had his mate back. He had Jack back and Jack was alright, so all was right with his world.

Chapter 12

The remaining few weeks of bull catching went by without injury. In spite of their injuries Jack and Alby loved the life, loved the job, and loved the team they worked in. They caught an average of four to five bulls a day. Wayne was right they had gone to ground, and the men were soon pulling in less than five bulls a day on most days.

On the third week back Jack learned that a team of drovers were coming to take the feral bulls to market. A beaming Bill approached Jack and told him it was his old outfit who were coming.

'The drive boss is Tom, I worked for him for nigh on twenty years. He's the one that you remind me of. So, you will meet him, Jack.'

Jack smiled, 'that's good mate I look forward to it. I would like to have a yarn with him and learn a little about droving. I'd like to sit and listen to you talk with them Bill. I'm pretty stoked and you must be to mate.' Jack slapped the beaming Bill on the shoulder now, 'and I can see you are.'

'Yeah, I am I haven't seen him for over three years, I hope the others are with him. Last I heard only one of the blokes had left. I'm hoping Fred is still with him he's a legend is Fred.'

Alby was wearing his characteristic wide grin, 'I want to meet em to now Bill.'

Wayne walked up, thumbing at Bill he said, 'so is he still jumping up and down about meeting up with his old cronies? I've met Tom a few times, nice bloke knows his business. I heard he's about the best in the business you know.'

Bill grinned, 'Yep, he's good alright and a damn good boss and a fine human being. A little like you Wayne.' This brought a guffaw from the big manager.

Jack asked, 'when are they likely to get here?'

Wayne answered 'should be here in the next few days. I'll be glad when these worrisome bulls have gone. Not a lot of drive bosses will take on a herd like this one.' Wayne looked at Bill, 'I rang the Mataranka pub and there was Tom thank Christ.'

It was three days later as the sun was getting low on the horizon that the drovers rode into camp followed by a truck. Jack watched as they swung down out of the saddle. He made Tom and was impressed by the man's easy manner and his greeting to Bill. Tom didn't hesitate as he threw his arms around Bill and a big, somewhat older man who Jack thought was probably Fred did the same. The rest followed suit and they milled around Bill talking excitedly. Every now and then giving Bill a shove or a touch or a slap on the back. Jack heard Fred telling Bill how long it was since they'd had a visit.

'Never seem to have time' was Bill's reply.

'Bull shit mate you got the whole bloody wet to come over' Fred laughed, 'we miss you mate.'

They walked into camp with Bill and shook hands with Wayne. Next, they were introduced to Jack and Alby. Tom gave one of his easy grins as he shook Jacks hand. 'If we have any trouble with these bastards' he thumbed to the holding yard, 'we'll come and get you. I take it you are the ball breaker, Jack.' He said to Jack and Alby. They laughed and Tom's face turned serious now, 'Jesus, he got you good mate. Is that the scar? Mind you, I would probably try and head butt you to if you kicked me in em.' There was more laughter and Tom said, 'I heard this team is one of the best and I can tell you now,' he ran his eyes round all the men now 'that this outfit is catching more bulls than any of the others.' Lastly, they met Charlie and Jimmy and Herbert.

The talk went on among the excitement and laughter. Bill stood beside Jack, he had loved Tom, but he was with Jack now. Jack and Alby and Wayne and his new team. The praise from his former boss was everything to him though. 'When do you blokes wanna pull out' asked Wayne?

Tom turned his attention totally onto Wayne and looked thoughtful. He switched his gaze to the bulls and lifted his hat, scratched his head, and replaced the hat with one hand. 'Looks like you got about sixty or more.' He turned to Wayne. 'Well, I'd like to get em on the move and out on the road by lunch time tomorrow. These bastards take a bit longer to round up. We brought some bulls with us to lead em, but they'll still need to catch on.' Tom looked down and said as an aside, 'never can tell with them though Wayne. But if all goes well, taking into account the number of bulls and how good my outfit is, we should be out of here by next week.'

The drovers all laughed and shouted him down. Tom took their derision with good humour. It was obvious that these blokes loved one another. But there was a bond here, an unusually strong bond. Jack could sense it, a bond he'd seen in the war. He knew it was Tom, these men were around for him. Fred and Ernie flanked him, they'd back him up every time and their faces said so.

Nevertheless, their overall demeanour was one of friendliness and professionalism. They loved this light-hearted banter they shared with their boss.

Tom smiled at Jack, 'you wanna come with us Jack?' Everyone laughed good naturedly and Jack found he liked the young man. Tom scrutinized Jack for a second and nodded, the grin slid from his face, 'job for you if you want it. You to Bill' he said and grinned knowingly at him.

'Hay hay hay' said Wayne 'you trying to poach my men here Tom.' The older man called Ernie grinned, shook his head, and went off to set up camp. The rest of them followed suit shortly after.

Jack was amazed as he watched them set their camp up. They were methodical and quick, and they travelled light. The way they cared for their horses was heartening and, unbeknownst to Jack, legendary. Wayne went over and asked if they wanted to eat with them, but Tom declined. He thanked Wayne sincerely and said they would come over for a coffee and a yarn after if that would be alright.

Bill said afterwards that they never ate with anyone as they found a break in routine was less than helpful. 'The old fellow Ernie is Tom's father. Those blokes have been together for over twenty years. Most of them.'

Jack was impressed by the aroma that was coming from their campfire and how quickly the food was made then eaten and cleared away. In fact, the men over there had to sit and wait politely, for them to finish.

They came over and all sat near as they could to Bill. Jack noticed how they seemed to reclaim him, he was still one of their own and he had their loyalty. The talk and the laughter went on into the night.

Jack was astounded every time Fred opened his mouth. The man was big and strong, as tough as old boot leather and wild as the country he inhabited, that was evident. But every time he opened his mouth a posh gentleman spoke.

Jack suspected he was ex-military, officer maybe, and that he was well educated. His intelligence was evident in his eyes. The little bloke Herbert seemed to gravitate to the older man.

Jack and Alby listened with fascination as the tales from these drovers went back and forth with bull catching. Jack was thirsty for knowledge from these blokes and felt let down when they had to go to bed.

They had an Afghan with them who was good for a laugh. Ernie, when he joined them was obviously the camp boss, no one back chatted him. In fact, the blokes treated him with a kind of reverence. Jack found he liked them all and was fascinated with their way of life. That they loved it, was evident.

Wayne spoke, 'I was bloody glad when the publican said you were in the other night Tom. If you hadn't come, we'd have waited weeks for a bloody truck.'

'Yeah, busy times Wayne. Nice little herd there, should get a few quid for em.'

Tom grinned at Bill now 'did you know me, and Emily had a baby girl?' He switched his gaze to Ernie, 'yep Ernie's a grand pa now.' Looking back at Wayne with a hard done by look and a whine, 'I've been trying to wet her head as best I can.' This brought a laugh from everyone.

Wayne shrugged, 'sorry to pull you away.'

'Congratulations' said Bill. 'Not to mention all her uncles here.' The drovers all smiled.

Tom smiled softly at Bill, 'you are one of those uncles Bill so don't be a stranger hay. Emily sends her best Bill.' Tom looked thoughtfully at his boots, 'I would like to speak with you Bill if that would be acceptable. Maybe at breakfast time?'

It was just like the man thought Jack to be up front about wanting to talk to his old mate. Jack admired the man and was flattered that Bill thought he was like the tall drive boss.

Bill nodded, 'sure Tom.' Tom flicked his eyes at Jack momentarily and knew instinctively that this man had taken his place. He smiled; he was glad. Glad that Bill was so happy. He had a woman to and apparently a very good one this time.

Jack saw it and saw the man switch his gaze to Alby and then back to Wayne. The smile never left his face and Jack knew they had got his approval. And for some reason Jack was glad. He knew that Tom had worked out the dynamic of the bull catchers' team very quickly indeed.

The next morning Tom took Bill aside for a short while and Fred got in the saddle with the ease of a man half his age. To Jacks dismay, he and one of the others whose name was Nevil, took up their whips, whistled a couple of dogs, and nodded to Eddy by the gate. Eddy opened the gate and the two drovers pushed through it. They pushed the four bulls they'd brought with them in to. Once inside these four bulls stood off by themselves and watched.

Fred rode slowly around the yard and as he went Jack noticed he had the bull's full attention. Unbelievably Fred started to talk to them, he talked to them in that voice of his. He talked about what was going to happen and what he expected of them, and he had complete silence and their full attention. So, he was an enigma to wild animals as well thought Jack.

Nevil rode beside him after a while and the bulls settled down. Fred whistled and the bulls they'd brought with them followed them.

Jack didn't know but these were the men who would receive these bulls straight out of the gate. They'd be familiar.

Jack and Alby looked at one another as a couple of the wild bulls started following them. Some of the other bulls followed them and then more of them. Jack saw in amazement as everyone in that yard relaxed.

Fred and Nevil rode out and got down to say hello to Jack and Alby. Jack realised that he had witnessed a master craftsman and he said so now. Fred chuckled and looked at Jack, 'well you softened them up for us see. I think one of those bulls is walking a bit funny.' Fred bowed his legs and he and Nevil laughed, and Alby joined in. Jack grinned good naturedly as was his way.

Jack shook his head, 'no I thought it would take all of us hours to get that sort of a response from them. And you were so calm.'

Fred started to roll a cigarette, 'yeah mate, that's exactly what they needed after what they've been through last few weeks. They're all young bulls and they are scared.' Fred looked apologetic 'I've done this work Jack. You have to push them around I know, but now they are ready to be led. We hope.' He bestowed his best smile on Jack and Jack was astounded at how it altered his face. The man looked years younger and quite handsome.

The little bloke Herbert came and stood beside the big man and Fred grinned down at him. Herbert grinned back and then grinned at Jack. 'The man's a genius' he said thumbing at Fred.

Jack found the little bloke to be a bit strange, but he liked him. Then it occurred to Jack that Fred and Herbert though very different physically were similar in their strangeness.

Bill and Tom re-joined the group, and they were smiling. 'I see you still got it Fred,' said Bill. He turned to Jack, and thumbing at Fed stated, 'The Pied Piper.'

Fred laughed, 'so have you got up to date on all the gossip Bill?'

Bill nodded and everyone laughed. Jack felt a pang of sorrow that they were leaving so soon. He could only imagine how Bill felt. Jack suspected that at least part of that conversation over there was trying to convince Bill to re-join his outfit. Jack knew instinctively that Bill shared that bond between them. Was part of it. Bill walked over and stood beside Jack and Wayne for one breathed a sigh of relief. Tom smiled; he sensed it.

A certain sadness assailed the drovers now as they actually embraced Bill goodbye. They tried to cover it up with a lot of bravado and back slapping, but it was tearing at them, and it was obvious. Bill couldn't speak after a while, so he just tried to keep smiling. Tom reached out and touched Bill's face, 'goodbye old friend, you're always in our hearts.' The drovers swung up into their saddles and Ernie got up in the truck. Jack saw the old man wiping his eyes as he started the motor.

Jack was astonished at how easy these drovers' showed affection and softness. Looking at them he realised that these blokes were so tough and strong and good at what they did, that they had nothing to prove. And not only that, but they had each other. And Tom, the boss, was so charismatic he was admired straight off.

When it was time to leave the yard Fred and Nevil got back in there and so did Tom. Tom waited at the gate and the four bulls followed him with Fred and Nevil to the side. The rest, encouraged by Jimmy and the dogs, all followed him out. Fred and Nevil flanked them as they spread out. As they came on through the gate the other three drovers fell into place and the whole thing went like clockwork with Jimmy the Afghan bringing up the rear.

Jack Alby and Wayne along with the rest of the men looked on dumbfounded. It was Eddy who, shaking his head said 'as often as I see it...... well it never gets old. They are bloody amazing that lot.'

Wayne turned to Jack, 'that is how they have such a good reputation for getting the stock to their destination in such good nick. There's no fuss and no stress and they don't hurry them along too much. There are none better at this than Tom and his men. It's a shame it's a dying art.' He walked away shaking his head 'bloody road trains. Cattle half dead when they get there.'

Jack and Alby stood and watched as the drovers took control of the rather large and wild herd. They took control and kept it. The whips cracked but not one made contact. Even the dogs were expert at what they did. Jack felt a pull, he wanted to be there with them, wanted to be part of it. Before it was too late.

Jimmy turned and waved a big grin on his face. Jack knew he was witnessing the end of an era.

Jack turned to see Bill smiling at him. He grinned back. 'Gets you in mate' said Bill with a faraway look in his eyes as he turned back and watched the herd move away. It was a couple of hours from lunch time, and they were on the road.

Jack said softly 'they are master craftsmen Bill, and you must have been just as bloody good. Otherwise, Tom wouldn't have taken you aside to try and get you back. Why did you not go?'

He sighed, 'Oh, you, Wayne Alby Hilda. Home every night. The rest of the boys. But I won't try and tell you it isn't hurting Jack.' He looked down at his boots, his voice so soft now that Jack had to strain his ears. 'And I can't be there when those blokes are put out to pasture.'

Jack hung his head, he felt like he'd been kicked in the guts.

The bull catchers spent another week out there and caught a few more bulls. These could wait for a truck to come, there were only twenty-two in all. They packed up and headed back to the station. They'd spend a couple of days unpacking and then they'd be off to town for a well-earned piss up. Jack was sorry it was over and so was Alby.

Bill was looking forward to being back with Hilda and the rest of the boys looked forward to the trip to town. Jack and Alby worked at unpacking and putting things away with heavy hearts. It was good, they had to admit, to sit down to one of Hilda's legendary teas. The talk was the drovers, the bull catching, Alby and Jacks injuries and of course the upcoming trip to town. The grog, the women......

When Jack got back to his room he sat on his bed in silence. He missed the camp and the hustle and bustle. Missed the camaraderie and sleeping outside. He got his writing materials out and turned his thoughts to Dan and Mary and home.

Jack realised with a start that he was looking forward to going to town. Wayne had told them all at teatime that he and Alby and Jack would be going out to Pimbara Downs station for the night on Saturday to look over some land and such.

He also informed Jack and Alby that they would be staying on for the wet. He told them that they would most likely be on a reduced rate of pay. Because of Nevil and Jim leaving and he said that Eddy would be off to his family in the gulf country.

Pete broke in and said that he had a job in Mount Isa for the wet season as usual. Said he preferred to be out of here for the wet.

'Geoff and Mike will head off in a month or so and they will come back in March. Now unless anyone has any objections, we will be off to town tomorrow for a wee drink and a good time.' The place was in an uproar.

After a while Wayne approached Jack and Alby, 'you do want to stay, don't you?'

They both nodded, 'shit yeah,' said Alby. 'We'd just have to find somewhere to go.'

'No such thing. You two are welcome to stay here for the wet whether you work or not. We don't kick people out you know, but if you're not working you get fed but you don't get paid.'

Jack was glad to be staying on, he didn't think he'd like not working though. So, he was glad he would be, glad he would still be earning. Jack knew he'd need the money. 'Thanks Wayne.'

Wayne stood a little closer and his voice dropped a little now, 'well we have a lot to do over the wet gentlemen. Fencing, erecting sheds, building a home, and moving into it.'

'I'm bloody excited Wayne' said Jack a grin on his face his eyes shining.

Wayne and Alby's faces said the same. Wane said 'I think young Mike is staying at the station here so we can throw him a few bucks to do some of the work. We'll get what we can out of the rest of them before they go.'

Jack's face turned serious now, 'you wanna buy this land Wayne or lease it?'

'Well, I was thinking we could lease it since there's an option to buy, and if everything pans out, we can buy it a bit later on.'

Jack went back to his room to write his letter. Alby said he was tired and went to bed. He sat at the table and brought his thoughts back to Dan and Mary and his home on the banks of the Murrumbidgee River. He thought about all the other people there that he loved, and a sadness engulfed him. He shook it off, he would see them all again he knew it.

Jack had reread Dan's letter. Yes, he remembered the starvation, the pain of it, the fear of it. He remembered the cold and the humiliation. He also remembered how they had all been brought closer together for it, had loved each other that little bit more.

Jack lifted his pen; it seemed awfully heavy. He filled it with ink and wrote:

13/8/1952

Dear Dan,

Thank you for your letter, Dan it was good to hear from you. I hope you are all well and happy. I know how much you enjoy watching the grass grow Dan, I only wish I enjoyed it as much.

Well, bull catching season is over for the year and I am already waiting anxiously for next year. I have never felt anything to equal it in focus and excitement. It is dangerous Dan as you say, and accidents do happen, but I loved it.

I would be overjoyed to have you come up Dan, anytime you can. I suppose during the wet would be the best time in terms of we are not usually busy then. Most everything comes to a halt in the wet which stretches from November to April. I have been assured we will work through it here on the station.

I met a team of drovers the other day Dan, they come and take away the wild bulls we catch. I found that I had the utmost respect and admiration for them Their life is not easy by any means, but I have never met such sincere and happy go lucky people. Apart from the team I work in of course, they are pretty rough and tough and yet very caring to Dan.

Some of the other blokes on the station here are talking about going into the business of bull catching full time and have asked me to go with them so I am excited and hopeful about that. There's a lot of money to be made.

I'm sorry it took so long for me to write after I left but I was traveling and living rough for a couple of months before I got the job up here. I thank you from the bottom of my heart for your forgiveness. I promise I will be careful Dan; you are not going to lose me. If I'd said goodbye I wouldn't have left.

Please give my love to Mary and the boys and Libby. And kind regards to everyone. I love it up here Dan and can't wait for you to visit, you and Wally. I talked to Wayne the manager and he says you can stay here. He says he'll put you to work. I believe he means it; you'll like him Dan. I have included phone number for station, in the address you can get me on that anytime.

I will close now Dan; I hope you write again I look forward to your letters. I may very well come home someday Dan and I will come for visits to. As you say mate, two planes two days. Bye for now, I remain,

Yours faithfully
Jack

Jack cried himself to sleep, it'll get easier he told himself, over and over. But for now, he had a dreadful feeling of homesickness that he hadn't had during his six years away in the war. For those six years he looked forward to going home soon. Now he knew he never would never could.

Jack didn't visit with Mary that night he was too heart sick. It wasn't getting any easier trying to give her up. Jack worried about Alby; he knew he was hurt more than he let on. Why had it to be so?

Chapter 13

It was time to get in the vehicles and get into town to the pub. As usual everyone was excited and jumping out of their skins. Alby sat in the back of the land rover with Jack. Garry got in the driver's seat as Bill was staying at home.

'Try and stay awake this time' they told him. Geoff got in beside Garry. 'See if you can keep him awake' they advised him. Alby leaned out over the back and sang out, 'Jacks driving home, you blokes.'

The mood was light and there was much laughter that morning. And despite his last trip, Jack was excited to, though he knew not why. Jack did however suspect he would probably do more drinking this trip. Christ he was thirsty. He hadn't been this thirsty since he got out of khaki. There was that and the business they had to do.

Mike the young jackaroo climbed in with Jack and Alby sensing the same in them as Russel had. Pete and Eddy got in the back of Wayne's vehicle, and they were off.

Bill stood at the gate waiting to close it, 'Gunna miss you old man' yelled Alby.

Everyone yelled their agreement and waved. Bill wasn't sad about not going he had to get his drinking under control. He was serious about making a go of it with Hilda. He laughed good naturedly and waved back closing the gate behind them. He felt a pang as he latched the gate.

Bill had told Tom of his relationship with Hilda and had told him how he didn't know if he was free or not. Tom had smiled and put his hand on Bills shoulder. 'Yes, I remember Bill, you telling me about it. I wrote a letter via a JP and sent it to the birth's deaths and marriages. Didn't hear anything for ages buddy. Then you left and not long after that I got a letter from them. Your wife divorced you back in '42. I sent you a letter, but I got it back, so I didn't know where you were. Well then, I forgot about it.' Tom smiled and handed Bill some papers.

'While I was at it, I got your certificates. That's what I wanted to talk to you about mate. I found out you were here last time we came though we didn't get to see you, and so I brought these with me just in case. There's a marriage certificate a birth certificate and a dissolution of marriage certificate. For your Christmas present, don't lose them, right?' Tom squeezed Bill's shoulder, 'we miss you, Bill. Anytime you want to come back alright?'

Bill was at a loss for words, he looked at Tom. 'Thanks Tom' he said softly, 'please don't ask me to go with you Tom it would make things too bloody hard. I miss you all. I am in a relationship now with someone I love very much.'

Bill had stopped talking and Tom shook his shoulder. 'Good on ya mate. Tell you what, next wet I'll come over for a few weeks hay? Me and whoever else. I'll give you a call a bit closer, I know the number here.' Tom watched as Bills face brightened and he knew he'd have to make good on his promise no matter what.

Bill mentioned the bull catching endeavour and was pleased to see that Tom was so interested. Tom told him that they could give them a hand even. And then Tom told him goodbye. And they were gone, and Bill had a lump he couldn't swallow.

And now Bill was closing the gate on his new family as they departed. He looked forward to spending alone time with Hilda though.

Wayne had suggested to Bill the day before that if it was their desire to live together there was another double room they could move into.

Other than the one Hilda had lived in with Nevil. 'You know' Wayne had finished softly, awkwardly.

Bill stood staring at Wayne and watched as the man grew decidedly uncomfortable. 'No, bugger that' Bill had replied at last, 'I'm moving into the house with you. Yes, indeed I am.'

'Oh fuck' Wayne had said and left him to it. He knew Bill was enjoying himself at Wayne's expense as usual. He stopped and turned around saying 'there are only single beds in there.'

'Yeah, I know' grinned Bill, 'already pushed them together.' Bill laughed hysterically at Wayne. The other blokes had heard it and they all laughed with him. Wayne hurried off shrugging his shoulders, there was just no arguing with Bill.

Bill walked back to the mess now in the lingering dust from the vehicles. When he looked up there was Hilda watching him. He walked up, a smile on his face and put his arm around her. 'Are you okay Bill' she asked, grateful he'd stayed yet a little concerned?

'Course I am love, course I am. I'm here with you girl. And we got the place to ourselves, what could be better? Did you think I would leave you here alone woman? We'll go into town one day on our own Hay. Have us a nice time woman, what do you say?'

'You could have….'

'I know woman and thank you. But I would rather be here with you. I bloody missed you; you know.' Bill took his woman in his arms and held her gently, 'you know I gotta get this drinking under control, don't you? I don't want to be a drunken husband, Hilda. You deserve better.'

Hilda kissed him and held him to her. She loved this man she really did. She did also realise how much he must have wanted to go off with Tom when he left.

She sighed and Bill tightened his arms around her.

The boys arrived in town at a bit after two. After throwing their things in their rooms they headed for the bar. They lined up on stools and grinned at the barman, 'line em up,' said Wayne, he always bought the first few rounds. He always put ten pounds on the bar, and he did this now.

Jack sat next to Wayne and Alby sat next to him. Mike lined up with them next to Alby and Geoff, then Pete and Eddy. Wayne got a whiskey and the rest of them got pints.

The barman looked at Jack as he put his beer in front of him, 'Jesus! Well, you don't look as pretty as you did last time you were here. Hay, wait a minute, you're the one, the one that kicked a bull in the balls.' He laughed and shook his head. 'Well did you learn anything son?'

'Yep' Jack smiled and nodded, he expected to get a lot of that.

'Well, what did you learn then son?'

'They hit a bit harder than I do.'

The barman laughed and told Jack 'The next ones on the house mate.' The barman eyed the tenner flicked his eyes at Wayne, then back to Jack. 'After you've finished this.' He picked up the tenner and left to get change.

The men sat and downed a few beers and started to get loud, the drink was affecting them now. Pete and Eddy spotted a couple of girls and went off to sit with them and Garry went to sit with an old mate. Geoff was in conversation with Mike, the two of them didn't know many people. So, when the boys over at the girls table sang out to them, they went and joined them.

Wayne sat forward and leaned on the bar; he'd switched to beer. 'I had a conversation with my boss the other day Jack, he rang me up to kick my arse on account of you two getting hurt this last two months. He reminded me that he alone was picking up the tab for all these injuries. So, anyway I reminded him what a dangerous game it was and how we always have injuries, just about every bull season.' Wayne took a swig of his beer downing half the glass and dropped it back on the bar.

Jack looked at Alby and back to Wayne, Alby was studying the ufo again. They waited sensing more was to come. And it did. Wayne took a deep breath and told Jack and Alby of his conversation with the boss, concerning the bulls. He said that he had suggested farming the bull catching out to an independent contractor.

The boss had said 'but we make a lot of money each year on them.' Wayne had replied that they also spend a lot of money catching them. 'Anyway' said Wayne now, 'he finally asked me if I knew anybody who would be interested in taking on a contract like that. I said yes, I do.

Then he told me to see them and hammer out some prices. He wants to make a little money on them he said.' Wayne smiled and went on, 'so it looks like we are in business gentlemen'. They raised their glasses quietly.

'So, we have to figure out the money side of it,' said Jack. 'How much money we'd make and how much money it's gunna cost us.'

'The other thing chaps is that my mate Stew says we can come out anytime tomorrow to inspect the shed. It's a good price really, the bloody thing is I think around three hundred feet by one hundred feet. There's a smaller shed that we could get that's I think one hundred and fifty feet by a hundred feet. We could cement them and use the smaller one for living quarters. We'd need to insulate it and petition it up into six bedrooms and a kitchen.' Wayne ordered another three drinks then looked at Jack, 'is tomorrow alright Jack?'

Jack nodded and turned to Alby who nodded, the ufo forgotten. 'Did you know that Bill is coming in with us Wayne' asked Jack?

Wayne nodded and Jack smiled. 'Well did you know he's bringing Hilda with him?'

Wayne grinned 'thank Christ.' He studied his beer for a moment and said, 'I guess we'll have to put in a real good kitchen.'

'Of course, she'll cook but she intends to negotiate Wayne.'

Wayne groaned and put his hand to his head. Jack tuned to Alby now, 'that's the dinner bell Alby, are you coming to get something to eat?' Alby nodded. Jack turned to Wayne who got off his stool finishing his beer. 'Yeah, I'll come with ya Jack.'

When the three men sat at the table, they ordered a meal and a beer and there they sat until the dining room closed, talking about the new business endeavour. Wayne said he'd get hold of the boss and ask him if he would sell them the vehicles and the gear since he wouldn't be needing it anymore.

Wayne looked at Alby and Jack and said quietly, 'are you two blokes sure you still want to do this? I mean you both got bloody hurt. Alby you could've got crushed and you Jack could have bloody well bled out. So, you might need more time to……. you know….'

Jack and Alby sat shaking their heads and Jack spoke. 'No, I love this life, Wayne and we got it down pat now mate. Mind you if it hadn't been for this here bull catching, I'd have run off with those bloody drovers. What a life they've got hay?'

Wayne was nodding a smile on his face 'I did it for a while Jack and I bloody loved it. If I thought, there was a future in it I'd be back out there tomorrow. But I give em about fifteen, twenty years and they'll be hanging up their saddles. I believe Tom has bought himself a station, so he'll be right, and he'll see all his blokes right to if I know anything. I did here a whisper that they were planning a sort of co-op, and by pooling their money, they'd be able to buy more and bigger. Tom'll be alright. And it's a crying shame, but I think the drovers will continue to pick up work doing local and cross-country trips for a few years to come yet and pick up some extra cash droving our bulls, hay. I hope so anyway.'

'They seem to have a very strong bond between them,' said Jack.

'Yeah, I heard what happened to them. They were droving a herd to Alice Springs, and they went into a place called the Devils Canyon.'

Alby sucked in air 'shit I heard about that, that was them?'

'Yeah, well when they came out after losing one of their number in there, they were all different. And they've stuck together ever since. And they have kept it to themselves.' Wayne looked at Alby.

'Devil's Canyon' asked Jack intrigued?

Wayne told Alby and Jack everything he knew and when he was finished Alby and Jack sat with their mouths open. 'Do you reckon there's anything in it' asked Jack? 'It is Tom and his blokes, and they all seem like really down to earth men.'

'Yeah' nodded Wayne, 'certainly makes you think. I wouldn't venture in there, just on their say so Jack.'

Jack looked around 'I think these ladies would like us to leave chaps.' They got up and went back to the bar. Jack knew why these men all stuck together now; he understood it. Like him and Alby, and Wayne and Bill from the wars. Jack wondered about Bill. He said this now.

'If you ask them, they just clam up and close ranks on you apparently. Best to leave it alone Jack.'

It was almost nine o'clock when Jack looked over and watched Sandy walk in the bar. Alby hadn't seen it he was messing around with Mike. Sandy walked over to Jack and Wayne 'g'day young lady,' said Jack. 'You wanna come and sit with us' and he patted the stool beside him? He felt immediately sorry for the kid she looked so young and startled.

Alby saw it and stood where he was ordering another beer. Jack thought the big man was going to ignore her. Sandy hardly took her eyes off Alby and looked nervous when he left the table and came over.

'Hello' he said quietly, his voice strained. 'How are you, Sandra?'

'I'm good thanks Alby. Can we talk? I got your letter......'

Alby bought her a lemon squash and took the girl to a table nearby and sat down. He leaned across and said quietly, 'what are you doing here Sandra? This is no place for a girl. Does your mother know you are here? Does she?'

Sandy put her head down and shook it, tears were forming in her eyes. Jack saw it in the bar mirror and his heart ached for them. He knew how they felt about each other. He leaned over to Wayne, 'do you think Alby's sober enough to drive?'

'Yeah Jack, tell him he can take the rover and take her home.'

Alby was at a loss. He said now, 'Sandy I explained in my letter. This between us cannot be. For one you are too young.'

'Yes, Alby and the next time you come into town I won't be. I just wanted to see you. Can't you even be friends with me Alby.'

'No Sandy, I can't.' Alby was getting flustered.

Jack arrived at the table and smiling he handed Alby the keys. 'Why don't you take her home Alby. This is no place.'

Alby took the keys and stood up, 'which one?'

'The one out the front mate.' Jack turned to Sandy his heart aching for the girl. If he was any guess, she had actually fallen in love with the big guy, but it was none of his business. 'It's very nice to see you again young lady.' Jack turned to Alby and saw a look of absolute adoration on his face as he looked at her. He went back to the bar shaking his head.

'Come on then' Alby said softly, 'I'll take you home to your Mumma. Are you going to introduce me to your parents Sandy?' Alby saw her drop her eyes; she didn't answer. He said now, 'you see girl? I'm not willing to sneak around. Now come on I will drop you home.'

The two left the bar. 'What do you make of it' Wayne asked Jack?

'It's a bloody shame. He's head over heels in love and so is she. It's just a month or so, a bit less, I think. At least that's what I think. Mind you he claims he needs more time to move on from Sue.'

Wayne shook his head and downed his drink. He got off his stool 'well I'm gunna turn in Jack, it's been a long day.'

'I'll just wait here see if Alby gets back.'

'Good man Jack, good man.'

It was nearly an hour before Alby got back and Jack could see at once that he was hurting. Alby came and sat on a stool next to Jack and Jack put his hand on Alby's shoulder 'wanna drink Alby?'

'No thanks mate I think I'll just turn in.'

Jack looked into Alby's face 'if she'd said she'd introduce you to her parents? What then Alby?'

A hint of a smile played around Alby's face. 'Well, that's just it, Jack, she did. They don't have a problem with it, in fact they thanked me for bringing her home. I had a bit of a chat and then left. Sandy saw me out to the vehicle. She kissed me Jack, I mean kissed me. I have never been kissed like that before, not anywhere near it. Now I know what the look on Russel's face was all about. It was close Jack; you have no idea how I wanted her.'

Jack chuckled, 'good on ya Alby, you decided what you want to do?'

'Yeah Jack, get the hell out of town and stay out.' The smile on Alby's face bespoke a different scenario on his mind.

Jack arrived in the dining room for breakfast, Wayne and Alby were already there. Wayne grinned at him 'saw you heading off to the bathroom and so I ordered you the big breakfast Jack. I've seen you eat mate you're as good on the fang as me. Should be here any minute.'

After they'd eaten Jack went to the shops and then the three men went to see the sheds. It was a drive of about a half a mile out of town. 'It'll take us a few weeks to shift these,' said Jack. The sheds were in good condition and the big one would hold all the plant including the truck. 'Was this an aeroplane hangar' asked Jack?

Wayne grinned and shrugged, 'looks a bit like it' he said. 'The doors on either side will come in handy Jack. Shouldn't take us too long to get it down move it and put it up again. We'll get everybody in here to help and we've got until next year or the year after. If you are up for it the bloke, I want to get the land from will see us this afternoon, anytime.'

'Yeah, no worries, Wayne. You in Alby?' Alby nodded his head Jack suspected the big man had had little sleep.

The three men arrived back in town the next morning and went to the bar to see if there had been any trouble the night before with the blokes. All was well so Wayne ordered three beers. They drank them and sat talking about the sheds. 'Bill told me that Tom and the boys had offered to come and help while they are sitting out the wet,' said Jack.

'That'd be good but even if they don't, we'll get it all organised. I want to get out there and mark out where we want the concrete floors. I'd like that done before the wet sets in. It's August now so we may have only six to eight weeks that we can be sure of.'

When they'd finished their beers, Alby stood up and leaned restlessly on the bar. Jack looked up at him smiling, 'well go on mate, we'll be still here when you get back.'

Alby looked down at Jack he smiled faintly. 'And where am I going Jack?'

'Jesus Alby, why don't you go and see the girl. Take her for some lunch or something. Have a conversation with her, get to know her. Her parents have no objections.'

Wayne slid off the stool and got the keys out of his pocket, handing them to Alby he said, 'go on son, go see her.' He smiled at Jack now and said, 'next time we come into town we'll have to clean the bloody thing.'

Alby looked down at the keys then back at Wayne, 'thanks mate.'

Wayne nodded and sat back down, 'we've got the other one if we need to go anywhere. If you prang it try and make it someone else's fault, there's a good lad. Have a nice time mate.' Wayne sat back down, he wasn't much at this fatherly stuff, and he knew it. He would never know how much it had meant to Alby.

Jack grinned at the look on Alby's face 'Buy her some flowers.'

So it was that, armed with a bunch of flowers Alby knocked on Sandy's door. He was breathless and wondered how he would even speak.

As soon as the girl opened the door her eyes widened, and her mouth dropped open. She gazed at the flowers Alby had pushed towards her. Then looking back up at him she grinned and took the flowers. 'Oh, thank you Alby, they're lovely. Come in. Mum and Dad are away till tomorrow and we...'

'No' Alby almost shouted and this brought a giggle from the girl. 'Well... that is I thought ...... I 'd take you for some lunch. You know... have a talk.'

Sandy looked doubtful, 'is it going to be a good talk Alby? A nice talk....? You know '

Alby looked at the flowers and back at her and lifted his eyebrows.

He took her to a café, and they talked for a couple of hours. By the time they left the café Alby was good and in love. His heart sang as it never had. And this beautiful girl held onto his arm and gazed adoringly up at him as they walked through the street. Alby was ten feet tall.

When Alby left her promising to come and see her as soon as he could, he took her in his arms and kissed her. His head swam and he got a feeling he had never thought possible. 'How I love you woman' he whispered, touching her face he walked away quickly.

He had reached the land rover when he felt her take his hand. Turning he looked into her eyes so full of love and desire. He knew instinctively that his were the same. Said the same. He also knew he was in trouble, big trouble.

Sandy slipped her arms around him and held him and shyly she said 'I know what happened to you, I know you've been married. I am so sorry Alby so very....... I can never take her place........ I......'

She was pulled roughly into his arms, and he said thickly 'hush now woman. I don't want you to take anybody's place. I just want you by my side. You hear Sandy?'

She nodded as she snuggled into his arms, 'Oh Alby, have I made you mad?'

'Of course not.' He kissed her and he felt her melt into him. Alby hadn't had the chance to get into bed with Sue, so this was all new to him. He told Sandy this now and she hugged him tighter.

He stepped back and taking her hand he took her back to the veranda out of sight of the neighbour's.

He was aroused and he knew she had felt it and hadn't pulled away. She reached up and standing on tip toe she kissed his neck. She murmured his name and a thrill surged through him.

Alby tried with all his might to tear himself away, but she wanted him with a passion. A passion equal to his own. A need equal to his. 'Oh God' he moaned and helped her to open the front door.

Chapter 14

It was getting on towards the end of September and the station was gearing down for the wet season. The work on moving the sheds was taking over all else. October was nearing and Wayne was anxious to have the sheds back up before the rains.

Alby had been back to see his sweetheart as she now was, every chance he got. Though the man was obviously very much in love he was always professional and stuck by Jack. He knew he'd always need Jack. Jack and Wayne understood him, and he could always rely on them and Bill. But Alby had to let Sue go. And Alby knew he loved the girl Sandra very much. She filled in the blanks and then some. But best of all she loved him in a way he'd never been loved before. And Alby liked it, he liked it very much.

The concrete had been laid for the sheds and they had finished pulling the bigger shed down. Wayne had a truck organised for two weeks' time. He wanted the small shed ready to go by then, Jack thought the man was possessed. Everyone thought he was possessed, even Wayne thought he was possessed.

It had occurred to Jack that it was another long hut. He wanted a good kitchen and a ceiling fan. He also wanted to build a veranda on and had started planning it.

Jack bought a Ute, it was a '48 Ford, two-wheel drive. It was handy for making the three-hour trip to town into a two-and-a-half-hour trip to town. The property had been sorted out and they had paid for the twelve-month lease. They had taken five thousand acres which was on the way into town. They would build their sheds about five miles from town. Amidst all this activity and excitement, Jack got a letter on the mail cart from Dan and found himself a quiet place. He opened it and read:

25/9/1952

Dear Jack'

It was good to get your letter and to hear you are okay. It was also good to hear that you have things to look forward to. Such exciting things at that. There is nothing like a new business venture lad. I am most glad to hear of your happiness Jack, nobody deserves it more than you. It does my heart good to hear of it.

I am thinking of coming up early in the new year. You know how Christmases are around here. With such a large family of kids it takes forever to plan and then do it. We have had another added to our number, a baby boy from Kath and Josh they named Jack. That gives us ten now Jack, under age fourteen.

Anyway Jack, I just want to say that I do understand why you left the way you did. No hard feeling mate, none at all. And I would have tried to selfishly talk you out of it. We love you lad. I was heartened at your words saying you may well come back someday. I will hang on to that Jack, thank you.

I will leave some room for Mary now Jack she wants to say hello. I will call the number you gave me soon and organise a date so I can organise tickets. Thanks Jack it's important to us so we can let you go. I don't think you are coming home this time. Well goodbye for now old man, see you soon.

Yours Faithfully
Dan

(Mary)

Dear Jack,

I just wanted to write a few lines and say hello. I am glad Dan is coming up to see you, I shall make the trip myself someday, that's a promise. I need to know you are alright. Please remember that there is a place here for you Jack, a place to call home. Forever Jack.

It was so good to hear from you after you left and to hear you love us. Glad you are loving it up there and that you are among friends. That's important, and I thank you for letting me know that. Write soon Jack, Bye for now.

All my love.
Mary

Jack held the letter pressed to his bosom until he could breathe again and got slowly to his feet. There was work to be done.

He walked around the side of the shed and there was Alby, waiting for him. 'How was it Jack' he asked quietly?

Jack couldn't speak of it, so he passed the letter to Alby. The big man scanned the page looked up and nodded. 'Shit mate' he said as he slung an arm round Jack. And like that they walked off to get to work on their project. Alby sniffed a couple of times, but they said no more.

Wayne saw them come out from behind the shed from across the yard. He'd seen Jack go behind the tool shed to read his letter. Looking at Jack now he knew it wasn't good. But Alby had him, Alby knew what to do. Fuck it all thought Wayne, why?

That night Wayne wrote to Rhonda, she hadn't answered his last letter, so it was just a note saying he hoped she was well. He also told her he was busy and would make this a short note.

Wayne had purchased fencing gear and had Alby and Bill out putting that up. They had taken their swags so as to stay out for a bit. The men had measured the five thousand acres off very carefully with the owner and everyone was happy with the arrangement. The yards that would initially hold the bulls would have to be made of sturdy stuff. They would use timber and iron.

There was an excitement building in these men. As soon as the sheds were up, they would take possession of the vehicles. The boss wanted the lot off the property, he'd got what he thought was a very fair price. Wayne spent hours with Garry sorting out his tools from the stations and found they would still need to acquire some more.

By Octobers end the men had the big shed up and had started on the small one. Bill had got a phone call from Tom, and they turned up early in November. The small shed was up and fitted out in a couple of weeks and Jack was very happy with it. Tom and Fred and Jimmy and Charlie had come. Jack couldn't get over the way they worked together. It was a pleasure to work with them and it had put a grin on Bills face. Jimmy and Fred ended up doing the fencing with Eddy and Pete.

It was a grey Sunday at the end of October and Wayne had taken a day to catch up on paperwork in his office. He also had been impressed by the drovers, their ethic and their intelligence and their willingness to just get on with it. The phone rang and as soon as he heard the man on the other end say hello, he knew it was Dan.

Wayne was at a loss, and he knew he was making a hash of it. It was like talking to God. 'Hello' he said when he picked up the phone, 'Wayne here, what can I do for you?'

Dan said 'hello, my name is Dan Roberts. I was hoping I might speak to Jack. I hope it is not a bad time to be calling.'

'Err…. No of course not. I'm Wayne the manager here….'

'Nice to meet you Wayne'.

The man's voice inspired a calmness in Wayne. Though flabbergasted he said, 'Look mate I am sorry, but Jack is out working at the moment, is there any chance you could call tonight?'

Dan laughed and said 'yes of course, thank you for your time. While I have you here Wayne, I would confide in you if I may.'

'Yeah, mate if I can help in any way, I know how much you mean to Jack.'

Dan laughed softly now and said as softly, 'he means the world to us mate. I'm glad he is happy there. I don't think from the sound of it that we will get him back this time. I wish to come up and see him you know just to be sure he's okay. We need to be able to let him go like, you understand?'

There was a tinge of deep sadness in the man's voice that affected Wayne. The three people were in a hell of a situation, and they all loved each other. Hells bells thought Wayne he didn't bloody know.

He said now, 'yes yes of course. He told me you would come and I'm glad you are. He has come to mean a lot to us here so you and whoever you bring will be very welcome.'

'Thank you very much Wayne. Now when would be a good time for you to have us about the place. The two of us.'

'Anytime at all. We could always use more hands. I don't know if Jack has told you we are embarking on a business venture.'

'Yes, the bull catching Wayne, he seems very keen. I can't remember when I knew him to be so keen on anything.' Dan laughed and went on 'I was thinking a bit after Christmas. I could narrow it down to January fourteenth. Will there still be plenty of work for us by then?'

'Anytime that suits you. I will tell Jack to expect you then. I will make sure you get a ride up here on the mail cart if you like and we'll pick you up in town.'

By the time Wayne hung up he had decided he liked the man. Dan had said he'd call back the following Sunday and he would call about seven o'clock at night. He thanked Wayne for his time and said that he looked forward to meeting him. 'Nice talking with you Wayne' he'd said.

Jesus Wayne thought, the man had made Wayne realise that his approval actually did matter to him. Yes, this was a man Wayne wanted to meet. This was the man who had brought these people, including Jack, through the depression and had saved Jacks life and that of many others. Women and babies, he'd heard, and a troupe of young men. And he'd done it all without raising his voice.

Wayne found himself wishing he could meet Mary. The man was a legend but so was his wife. Poor bloody Jack. Yet, Wayne thought now, lucky bloody Jack. He couldn't wait to talk to Jack now.

❋

Tom and the boys left just after halfway through November. The sheds all up, the smaller one lined and sectioned into living quarters. Jack had insisted on insulating the living quarters. There was still a lot of miles of fencing so they promised to come back after Christmas, and they would finish the yards as well.

When Tom met Hilda the two of them hit it off at once. And when Hilda met Fred, she was enthralled, falling under his spell like most women did. Bill was pleased that she liked them all even Jimmy and Charlie. Herbert he wasn't familiar with, but Fred liked him so... Hilda could see how much good it had done Bill to have them around. When they left, promising to return in a couple of months, everyone was sad to see them go.

Jack asked Tom where he had bought his station. 'I got five hundred thousand acres just across the border about three hundred miles, it is a long narrow piece of land. So, we will be a lot closer. We are working now to put cattle on it.' Tom grinned. 'I hope your enterprise here takes off for you, I am happy for Bill for his part in it and his new relationship. She is a lovely woman.'

'Well, it is good of you to help us with all this' said Jack running his eyes over the living quarters.

Tom smiled 'we are busy doing this very same thing Jack. Not a long hut but a few smaller huts.' He clapped Jack on the shoulder, 'glad we could help. Glad Bill has got you Jack.'

Jack had an excitement growing in the pit of his belly. The living quarters were done complete with a shower at the end of the veranda and two toilets off the end of the veranda. Bill was busy in the big shed, building Hilda's kitchen.

The day he'd got home, and Wayne told him of his phone call with Dan, Jack had been ecstatic. Dan was coming and Wally to. Jack's hand went to his face and his fingers traced the jagged scar.

Wayne saw it and the grin dropped from his face. 'What do you think he'll make of it, Jack' asked Wayne touching his own face?

Jack smiled ruefully, 'he'll probably wonder if I am any good at catching bulls. And if he finds out that I kicked it in the nuts he'll wonder if I had too many bombs dropped on my head in the war. He will be concerned Wayne; he worries about those he loves.'

'Well, I'm glad he's coming. And this Wally he is bringing with him?'

'Yes', said Jack, 'Wally lost the use of his left arm in the war. He can still use it a bit but not enough to get back to his job. But Dan has found an occupation for him, and he loves it. He's happy where he is. Dan was a big help to him when he got home as he was to me, he's only about twelve years older than us but he's a mother hen. But I love it up here, I doubt I will ever go back for longer than a wet season.'

Wayne smiled, 'you are lucky to have had him Jack very lucky. And he was lucky to have you to lad. Don't forget that, Jack.' Wayne stood up to go and looked back 'Christmas is just round the corner, and we have a lot to do.' Wayne turned and looked squarely at Jack, 'is this visit with Dan likely to dredge up painful things for you Jack?'

Jack smiled up at the man he had come to admire, 'not unless he brings Mary with him.' He got up to now, 'we have got a lot more done than I thought we would Wayne. It's just the fencing that worries me now.'

'Yeah, we've done better than I thought. By February or March, it should all be finished. We should be in by next bull catching season. Of course, we are going to need jobs until then, aren't we?' Wayne smiled his characteristic smile you couldn't help but answer. He went on, 'I'll stay on here as manager and you boys can work here when you're not catching bulls. But there will be plenty of work for you to do when you are here. It'll be catch up Jack.'

Jack grinned at Wayne, the thought of working long hard hours was more of a comfort to him. Wayne knew it only too well.

Christmas came and went, and Wayne and Hilda had excelled. Wayne gave all the men a bottle of scotch for Christmas, Bill got a bottle of lemonade and Hilda a box of chocolates. Hilda had put on a spread that was better than a fancy hotel thought Jack. She had done ham, turkey, roast beef, and gravy.

There was Christmas cake and pudding with custard.

She had also served up salad as well as the roast vegetables. Fruit and lollies and nuts were put out on the tables. Jack sat and stared at it, the tables laden with food and drinks. It took him back to Christmas at the long hut. Jack said this now and found himself explaining the long hut to Wayne.

There were just six of them there for Christmas dinner as the rest were away. There were only him, Wayne, Hilda, Bill, Alby, and Mike. Jack began, he felt as though he was the entertainment. He took his time.

He told them of the years on the road after his father had died after the bank had taken the farm. He told them of the state he was in when Dan found him on the side of the road. How the man and his dying wife had cared for him, loved him. He told them of the others the women and children and old men. Told them of his family and his love for them. He went on. Alby listened and watched Jack with hooded eyes, he knew the pain all too well.

'When we arrived in Balranald, we were starving and had little to our name. We had only each other and Dan. The townspeople weren't happy at our arrival. We camped on the outskirts of town, but the council came and moved us on. We did find out later it was just a few of them making it their business to hassle us. Well moving wasn't really hard, we had probably four tents some tarpaulin shelter and pots and pans. We had very little bedding, and very little else.'

Jack stopped talking to eat for a while. He was reliving every bit of it and trying not to let his feelings show. Wayne spotted it, they all spotted it. 'Must have been bloody hard Jack. And you had old people and babies' Wayne asked?

Jack nodded. 'Yes, we lost two babies and three old people on the road. Anyhow we moved on to the commons and thought we'd be right for a while. It was March and winter was approaching. The winters are cruel there, the cold will kill you quick as the heat.'

Wayne nodded and kept his head down. 'I know Jack, quicker even. I spent a winter there after the war. That was enough for me.'

They waited for Jack to continue. He did, 'We didn't know how long we could last. The children were getting weaker, and we all fed the poor little blighters from our meagre plates. Dan had got us there; the man took people into his tent when it was so cold lives would be lost outside. He worked tirelessly to keep us sheltered and fed. He planted what he could and caught what he could, but he had little to work with. And nobody cared. Government assistance was almost nothing, the old fellas gave what they got. We were just hanging on by this, trying to stay alive.'

Jack had to stop his throat was hurting and his voice failing. He daren't put anything in his mouth as he let a tear fall. Bill put his hand briefly on his shoulder. Surprisingly he said softly to Jack, 'go on get it all out man.'

Jack nodded, 'then one day Mary shows up. Pulls her cart up out the front of Dan's tent and starts pulling bags of produce from her farm out of the cart. Potatoes, carrots, onions, flour, milk, and such. She had picked up three of our thin kids and brought them home see'. Jack breathed deeply.

'Then she marches up to Dan and says she had a proposition for him. And the next day we had bags of seed and an acre to plant them in. She gave us what we needed to feed ourselves, it was unbelievable. She even let us use her plough behind her horse Lilly. She gave us traps and fishing lines and we were never starving hungry again.'

Everyone at the table had stopped eating and you could hear a pin drop. The tale Jack told was unbelievable, but they all knew he spoke the truth. The emotion in his voice spoke of his deep feelings, his treasured memories. The tears in his eyes told them of his pain and his loss.

Jack went on 'then, you guessed it the council told us to move on they didn't want us there either. Mary told us this and then she says to Dan, 'I will give you another acre to use. We'll build a long hut she says, just like the Vikings used to make. And we better get moving the winter is almost upon us. And we built a long hut measuring I think around thirty feet by seventy it sort of grew as we built it and then some of the blokes put up smaller rooms to sleep in. Anyway, the blokes slept one end and families at the other and a big kitchen in between. Many good and happy meals we ate there all together and Mary joined us, and we became a real family. We salvaged materials from the dump for the build. We all moved into it and never lost another soul, we slept warm, and we were all fed adequately. Dan lost his wife she had been dying for so long it was a blessing, and the man had never left her side. He has a way with his people he will muck in when the work needs doing. Then he's soft and tender when you're hurting.'

Jack kept his eyes fixed on his plate. 'We all love him and Mary. They all still live together you know. When Mary married Dan, she moved in with him. She moved out of her little house and moved in with him. Some of them have made their own bedrooms onto the long hut, Mary and Dan included, but they still eat together and live together. I don't think they could do without each other now.'

Jack heaved a sigh, 'In the end Mary signed four acres over to us all so we could feel safe and secure.' Jack gave a laugh now, 'Mary never liked councils much.'

A pain crossed his face now, 'some men from the council hurt her once, broke into her house and hurt her. Well Dan set forth on a trail of revenge and not one of them still resides in Balranald. And not one of them doesn't know he's lucky to be alive, with the scars to prove it.'

Jack put his elbows on the table and drew a deep shaky breath. Hilda eyed him for a moment then said, 'thank you for sharing that Jack, I know it was hard. We really ought to be very grateful. Now they are all in and out of the weather and have plenty to eat. I would like to meet them. Every one of them and I can't wait to meet Dan and Wally. I think you are fine people.'

'Thanks Hilda,' said Jack. 'Dan and Mary farm wheat and make good money which they share with everyone, and Dan and Mary and the others also grow market gardens which they sell at the markets in town. Their produce almost always sells. Some of the women make pickles and jams and such and the old fellows make wooden furniture and even plates and cutlery, just out of second hand off cuts. The profits mostly go to the community. When they have pigs, rabbits, or fish they smoke or salt them and sell them to. It seems like they fed the whole town during the hard times, they never raised their prices see, Dan wouldn't hear of it. They sell milk and lamb to. The towns people wouldn't have fared so well without them. Some of the people work and they all hand most of their wages over to Dan. He sent all the kids to school; they have toys now. He does improvements to the hut; you'd never know it was all built from cast offs.'

'Hell' said Wayne at a loss for words.

Alby sniffed. 'That's a family I'd have bloody liked to have been a part of Jack.'

The rest of dinner went off without a hitch. Wayne asked Jack some questions which Jack didn't mind answering. Wayne said 'well I take my hat off to Dan and the rest of you. And I take my hat off to Mary to, what a generous soul. You all came through it none the worse, I think. Maybe even better for the experience Jack. If you just hadn't fallen in love with the same girl you would agree, wouldn't you?'

Jack looked at Wayne and noticed the lack of malice and even the love in his face and nodded. 'I do Wayne'.

Wayne put his knife and fork down, 'now for some of that lovely pudding you make Hilda.' Wayne smiled at her. He looked at Bill now 'how's that kitchen going Bill?'

'Yep, it's ready to go in.'

'Good, good. You might like to swap over onto beds Bill. Make em all doubles my friend.'

Bill cleared his throat, 'have to order some mattresses up.'

'Already done mate' Wayne smiled rising out of his chair. He dropped his voice, 'I hope you have made a lovely kitchen for Hilda.'

Hilda shouted from the kitchen, 'that won't save you from paying me a decent wage Wayne. So don't think it.'

Wayne sat back heavily in his chair. Bill grinned at him, and it was kind of malicious.

Jack looked at Alby now and said simply, 'you to Alby?'

Alby nodded 'yeah mate. We got kicked out of the house and went on the road in a tent. My old man went after the rabbits a bit farther North than where you were. He had an old ford and he managed to keep us fed reasonably well. One of my sisters died but.'

'I'm sorry Alby. What family do you have left Alby?'

'Well, my dad died and so I got an old mum down in Cunnamulla but she's in a nursing home now and doesn't have a clue who I am. I got a sister married in Long Reach, she goes to see her, but mum doesn't know her either. Jan, my sister lived in Blackall before that, and she was a nurse there. She has two kids; I haven't seen them for a few years. Her husband doesn't like me, and I only cause trouble for my sister. This is the first Christmas I haven't been alone in a lot of years.' Alby looked down 'I get a card from Jan and the kids every Christmas, but they usually take a while to catch up with me.' Alby looked down, 'I write once a year and let her know I'm okay.'

'Yeah, well that's gunna change son, no more eating alone Christmas day or any other day really,' said Wayne. He raised his glass 'to family mate, our bloody family.'

He winked at Jack and with raised glass he said, 'and here's to our very own long hut.'

That night when Alby got back to his room he wrote to his sister with pen and paper he'd borrowed from Jack. He poured his heart into that letter. He promised her he would visit mum soon and he would call on her. 'I will stay at a hotel' he told her. 'So as I don't antagonise your husband. I do know he is good to you and the kids so he's alright with me. I have grown up a little, sort of getting over things. I love you sis and the kids.' He went on to tell her of his new venture and the friends he would go into it with. He spoke to her of Jack and Wayne and Bill.

He told her he would send her some money for the kids for a present. 'I hope twenty quid is enough, I'm not sure now a days.' He told her he hoped she would not send it back. 'I know I haven't been the best brother, but I want to change all that.'

Alby found he couldn't see for tears at one stage and stopped writing for a bit. He picked the pen up and finished his letter.

'I love you sis, I always have. Please let me try to make it all up to you. And sis, let me know if you ever need anything, I am here.' And he signed it 'your loving brother Alby.'

Alby included the telephone number of the station in his address. He closed the letter with kisses and folded it. Putting it in the envelope, also from Jack, he sealed it down.

He got into bed and in the darkness, he thanked God for Jack, and for the fact that he could write it.

Wayne got into bed and for once he tossed and turned for a couple of hours before he went off to sleep. His mind was in turmoil and jumped from one thing to another. Wayne worried.

He worried about Jack and his broken heart. Worried that Jack might be tempted to go home with Dan when he went home. He told himself it was just as well to know and to find out sooner rather than later. Wayne worried that Alby would go with him. Wayne couldn't see those two ever parting company.

Wayne worried about Alby and his very young love. Alby and Jack had both changed since arriving there, had both brought about an improvement in their lives and characters. They had taken on a peace that most people would have envied if they only knew it. In their short time on the station, they had affected change in them all.

And yes, Wayne had to admit even in himself. Where would he have got the guts to tell the boss he was leaving to go bull catching? And where indeed would he have found the courage to leave Margo and just be by himself? And Wayne had a good sort of hunch he'd never have written that letter to Rhonda either.

That Wayne hadn't heard back from Rhonda was disappointing but at least he had tried. He had taken up the pen and tried to rekindle his first love. He would no longer regret that he had done nothing, whatever the outcome. He knew he wouldn't have so much to look forward to had it not been for both Jack and Alby. Yeah, Wayne was a new man, and he knew it, and every day he got a measure of his self-respect back. He got a measure of his peace of mind back to.

Wayne found time there in the dark, to worry about Bill and Hilda. What a mess he thought now if that didn't work out. And Bill doing so well off the drink. That was one thing Wayne counted as a blessing, he was getting his mate Bill back.

Yeah, Wayne hoped against hope that Jack and Alby would never leave. And these new blokes in his life, he wondered if he'd have gotten to know Tom and his crew if it hadn't been for Jack. What a wonderful bunch of characters they were.

Wayne knew they'd never have been so close to finishing their new home and business if it hadn't been for them. The new friendship was a good one all round. He found he was glad for them to that they had a new enterprise to look forward to.

And that this new enterprise encompassed so much of their old life, their old ways was nothing short of a blessing. Because Wayne also grieved the loss of the humble Aussie drover, for lose them they would. And with them would go a most noble and heroic Australian. Everyone in the business of raising livestock would suffer this loss as Wayne saw it. And not least the livestock themselves. And Wayne knew sadly that it would be the same the world over.

And the role of the ringer, the stockmen, that too would be changed for ever. And what would happen to the noble yet humble stock horse when the motorbikes arrived?

It was the end of an era, a way of life. And Wayne fell asleep with a lump in his throat. What could he do?

Chapter 15

When Wayne arrived in town to pick their guests up from the pub, he found them sitting on a bench seat out the front. As he parked the land rover and got out, he kept his eyes on them. Dan stood up. Wayne noted the tall well-built stature of the man and his straight back and dark good looks. He wore no hat, and his dark hair was close cropped and neat.

Wayne walked towards the man as if he were about to greet royalty. Of all that he had expected, the man lived up to it and more. The man beside him, Wally was equally impressive. He was a little taller and built like a brick wash house. He was easily recognisable for the way he carried his left arm.

Dan stepped towards him smiling and offered his hand. 'I'm Dan Roberts and this is my mate, Wally.'

Wayne took his hand and shook it and then shook hands with Wally. 'Wayne Strawbridge mate nice to meet you. Jack talks about you and I am looking forward to getting to know you. I'm sorry it's me picking you up but I had to come into town see. A bit of business.'

'It's very kind of you Wayne. It is also very kind of you to put us up. I can't thank you enough.'

'Aww its nothing Dan. We think the world of Jack and it'll be a pleasure.' He turned to Wally who was putting their bags in the back, 'you wanna ride in the front mate or in ....' Wally jumped up in the back and grinned at him. Wayne found himself grinning right back. 'Good on you lad.' He got in the front with Dan.

On the way home in the car Wayne struck up a conversation about farming. He found the man was enthusiastic about the subject and, much to Wayne's relief, went on at length. Wayne told him he didn't know much about it. They got on to truck driving and then on to station life. They touched on bull catching but Wayne was not very forth coming, and the subject dried up. Dan noticed it and wondered.

Wayne thought that the man beside him was nervous. 'Will we see Jack today' asked Dan anxiously?

'Yeah of course as soon as he gets back. He might even be home by the time we get there.'

Wayne was loath for this man to get sight of Jack. How was he going to take to the mess Jack's face was now? And the fellow up in the back, Jesus if he went off. Dan kept looking back to check on him, mother hen was right.

Hilda met them at the front of the mess when Wayne pulled up, and when Dan got out, she could see what the fuss was about. He was a remarkable man and he looked it. Wally grinned at her, and she had the urge to feed him.

Bill came out and held his hand out to him, 'I've been waiting to meet you Dan' he said with a friendly grin, 'I'm Bill,'

Dan took his hand and introduced him to Wally. 'It is very nice to be here and to see the place. I know now what Jack was on about in his letters home. The place is wild and beautiful just as he described it. I am more at ease in the gentler slopes to the south unfortunately.' He grinned to take the edge off his words.

Hilda almost yelled when she saw the land rover drive up. 'Here he is Dan. Oh here's Jack.'

Dan smiled at her and then turned to watch Jack get out. And Wayne watched Dan watch Jack get out. He watched the man's face, very carefully.

Dan was horrified when Jack got out, he had to stifle a sob as his hand rose towards his face. 'Jack' he breathed, dropping his hand to his side. Jack walked right up, and Dan took Jack in his arms and held him. Rocking him as you would a small child. As if his face had just happened.

Wayne watched on, his heart in tatters for some reason. He saw the tears running down Dans face and the tears also on Wallys as he sobbed Jacks name.

'Your face Jack' said Dan softly, 'your poor bloody face.'

Wally put his hand out and touched Jacks face just as a tear spilled down his cheek. Jack looked at Dan as a child would gaze at his father.

Wayne signalled the others, and they drew back onto the veranda. This was a family meeting, a very emotionally charged family meeting. It was no place for gawking strangers, he told Hilda and Bill softly as he ushered them into the kitchen.

Bill turned to Wayne 'he's not impressed.' Wayne nodded.

Outside Dan held Jack at arm's length and said, 'the bulls jack?'

Jack nodded. He looked into Dan's face and broke down and cried. 'It's good to see you two.'

Wayne watched out the window and listened intently as he heard what Dan said next.

Dan said softly, 'won't you come home boy? Jack? Come home?'

Jack grinned through his tears and shaking his head he said 'Hell no Dan. This is my life. I got in the way Dan, I was inexperienced. It won't happen again.'

Dan touched Jacks face now, 'and your nose was broken to Jack?' Jack nodded. 'I'm alright Dan, I don't want you to worry.'

Dan just stood for a moment nodding at Jack and asked incredulously, 'you don't Jack? You don't want me to worry?'

Wayne turned to look at Hilda she was sniffing and wiping her nose. He told Bill to take her away and noticed Bill was weepy to. So, Wayne didn't feel so bad about his own teary eyes. You couldn't help it, not when you knew the whole story. And these blokes were family, there was no mistaking that. A bloody close-knit family at that, thought Wayne.

Dan stood back and Wally took Jack in his embrace and when he stood back, he smiled at Jack. 'Jesus Jack. You must have done something to piss him off hay?'

Jack smiled ruefully and shrugged 'mayhap.'

'Well,' said Wally with his half grin, 'what happened?'

'He had my mate Alby pinned against the rover squashing him, so I out and kicked him in the nuts.'

Wayne stood astounded as Dan's head went back and he let out a bellow of a laugh. He laughed with Wally and Jack. Dan doubled up and he and Wally held onto each other. Wayne breathed a sigh of relief, but he wouldn't be sticking his head out just yet.

'Oh Dan' said Jack now, 'this is my mate Alby' as Alby strode up.

Alby shook hands with the two men. 'Yep' said Alby stepping back now to stand beside Jack, 'fair in the bloody balls. There isn't a man jack alive from the black stump to Kingdom come not talking about the crazy bastard that kicked a bull fair in em. A big two-thousand-pound wild as the hills, feral bull. He's notorious now is Jack and no one wants to try him on. Blokes put ball guards on when he walks in the pub, fair dinkum they do. Bull guards they call em now. Don't they Jack hay?'

Dan was laughing and shaking his head, so Jack really was at home. Dan didn't quite know how he felt about it, but Jack had made this place his own. And when a man did that, you had no call to go interfering. Dan would just have to let go, let go and hope for the best. He pulled Jack into his embrace once more and said light heartedly, 'guess you showed him buddy. And all you got was a broken face hay.' The four men laughed some more. And Dan had noticed the scar on Alby's arm. It had been stitched and Dan knew immediately it would be Jack's work.

The grin slid from Alby's face as he said quietly, 'if he hadn't, I'd have been deader than a door nail and no mistake.' He nodded at Dan to give emphasis to his words. Dan nodded back, his gratitude on his face. Alby said softly 'we saved each other Mister Roberts.'

Wayne sidled back out the door thanking God for Alby as he came. The kafuffle was over, the debacle was well and truly debunked. All the same Wayne stood next to Alby.

❖

Dan and Wally settled into station life; they were staying until January the thirtieth. They had taken the room next to Alby and Jack and they ate at the mess with everyone. Dan was amazed at the food Hilda dished up and he told her so.

She smiled down at him, 'thank you Dan. I can see where Jack gets his lovely manners now.'

Jack and Dan went for a long walk after tea the first night and Dan filled Jack in with all the happenings at home. Jack was sorry to hear that Samuel was still ailing and appeared to be suffering from dementia.

Wally sat at the table talking quietly to Bill and Wayne. Wally said excitedly, 'I can see what Jack loves about the place. I think if I had two good arms I'd be looking to stay to.'

Wayne grinned at the young bloke's enthusiasm. 'Well, wait until we get settled over at the other place and you could at least come up for the dry. Can you drive?'

'Yes,' said Wally eagerly. He bestowed one of his wide grins on Wayne and nodded his head, 'you're on' he said, and they all laughed.

Bill liked the two blokes, and he could see where Jack got his attitude. Nobody had it easy during the great depression, but these blokes had done it bloody tough by the sounds of it.

He said softly now, 'That's what Jack does Wally, he drives the catcher vehicle. He secures the bull to the vehicle by a mechanical arm and then Alby gets out and ties it to a tree by the horns. We'll see if he'll give you a ride in it tomorrow hay. Alby was tying a bull to a tree that day and the bloody thing was too quick and had Alby pinned to the vehicle. It sounds funny but make no mistake that bull would have crushed the life out of him if Jack hadn't done what he did. Jack is a hero, and everyone knows it. Well then when Jack was laying on the ground unable to get to his feet Alby rushed in and pulled him to safety. They saved each other that day and they are both heroes Wally.'

Wayne chimed in now and said, 'and Bill here took out half the fencing on the place getting his mate to the helicopter.'

'A few gates Wayne' grinned Bill.

He went on 'And Wayne there also saved Jack by stemming the bleeding. Jack could have bled out if not for him. Teamwork Wally it's what gets you through. You blokes know all about that hay?'

Wally looked, wide eyed from one to the other. He let out the breath he hadn't realised he was holding. 'Alby and Jack' he breathed 'heroes.'

His eyes widened in wonder, and he waved his hand around at them, 'all heroes.'

Bill smiled softly and nodded at Wally's arm, 'you to I see mate.'

The next day the men all got Betsy out of the shed. Dan couldn't believe his eyes. Jack drove it up beside the man he idolised and with a grin, 'care to step into my office Dan?'

Dan got his mouth closed and shook his head, 'not sure Jack' he said looking her over.

With a lot of loud encouragement from everyone he got in the seat beside Jack. Jack put it in gear and let the clutch out. He idled to the gate and leaned across and told Dan to hang on. Dan was already hanging on; an excitement was making its way into his belly, and he began to understand. They were still in first.

Jack planted his foot and roared out the gate. He'd seen some cattle over to the west the day before and so, about a kilometre out he shouted again to hang on. Dan found himself loving it, no wonder he thought a grin on his face. Jack had seen the grin and that was enough for him.

Jack didn't slow up he just left the road, the two men bouncing in their seats, and headed off to the west where he knew the herd was. Dan hung on; he knew an adrenalin rush he had never known before. He watched enthralled as Jack charged through the scrub. What he didn't miss he flattened. Dan realised this could very well be addictive.

Dan spotted the herd of huge wild cattle with great long horns, and it took his breath away. The next thing he realised was that they wouldn't be avoiding them as they hurtled through the scrub towards them.

'Jesus', he yelled as Jack went after them.

Jack singled out the massive bull and cut him from the herd, round and round they went, and Dan began to feel dizzy. Dan held on, his knuckles white, as Jack chased the wild beast and got him on the front right-side fender. Through the bush they went at giddy speeds ducking trees with breath taking closeness.

Dan had to duck low branches and landed back in his seat several times when they hit bumps and ruts. At one stage Dan found himself flying through a creek with Jack, they were air borne for a few seconds. He knew it would do no good to object. Hell, he didn't want to object! He loved it. Dan, like Jack had thrown caution to the four winds. He had a newfound respect for the man beside him and wondered at it. Why hadn't he seen it before, maybe he'd been too busy treating him like a baby.

Jack had the bull sitting nicely on the fender and Dan could hear the beast puffing and grunting above the thunder of his hooves and the motor. He felt fear but it only added to the exhilaration.

Jack hadn't planned to do it, but he found he had to, knew Dan needed to see it. Experience it. He brought the vehicle in close to the bull lining his neck up with the arm. Dan held his breath he knew what Jack was going to do. Dan felt an excitement tear through him, it was tremendous. Jack, he sensed, was very calm.

Jack leaned left slightly and held his thumb on the switch. The bull stayed nice and straight and steady. Jack pushed the button, and the arm came out and trapped the bull holding it against the vehicle. Jack had both hands on the steering wheel now as the rover rocked and bumped with the movement of the bull. He applied the brake bringing the bull slowly to a bucking bellowing halt.

Jack brought the struggling bull to a sturdy tree now and gently pulled up in the shade. 'There you are Dan. At this point, Alby would get out and slip a rope over his horns and tie him to that tree.'

Jack released the hold on the bull and the animal tried to gouge him before it took off. Jack deftly backed and kept backing away to the left until the bull lost interest and ran off.

Dan couldn't believe it; he sat realising that the both of them were panting heavily. He had never dreamed this would be so physical. He said now, 'is it always like that Jack?' Dan knew he was trembling inside.

Jack smiled and nodded, 'It's always a thrill Dan, always an exciting ride. And the ending is always uncertain. Sometimes the bulls win Dan' Jack grinned and touched his face. 'You wanna drive her home, Dan?'

Dan could only imagine what it would be like to go ahead and tie the bull to a tree. This was a dangerous game here.

Jack was delighted when Dan nodded and got out to switch seats. The roar the men let out as Dan brought her in the gate was a feeling all on its own. The adulation and the camaraderie. Dan got out pumped and somewhat sad it was over. He still had a wide grin on his face and when he turned, he looked at these blokes a little differently. These were ordinary blokes doing extraordinary jobs. Dangerous jobs and they took it all in their stride. And these blokes were happy, they loved it.

On the way back Jack had explained the procedure to him, Wayne's role, and Alby's. Then Bill and the blokes who had the job of getting these monsters, hostile monsters, into a truck.

Wayne stepped up 'reckon you'll make a bull catcher out of him Jack?'

The men laughed and Wayne turned serious, 'next time come up in bull catching season mate, we'll all be out there. You wait till you get a go at it.

Dan nodded and grinned at Wayne. He patted Wally on the back as he got in. 'Hang on' he said to the youngster. 'Just hang on.'

Wally came back white and grinning from ear to ear and Jack hadn't caught the bull this time. Wally drove it back and enjoyed all the fuss. Under Jack's supervision he'd tried it all out and found with practice he'd be able to manage it.

The next day when Dan was taken to the living quarters, they had made out of the shed he smiled knowingly at Jack. Jack nodded, 'our very own long hut Dan.'

Dan whistled and said, 'what an amazing job you've all done Jack.' He looked around, 'I hope this place will be every bit as happy for you all Jack.'

Wally slapped Jack on the shoulder 'me to mate. I know it will be Jack.'

'It's not going to be as big Dan. I think what we had was unique and you guys are still all together, so you've all made it work.'

Wayne and Bill were a little overcome with a feeling of gratitude. They were all encouraged by the talk. They all had some of Hildas lunch and set out to do some fencing.

As they ate, Wayne said quietly, 'yeah, it's a testament to you Dan. You people built a long house from nothing. My hat off to yous Dan.' He looked around their own long hut, 'I take my hat off to you. All of you. I know the story.'

It was on the twenty first when Bill came excitedly into the mess for tea.

Everyone else was already there but Bill had got a phone call from Tom. He sat at the table now and plonked his plate down in front of him losing some of it over the side. Dan smiled kindly at him; he looked like the cat that got the cream. He liked Bill, and Jack had told him that the man was ex light horseman and a good friend to Jack.

Wayne looked at him, 'well go on then mate, when are we getting another visit?'

'They'll be here in a few days Wayne' he looked at Jack. Bill did his best to remain calm.

But then Jack got excited to, 'That's great Bill, Dan and Wally will get to meet them.' Jack turned to Dan, 'the drovers I told you about.'

Wayne, also excited, said 'we should get the fencing all done. We should throw our swags in the rover and camp out there. The bureau tells me that there's no more rain in sight for a while yet.' Wayne was cutting his steak, 'the boys here could get in some fishing out there. Though I suppose you don't get really excited about that living on the great Murrumbidgee hay?'

Dan shrugged his shoulder and looking at Wally he said, 'there are some who get excited about fishing even when they're fishing and when they are asleep as well.'

Everyone laughed. Dan turning serious said to Wayne, 'you know, next year I think we will come up for some of the bull season. That's if it's alright.'

'Hell yeah,' said Wayne. He grinned knowingly at Jack. 'Bloody bug bites everyone Dan.'

Dan had realised and recognised that fact.

There was much excitement the day Tom and Fred turned up. Dan saw immediately what Jack was on about. He had never met nicer, happier people in his whole life. In fact, he thought, everyone here was good. Good people, he looked at Jack who was being slapped on the shoulder by Tom who was teasing him about being a ball breaker. 'A bull ball breaker no less' he finished amid joyful laughter.

Fred spoke now in his most surprising voice and posh accent. 'We even heard about you over in the Mataranka pub Jack, fair dinkum. You are a legend.' He turned to Dan, and laughing he said, 'you'll no doubt hear the stories floating up and down the Murrumbidgee before long.'

Dan nodded and laughed. Yes, Jack was at home here thought Dan swallowing a lump. The conversation and the laughter went on into the night. Dan realised that he and Wally had been taken in here and treated like family same as Jack. Much loved family at that.

Dan thought he'd like to bring Mary up here but knew he never could. Jack looked so happy now. Happy and at peace and Dan was happy for him. He couldn't do anything to jeopardise that. He had known why Jack ran off; he wasn't blind. The only blight on Dan's happiness was that it was at the expense of his beloved Jacks. The price tag had been a heavy load for Dan.

Jack caught Dans eye and gave a shake of his head, he wasn't blind either. Dan smiled at him, and Jack nodded faintly.

The holiday went all too quickly for all of these men. New people met; new friendships forged. They all worked well together and treated each other with care and respect.

Dan was glad he'd come and met them all. He'd never met people like them, and he knew that these people followed and fell under the influence of Tom and Wayne. These were great men indeed and Dan knew Jack would flourish under their care. They worked hard and had no real need of each other except for friendship, love and support, and an enjoyment of each other's company.

Dan looked at Wally now, the lad was star struck, the admiration he had for all these blokes was evident in his face. Dan felt for him, he didn't stand much of a chance at this life with only one good arm.

As if he'd caused it Tom asked Wally about his arm now. Wally told him what had happened. 'I'm sorry to hear it mate,' said Tom. 'How are you coping with it?'

Wally talked for a while and then Tom smiled and said, 'you're not letting it stop you mate, that's good.' Tom sat and told Wally briefly about his wife Emily. Wally and Dan both were amazed. 'So don't think you can't mate because you usually can. My Emily dances with me and she drives the car and runs a very busy shop. You got a bull catcher in you if you want it enough.' He grinned now, 'or a drover. We'll get you up on a horse next time and rounding up some cattle'. Tom smiled at Wally, 'we don't really work in the wet but come back in the dry and you'll see a different top end.' He nodded to include Dan.

Dan could see Wally start to dream, and his heart went out to the lad. But alas Wally was no lad, he was a big strong man. Maybe he'd been holding Wally back to. Maybe Wally would be up on that tractor from now on. But Dan had shut the poor bloke away in a paddock with a few sheep to look after. He put his head down. He'd neglected Wally but he would no more.

The talk went on until it was time to climb into their swags. Dan spoke to Jack briefly and told him he could go home happy now. 'I know you'll be alright, but I will be praying you don't get hurt again though.' Dan smiled 'I can see why you do it though Jack. Never felt anything close to that and Wally hasn't stopped talking about it.'

Jack grinned at Dan, but he saw the worry lines deepen on his face and he thought he knew what they were. He said, 'you'll never lose Wally Dan, not for long. He's not like me Dan.'

Dan reached out and hugged Jack, and Wayne felt his pain from across the room. 'Bloody Hell' he said to himself.

The day came for Dan to leave, and everyone took the time to see him and Wally off. At Wayne's suggestion they had gone to the pub for lunch and a few drinks which Wayne shouted. No one let Dan or Wally put their hand in their pocket.

Dan wasn't a drinker, but he had a couple of beers, he was dreading saying goodbye to Jack. 'We can keep in touch by letter though son. write often Jack, I need to know you're alright. And I won't be telling Mary about this,' he indicated Jacks face. 'She'd come up here and march you right home. She's expecting me to bring you back you know. She told me to talk you out of this madness Jack. But in fact, I think you should stay here, you suit this place, and it suits you. And I will attempt to tell her that Jack.' Dan laughed with Jack. Dan went on 'I do want to come back for some of the bull catching season mate.'

Wayne had been standing listening to this 'do you ride Dan' he asked?

'I do a little Wayne, not like these blokes though.'

Tom said, 'a day in the saddle Dan and you will be.'

Wayne took a gulp of his beer, 'I for one am very glad you all came, we are almost ready. And thank you Dan for driving the catcher vehicle to the long hut, there I go now 'long hut'. Anyway, I just wanted to say how grateful I am to you blokes.'

Bill stood back a half grin on his face now, 'you can do better than that Wayne. You can show us your gratitude. Line em up, go on.'

'Oh, fuck me drunk,' said Wayne.

'Well, she'd have to be drunk wouldn't she Wayne' said Fred a superior look on his face? Wayne stood a smile on his face as the place was filled with laughter. Dan laughed and banged his glass on the bar.

Wayne looked at the barman, 'yeah go on Ross set em up.' The barman put the drinks on the bar. Wayne said 'here's to us, from all corners of this country, sharing a drink or two hay. And thanks to all of you for your help.'

'Here, here' from everyone and they drank.

Dan spoke, 'It was our pleasure Wayne and I'm mighty glad we came. We enjoyed every minute of it.'

'Don't be strangers, mate' Wayne cleared his throat. 'We could put you to good use Dan, you to Wally. So come for a month or two or three.' He took a swig of his beer, 'pay's lousy though.' There was much laughter.

The mail cart pulled up and Dan and Wally had to go. Dan embraced Jack and tears blanketed his eyes. 'Please look after yourself a little better Jack. Try mate.' Jack nodded and gazed at the man he had loved above all others. The man who had taken him in and treated him like a son. Had probably saved his life.

Alby felt his pain and stood close by. He shook hands quietly with Dan. He was overcome with feeling and Dan could see it. He said softly now 'I'm glad Jack had you Alby, all through those dark years of the war and I'm bloody glad he's got you now. And I heard the story of how Jack saved you and then you saved him and that's only the time we know about. And remember our home is your home if you ever want to visit us.'

Fred stepped up and slinging an arm around Jack he said, 'we'll look after him Mr. Roberts.'

Dan grinned and said, 'thank you very much Fred.' He shook hands with them all and climbed into the truck. Wally stood looking into Jacks face shook his head and embraced his long-time friend. 'You are my brother Jack and I bloody love you.' Wally turned and got up in the back. He looked down at the blokes and then to Tom, 'maybe Tom, maybe.' He grinned and Tom knew the man was goodness all through.

Tom grinned and threw his hand out to Wally who leaned down and took it.

'Never forget Wally, never forget Emily. And when you come up next time, we will meet again, and you will meet Emily. That's a promise man.'

'Thank you, Tom, I would be honoured.' He grinned, 'maybe she could teach me to dance hay.'

'Yes, she could Wally, she sure could. She taught me.'

Wayne stepped up to the window and spoke to Dan 'for the next four or five months you can ring him at the station. After that we may put the phone on at the long hut, but we'll keep you posted mate. And don't forget you are welcome there anytime mate and you can stay as long as you like. You did a bloody good job with Jack here Dan he's a fine man.'

Dan smiled at the man; he liked Wayne. 'Thanks for that Wayne, thank you very much.' Dan swallowed and went on, 'we'll ring about seven on a Sunday if that's okay. And our home way to the south is your home to.' He looked around now 'you are all welcome at our humble abode. I'm glad he has you Wayne I'm glad he has all of you.' As the truck pulled away Dan hung out the window 'See you next bull catching season little mate.'

Tom smiled at Jack. You needed a father no matter how far away they are and whether it's by blood or by life.

They watched the truck until it was out of sight and Wally was waving back to them. Jack could hardly see.

Alby knew and he led Jack back into the bar. 'Where are you two going' asked Wayne?

'We need a bloody drink, Wayne.'

'Okay' said Wayne. Tom and Fred were on their way back to the bar followed by Bill.

Wayne lined up with them and said to Ross 'one more thanks Ross.'

Jack had mixed emotions. Though he was sad at their departure he was also very glad they had come.

Tom had sidled up beside Jack and he said quietly now, 'You know I only found out that Ernie was my dad a few years ago. But he'd always been my father, Jack. He'd always looked after me. He even looked after my drunken no-good stepfather so as he could keep an eye on me. I can see Dan looks on you as a son even though he's not that much older than you. You are lucky Jack he's a fine man. And so are you so he's done his job well. He took on the task you see Jack; he wasn't lumbered with it. He wanted it.'

Jack knew every word of it was true and he stood there nodding, his heart in tatters. 'Thanks Tom' he said simply.

'Jack, I know of your complication I made it my business to find out. I think it involves Dan's wife. I'm sorry Jack, heart sorry mate. I have no words of wisdom Jack, there are no words. I had my own share of complications, challenges in that area.' Tom clapped Jack on the shoulder now. 'Some day man. Some day a lady will come out of fuckin nowhere and knock your socks off. You can't stay lucky forever mate hay?' The two men laughed and downed their drinks, banged their glasses down and sucked froth from their top lip.

Tom said, 'and we're all here for you brother.'

When it was time for Tom and Fred to leave, the boys went to the pub the night before. Tom, Fred, Wayne, Alby, Jack, and Bill. Sandra joined them and was introduced to Tom and Fred. Once again it was Fred who impressed the young girl the most. Jack thought the man was an enigma. Fred the enigmatic ladies' man he smiled to himself. You couldn't help liking the man, no one could.

Tom was also taken with the young girl, and he told Alby he was a lucky man indeed. He turned back to Wayne now and said, 'when you catch those big bloody bulls don't forget to call us when you want em moved.'

Wayne assured him they would. 'What about the other stations Tom do you want me to drop your name around the place?'

'You know it buddy,' said Tom with a wide grin. 'Give us as much notice as you can so we can be free and get over here.' Tom sipped his beer, 'have you got any other stations to contract out their feral bulls to you Wayne?'

Wayne smiled at the young man he had taken a liking to, 'Two others are considering us. Now it's the Mataranka Pub hay?'

'Right again mate.' Tom took a pencil and paper from his pocket and wrote on it. 'If you can't get me there, ring this number. Emily will soon tell you where I am.' Tom looked thoughtful, 'I could drop your name around about Wayne.'

Wayne nodded and thanked him and picked up his glass. 'Well anyway Tom, while we're all here and our glasses are full… I'd like to take the opportunity to wet that babies head.'

Every man there raised his glass and drank. Tom said now, 'allow me to raise a glass to new friends, new family and new alliances.' His eyes came to rest on Jack and then Alby and he smiled. He liked these two men from the southern land and the banks of the Murrumbidgee, and he raised his glass again. 'To the Murrumbidgee.'

'To the Murrumbidgee.'

Fred took his turn now, 'and allow me to announce that Janet and I are engaged, and we have set a date.' He smiled at everyone 'it's the end of next wet and you're all invited.'

Tom stood starring open mouthed at Fred, 'by hell Fred, you kept that a secret.' His eyes narrowed as he gazed at the man he'd known since he was a small boy. 'You Fred, a confirmed bachelor?'

'Yes, me Tom, but I am no confirmed bachelor. I got married when I was nineteen. When I got home from the war, I couldn't wait to see my lovely wife. I hadn't seen her for over a year and so it was with great anticipation that I opened the door. And there she was waiting for me, alas, with a bloke to keep her company. I could never quite find a vision to replace it with.' He smiled at Tom. 'Until now' he finished as he raised his glass to the woman he loved. 'To Janet, my Janet.'

'Fred' breathed Tom. He walked to his oldest friend and embraced him. 'Fred!'

Bill stood open mouthed 'I just can't get over it, Fred. I remember the subject was discussed but I didn't think it would come to anything.'

'Well neither did I Bill. But she loves me and well she's a good woman. She suits me you know?'

'To Fred and Janet,' cried Wayne.

By the time the toasting was finished they'd had to get Sandy to drive them out to the long hut.

Jack lay in his bed that night he was still smarting from Dan going home. Now these drovers were going as well.

Fred had made him promise he would come to the wedding. Then Fred had studied him through narrowed eyes and then smiled. 'You are a good man Jack, none better. But you are lonely. I know loneliness when I see it because I spent so many, many years there myself. You think you've found love and then it is snatched away from you. Your heart will mend my friend, in time. You did the right thing getting out Jack. Maybe your next love won't be the deep all-consuming love like the last one, but you will find love again. And when you do you will understand the meaning of true love. When you meet a woman who you just fall in love with, fall in step with, nice and easy. Someone you can talk to nice and easy and laugh with and share anything with. That's the woman you want, the woman who loves you. And it can be around any corner Jack my old mate so stay fuckin alert.'

Jack had to laugh but he nodded his understanding. 'Thanks Fred.' Jack turned over and closed his eyes a smile on his face. Maybe!

Chapter 16

It was the end of February, almost the end of the wet and the men had gone home to the station to catch up on some work around there. The other boys would be back soon, Geoff, Eddy, and Pete. Mike had stayed on at the station and did most of the work around there. They all knew to be back the first week in April for mustering and branding.

The long hut as everyone called it now was finished. There was a nice big kitchen and six bedrooms all the same size and all sporting a window, double beds, and new mattresses.

Jack and Alby had built an outside area off the veranda which would be their sitting area it measured twenty feet wide and thirty feet long. It was a roof and on the opposite side to the long hut was a wall and so was basically an extension of the veranda. The other two sides were open, and the floor had been cemented all built of corrugated iron. The long hut would do them for years to come.

They had got a lounge suite sent up from Mount Isa. It was a nice brown leather one and would be less likely to spoil. The area would double as a guest room.

The men Bill, Wayne Alby and Jack had taken Hilda to see it. They had made the beds up and washed the lino floors. Hilda had chosen the lino from a magazine it was a rich cream with some brown and here and there a gold fleck. The place looked lovely. They had also got hold of a wooden table and chairs and put that on the veranda just outside the kitchen and polished them. Camp chairs were placed along the other end of the veranda.

Hilda sat in one now gazing, wide eyed about her one hand over her mouth. Bill hunkered down in front of her while the others looked on. 'What is it love' asked Bill? 'Don't you like it? Why not look at the rest of it? Come on love.'

Hilda stood up and put her arms around him. 'Oh Bill, I love it. It's a home darling, our home.' She reached up and kissed him, 'I love you, Bill.'

Red faced, Bill held her for a moment and said 'come see your kitchen. I made it with my own hands.'

'Oh, Bill look at that beautiful sitting area. I..... we can sit out here in the evenings. What a lovely place for you men to have coffee and talk and start your day.'

Bill grinned, 'with one of your marvellous breakfasts Hilda.'

She walked into the kitchen and looked at the cupboards of polished wood, the double sink and six burner range. It was red and complimented the wood. She was speechless and stood looking from one to the other. There was a wooden stool at the end. 'For you when you feel a bit-tired love. I made it myself.' Bill got another kiss.

She was shown to her bedroom and was surprised at how roomy it was. All the bedrooms were equal in size to the rooms on the station. Bill said now, 'we'll get a dresser and a wardrobe love we just haven't got around to it yet.'

'Oh, it's beautiful boys I love it. Oh, I do Bill, I do.'

Wayne came up beside her, 'we can put in a garden Hilda and a lawn. Some trees and shrubs. We'll make it a home Hilda.'

Hilda hugged him and then the rest of them in turn. She turned and went back to the kitchen and out on the veranda. 'We have a table to sit at. And eight chairs, we can all sit down to eat. We will need a side table for the dishes.' She walked to the end of the veranda, 'what do we have here' she said and opened the door.

Bill was behind her as she stepped back, his hands came up to support her. She turned her head to look at him, 'oh Bill a bathroom. A shower Bill. It's beautiful, the whole place is beautiful.' She turned to Wayne who was standing away a little, 'yes Wayne I would like a vegie patch.'

The station was getting back to normal, most of the work at the long hut as they all called it now, was done. Hilda was happy with it and that was the biggest worry out of the way.

Pete arrived back from Mount Isa, and they expected Eddy back any day. Geoff had been back for a week and had jumped in to help finish up at the long hut.

Mike the young jackaroo had started pestering them to be taken with them when they went over to bull catching. He asked Jack but Jack didn't want to deal with it. 'Go and ask Wayne,' said Jack.

'Why' asked Mike? 'He just fobs me off same as you.'

Jack sat down and told him about Russel and how he had died. Mike shrugged, 'but that's not me Jack. How is it fair to say no to me because you are all feeling guilty about Russel.'

'Let me think on it, Mike and if we need another bloke, I will make sure you are given due consideration.'

'Hay?'

'Just leave it with me Mike and we'll see.'

The men had all been back for a week and back at work Eddy had let them know he'd be back in a few days. Most of their time was spent on preparing for the muster. This was the other thing that these ringers lived for. The big musters which happened twice a year usually.

Wayne had delegated Mike and Garry to stay back at the homestead. It was time for branding. This would be done in mid-April, but they would have to muster cattle for over hundreds of miles. From the four corners of the station, they would bring them, the young and old, big, and little male and female.

In the meantime, vehicles needed maintenance and servicing. Horses needed to be shoed and checked. Geoff would need to make himself ready with his kitchen and his plans.

Swags needed to be aired and boots repaired. Saddlery gear would have to be checked and oiled. The station was a hive of activity. There were some station maintenance jobs which had fallen behind, so Wayne had to pick someone.

He sat at the table at breakfast and told the men he had chosen Jack to go around the station and check the fencing. 'Just the boundary Jack, do you think you can manage that?'

Jack nodded. He knew he was familiar enough with the property to find his way around the boundary fence.

'Good opportunity for you to familiarise yourself with the place a little more Jack. Any repairs needed just make a note of where it is.'

'Alright, thanks Wayne,' said Jack. He did look forward to getting out there in the bush alone.

'Bill, can you race about and check the bores. That way you'll be back in a few days, and we can finish getting ready. Meanwhile the rest of you go about getting ready. You all know what to do don't you?'

Everybody said they did. Wayne turned to Jack and Bill 'Bill, I'd like you to get going tomorrow morning. Jack you'll have to go a day or two later I'm afraid. I'll need your help here for a bit and the rover won't be ready until then. Alright then lads' he said as he rose from the table, 'let's try and be ready to go in two weeks. We'll start as usual and round up from East to West, North to South.' The men got back to work.

Wayne found Jack and Alby and spoke to them about their plans. 'I don't know how you are situated men, but I would suggest you go on taking on the work here during the wet. I'll stay here for a year or two and in the bull catching season we will stay over in the long hut.'

'That sounds fine to me Wayne.'

Alby nodded and said 'when Sandy and I are.... Are '

Wayne smiled at him, 'yes, you can bring her to your home Alby. Your room is your business mate. Now, Eric to the North of here has given us the contract for the bulls if we want it. We can discuss that later okay boys. We'll go and see him and have a discussion about price etcetera.'

Alby and Jack both nodded. Jack was glad they would be able to stay here and work during the wet.

The mail cart had been and there was a letter from Dan. Jack got back to his room and opened it later that night, it was just a note, but it was from home.

29/3/1953

Dear Jack,

Just a quick note mate I'm afraid. Just wanted to let you know we got home safely, and everyone was happy to see us and hear the news from your part of the world Jack.

I told them how beautiful it is up there and how wonderful the people are. Jack I was overwhelmed at how those people welcomed us in and treated us like family. It was the best holiday, Jack. I also told them what an exciting life you have. Bryce is all talk now about going up there and being a bull catcher.

I think most of the people here are simply amazed at how well Wally and I were treated up there. To stay at the station and be fed and cared for like that. I was amazed and I am grateful you are with them. One less worry Jack.

I cannot tell you how much that ride in the bull catcher with you affected me. Going after a monster of a bull, can't wait to be there when Alby ties it to a tree. And the day I drove it to your long hut Jack, that was incredible. Thank you.

Anyhow I must go now I will write again soon. Until then, I remain,

Yours faithfully
Dan Roberts.

Jack put the letter down on his table and sat back in his chair. He felt much better, much calmer now he had seen Dan and knew he had his approval.

The men got back to work. Wayne needed Jack to help Alby with the station truck, the gear box was giving trouble again. It was heavy work and Jack and Alby worked well together.

Bill left the next day in the four-wheel drive that Gary had finished giving an overhaul. The next one would be ready in a couple of days. Jack would take that one.

Three days later Jack threw his swag in the back and left the station. He had a radio with him, and he had instructions to call Wayne on it every day at six in the morning and at night.

He had a tent with him and enough food for a week Jack thought. He also had a first aid kit. In addition, he had a drum of water and drums of fuel. Jack jumped in the front seat; he was excited. How he loved this life. Loved the bush, it calmed him and kept him focused at the same time. It was everything to him.

Chapter 17

Jack was ready to pull out on a Tuesday morning. He had said goodbye to everyone and jumped in the land rover. Wayne walked up to the window and handed Jack a rifle and a box of bullets. 'Just take it son, even though you probably won't use it. You never know you might spot a bush turkey or some such. If you do bring it back, will you? But nobody goes out on these runs without a firearm Jack. And I don't need to ask you if you can use one.'

'Sure,' said Jack a grin on his face. He wanted to get going.

Hilda ran out 'just a little something extra Jack, I made it last night.'

'You are too kind Hilda' Jack said and as an afterthought he said, 'what is it?'

'You'll see, it's your favourite Jack.'

'You know my favourite?' Jack smiled.

'It appears I do. You tell me when you get back if I was right.'

Amid laughter and advice to take care Jack left the station. Alby ran up to the window as he was nearing the gate, Jack stopped. Alby looked at Jack. 'Listen mate, be bloody careful out there, hay.' He stepped back, 'Just be careful. I mean it Jack… please.'

'I will mate,' said Jack. 'I'll see you in a few days, okay?'

And Jack was gone leaving Alby standing in the dust, a terrible feeling in his gut.

Wayne decided not to go straight back to his office he had a couple of jobs to do. It was a beautiful day, the sun shone, and the Sky was a deep blue already. It was nine o'clock. Wayne whistled as he went.

Wayne was nearly finished dragging saddles out onto the floor when a deep rumbling noise caught his attention. You could only just hear it, but he knew it was thunder. That's funny he said to himself, there's nothing forecast. Wayne put the saddles along the wall inside the stable. Probably just an electrical storm he told himself.

Just a few minutes before lunch time Bill came in the gate. Without preamble of any sort, 'where's Jack' he asked Wayne?

'He left about four hours ago to run the fence. Why?'

'Well, it looks like weather coming Wayne.' Bill sounded edgy.

'Bull shit' said Wayne walking to the door. He couldn't believe it, the northeastern sky was black, and the rumbling was getting louder. 'Shit' he said and hurried off to the office. Bill followed him and Alby who'd come out of nowhere. Alby felt sick. He had a storm in his gut, and he couldn't really, fully understand it.

Wayne couldn't get any body on the phone 'the phone lines must be down' he said feeling a little sick himself.

'Jack' said Alby.

Bill turned to him, 'he'll be alright mate. How far away could he be Wayne?'

Wayne looked at Bill, his face had paled considerably. 'The way Jack drives? He could be nearly a hundred miles away. And I can't send anyone after him because we don't know what's coming and they would probably just get bogged. Well then, we'd have two men out there in the storm. That fuckin down pour is just minutes away. I'll try and get him on the bloody radio.' Wayne sat down behind his desk. 'He needs to stay out of the creeks by the look of it and he's probably crossed two or three already.'

Wayne turned the radio on and turned it up. All they got was static. Wayne tried to get through to Jack. A voice came on the radio with a weather alert.

The tail end of a cyclone which it had been thought would pass a few hundred miles to the North had veered to the south.

'Shit' Wayne said now. He kept trying to get Jack. Unseasonal storms were often times, the worst storms.

'What are we gunna do' barked Alby? Wayne looked; the big man was as pale as a ghost but sweating liberally. It ran down his face, Bill put his hand on Alby's shoulder to comfort him.

Bill said 'but if he sees it, he'll come right back. He could be here any minute. Come on Alby, Jack's no fool.'

Alby proved inconsolable and Wayne said to Bill on the quiet to make sure no keys had been left about.

Wayne said also on the quiet, 'he probably hasn't seen the damn storm, it's behind him. He probably hasn't heard it either. Jesus Bill, how the hell could I have been so fuckin slack.'

The radio crackled and Wayne pounced on it. 'Wayne here mate.'

It was Bob, a neighbour, 'Yeah Wayne, I heard you trying to get somebody. You got somebody out there Wayne?'

'Yeah, young Jack is out there.' Wayne drew a breath 'what's he in mate?'

'Jesus, nasty one. Try and get hold of him and tell him to stay out of the bloody creeks. Has he got a radio with him? Tell him to dig in till it passes. Preferably on high ground. Eric reported rain coming down in sheets farther north.'

'Okay mate thanks.' Wayne went on trying to get Jack on the radio without success. He looked helplessly at Bill and Alby, 'he's on his own gents, we can't get to him. The poor bastard's on his own.' He put the radio down 'all we can do his wait and pray. Can you blokes go and help batten down. I'll stay here till I hear from him.'

Jack had covered a lot of miles since he left the station, so he stopped to eat his lunch. He went to turn the radio on and then thought better of it. He'd call in at six as planned.

He got out of the rover and lit a fire to boil the billy. After he'd eaten his lunch, he got back behind the wheel and went on. It was almost two o'clock. Jack had to pull over an hour later when the storm hit. He had heard how fast these storms could come upon you, but he hadn't expected this.

The storm, the thunder and the lightening and wind and rain didn't let up for almost two hours. Jack decided to abandon his mission and head for home. He turned the rover about and set off.

When Jack got to the first creek it had about a foot of water in it. He knew it would be alright, he had to try. His inexperience showing, he slipped the rover into gear and into four-wheel drive and eased into the creek.

Jack had thought himself through the creek when he felt the vehicle sink, she sank down to the axle. Jack was stuck fast and he new it. He had a shovel he'd dig himself out. As he was getting out of the vehicle, he heard a slight crackle on the radio.

He got out and had the presence of mind to take the food his swag the rifle and the tent and water out of the back and put them up on the bank. He didn't know how long he was stuck for.

As an afterthought he reached in the front and turned the radio up. To his horror he heard Wayne shouting at him to answer. He lifted the handset and said, 'hello Wayne.'

Wayne's voice came back, 'thank Christ Jack. Are you okay mate?'

'Not really mate the storm caught me by surprise. I'm stuck in a blasted creek and I'm gunna try and dig myself out.'

'Listen to me Jack. Get out of the damn creek, there's a few feet of water coming at you and it's coming bloody fast. Get out of the creek Jack but tell me very quickly, where are you?'

'I'm still on the East boundary about three creeks in. Must be about a hundred or so miles Wayne.'

'Right Jack we'll be there as soon as we can. The storms pretty much done but there's that wall of water. Get out Jack and sit tight.'

'Righto' said Jack, but before he could say goodbye Waynes's wall of water rushed around the bend in the creek and came straight at him. Jack's mouth fell open.

Wayne even heard it on the other end, he heard Jack shout 'shit……' Wayne yelled 'Run Jack, run.'

But Jack hadn't released the talk button and didn't hear it. But Wayne heard the wall hit the rover and the shout from Jack. Then there was silence, a thick sickening silence.

Wayne turned to look at Alby who'd taken up residence in his office. Alby was as white as a sheet. 'I'm going out there Wayne.'

Wayne nodded, 'as soon as the storm is gone, and the creeks have all run themselves out you can Alby. And I will help you. But for the minute all we can do is pray.' Waynes's heart ached for the big man. 'Alby, Jack's either alright or he's not alright. Either way we can't help him, we can't get there in time even if we could leave now.'

From what they'd just heard he didn't think Jack was coming back. Wayne had to stifle his tears, his sobs, and call it in. They were missing a man and they suspected he'd got caught in a flash flood. The nightmare of the outback. Sadly, Wayne gave search and rescue Jacks last known position. He was told to sit tight. Wayne shook his head, they had horses. 'There will be no sitting tight' he told Alby now.

Alby got up and walked out as Wayne got on the radio. Alby went and told Bill the grim news. The station was in shock.

When flash floods came, they came out of nowhere in no time. No one had ever tried to measure the force of the water, but it was usually a force greater than mans.

Jack had felt the water hit the vehicle and had tried to avoid being swept along with it. But inadvertently Jack had landed in the back of the rover. The vehicle rolled and tumbled, and Jack was soon thrown out into the raging swirling torrent of water. Jack fought desperately for air; it seemed like for hours.

The last thing he felt was a crushing blow to his side and he felt a searing pain in his shoulder. He dropped some distance and expected he'd been dumped back in the water. He knew he couldn't take much more of that.

Instead, he felt solid ground underneath him, he must have been thrown out onto the bank. He rolled over and lay still, as the blackness engulfed him. Jack, after five to ten minutes in the rushing swirling water had no fight left in him.

When next Jack opened his eyes, it was nearly dark, and he was cold. He lay shivering wondering what to do. He couldn't move. Jack heard a noise which was strangely familiar to him in a terrifying way. He lay listening to it, his heart beating like a drum. What the hell was it?

Jack couldn't see very much, and he suspected if the moon wasn't above him, he'd see nothing. Then Jack heard a grunt he knew all too well. Bulls! The bulls had come for him. Had they come for revenge, to kill him as he lay helpless. Or had they come to take him home? To take him to that great never, never in the sky. Jack knew it was no use to try to run or fight them, so he remained still.

He wondered vaguely if the afterlife he was going to would be just all bulls. 'Oh Christ' he murmured and closed his eyes.

He felt the hot breath of one of them on his cheek. How many of them there were he didn't know but he felt there were a few. One of them nudged him and he tried to shift away, it was an instinct to try and avoid them. Now the blackness was nudging at his brain, and he gave up.

Jack smiled at the irony of it and passed out. Well, he'd arrive in heaven in style. He heard a sweet voice and knew he'd got to heaven, and a peace enveloped him.

Wayne had called the police station to ensure they got a search underway as soon as they could. He went to the mess for tea and sat in silence with the others. He was thankful that at least the phone was back on, but you never knew how long for.

Alby broke the silence. 'We shouldn't be sitting here safe and dry, eating bloody food with Jack out there. He could be laying hurt somewhere.'

Bill looked at the big man and said softly, 'is that what you think Alby? That Jack is hurt but alive?'

Alby nodded, 'I think so Bill.'

'Well, that makes me feel better Alby.' Bill put his hand on Alby's shoulder 'won't do any good if you're laying out there to buddy. Let's get some rest and get out there first thing hay. Come on mate, big day tomorrow. He's probably in the tent in his swag worrying about us. He'll be hoping to see us.' Bill helped Alby to his feet.

Wayne couldn't eat, he got up and mumbled, 'I wonder if this is on the bloody news.'

When he got back to the office, he got his answer. The phone rang, it was Dan.

Wayne found himself consoling the man and explaining himself at the same time. 'I'm very sorry' he finished.

Dan heard the grief in the man's voice and said softly. 'Not your fault Wayne, you don't control the weather.' He drew a deep breath and said 'what's the situation Wayne? Can we hope he's still alive?' The pause on the other end of the phone nearly stopped Dan's breath. He looked at Mary who was on the verge of tears. He put his arm around her and held her. Everyone sat silent and Dan knew this would turn into an all-night vigil. These people would sit vigilant for as long as it took. This was one of their own, Jack mightn't be in the room, but he was in their hearts.

Wayne's voice came back, 'I just don't know Dan, Jack is a strong, smart man if anybody could survive this it's him. But we'll be organising a search party tomorrow. We'll go out on horse back and look for him.'

'Should I come up there Wayne?'

Wayne advised him to sit tight that they had enough men, and the search would begin in the morning. 'We know pretty much where he was when the storm hit so we will start there.' Wayne paused and swallowed 'they'll get a plane out to try and spot him or the vehicle. I'll keep you informed mate. It'll have to be through Hilda, I'll be taking a radio.'

The next morning, they were getting the horses into the truck they figured they would get them to number two bore there was a fairly decent road to that.

Jacks last position was about fifty miles on from that and it was just a track. They'd use all the gear they had ready for the muster, and they'd just need water and food.

They were busy with what they were doing and didn't see the man walk up. 'G'day.'

Wayne swung around and smiled at Eddy, 'you're back, thank God.'

'Yeah, heard on the radio Wayne, thought you might need a tracker. You got a horse there for me?'

'How'd you get here Eddy' Wayne asked puzzled?

'Got a ride to the turn off and walked all night. Ran some of it.' Eddy grinned; he looked tired out.

'Go and get some breakfast and some coffee. We'll get your stuff ready.' Wayne smiled sadly 'we're gunna need all the help we can get Eddy.'

By eight o'clock the boys were ready to go. Wayne was leaving the office when the phone rang. It was Tom. 'Heard about Jack mate we'll be there in a few days.'

'We're just heading out now to look for him. You can talk to me through Hilda.'

'Okay mate we'll have a radio with us, talk soon. And the best of luck Wayne.'

Wayne thanked him and put down the phone. It rang again, it was the neighbour, 'Where abouts was he Wayne?'

Wayne told him. His neighbour Eric's voice came back, 'listen we'll head out that way and we'll probably meet up with you somewhere along the line. We'll scout round down this end of the creek.'

'Okay, thanks a lot mate we appreciate it.' said Wayne.

He walked outside and there was Jim with his own horse. He hadn't seen Jim since he'd run him off. Wayne didn't bother to argue, 'come on then' he said. They dropped the tailgate and put Jim's horse up in the back. They were off, they had enough provisions to stay out a month.

Hilda fussed about what to give the boys to take to Jack. Medical supplies were uppermost on her mind. She couldn't think of Jack as being dead, he had to be alive. But she knew he would almost certainly be hurt. He'd need dry clothes and a blanket.

Wayne had grabbed a spare swag for him and some dry boots. He packed a hat and flask of whiskey, unbeknownst to him that was the fifth flask on the journey. Wayne couldn't bear to think of not seeing Jack alive again, not talking to him, listening to him laughing with him.

Alby had a flask in his saddle bag. Alby was almost certain they would find Jack alive and not just because he needed it to be so. He was certain he'd feel it, if Jack was gone from this world, he would feel it. And he didn't.

Bill had another flask for Jack in his saddle bags and he had a hope in his heart. He stood cuddling with Hilda; he couldn't quite bring himself to say that everything would be alright.

Wayne carried a hope in his heart because he couldn't get through this time without it. Wayne wasn't coming home without the much-loved Jack, dead or alive. He needed Jack. Needed him to be alive, he looked at Alby.

They climbed up in the truck, they had the horses in there and they pulled a trailer with their supplies. Wayne started up the old blitz and they went in search of Jack.

Chapter 18

Jack woke up in a tent, it was morning he thought. He wondered if he'd lost his memory or something. He lay there his head hurt like hell. Must be alive he told himself somewhat surprised.

He tried to look about him, but it was a huge effort, and he gave it up and closed his eyes. Jack suddenly had a memory of some one handling him during the night. Maybe the boys he thought and then remembered the hands had been so gentle he'd thought himself in heaven for sure. Yet how could some one so gentle have wrestled him away from those bloody bulls?

Some one during the night had forced him awake and to drink, he was sure. The blackness was nudging at his brain again. The last thing he saw was the roof of the tent and knew either someone had found him and put him in a tent, or he was in heaven.

Next time he came to it was to a heavenly smell. It was steak, steak and coffee. Jack tried to sit up, he needed some of that. He was stiff and sore all over and the effort was too much.

Wayne and the boys reached the number two bore by ten o'clock and unloaded the horses. They transferred their gear to the three spare horses and set off to Jacks last known location.

By dark they were still ten miles shy of their destination. The men, Wayne, Alby Bill, Eddy, Jim, and Geoff reluctantly made camp. They'd left Mike at the station with Hilda, and they left the truck at the bore. Wayne could see as they went along that they wouldn't have got a land rover through this.

It was almost cruel for these men to have to wait until morning to reach the sight. The feeling of dread ran rife through the lot of them. But somehow, they ate, got into their swags, and slept.

Jack had lain in a strange swag and waited for someone to come through the flap. He had to know who had looked after him, maybe the boys had brought Hilda. He heard some one walking towards the tent and waited, he was nervous. He was helpless.

The person coming through the tent flap was a woman, she had to duck her head and he saw she had light brown hair a little lighter than his. She looked up saw he was awake and smiled. Yep, Jack told himself he was in heaven. The woman coming towards him was so beautiful she had to be an apparition. She was all the beautiful women he had ever seen rolled into one.

By the time she reached his swag and hunkered down with the aroma from the plate of steak wafting up his nose, he was in love.

'Glad you are awake Mister. You had a close call. Do you think you can eat I cut it up for you.'

'Who are you? Where am I?'

'Eat' she said with a smile that lit up the tent and the universe. A smile that altered your chemistry so much it made your heartbeat like crazy.

He took the plate, 'thank you. Are you alone here?'

'Yes I am. Eat.'

As Jack ate the woman told him she had been on her way home when she saw the rover flash by on the current. 'I knew someone was in trouble, so I followed the creek back. I found you on the creek bank. My bulls almost ran right over you, but they stopped. I couldn't get them to go on, so I got down to investigate. Well, that's when I found you. Eat.'

'Going home where? I didn't know anyone lived here abouts.'

'My property borders Mable Downs for a bit. I have a narrow strip of land I bought from Bob. It's just one hundred by thirty odd miles. But it's mine. In answer to one of your questions, that is where we are now. I brought you home Jack, I wasn't sure where to take you or how far or even how badly hurt you were, so I brought you here.'

Jack was busy gulping at the steak and eggs. 'Your bulls?'

'Yes, it was Caeser who refused to walk over the top of you. He's a gentle soul, a bit of a sook.'

Jack touched his face and went on eating. He laughed and said, 'I thought the bulls had come to exact revenge or take me to heaven.'

'Was it bulls did that to your face?'

Jack nodded, 'Tell me, were you riding a bull?'

'No, I use the bullock team when the ground is wet. If the worst comes to the worst and I get bogged, I just unhitch the cart and ride them home.' She smiled that dazzling smile that made Jack feel faint.

'Anyway, my name is Jack, and it is very good to meet you.'

'Nice to meet you to Jack, my name is Mary.' She noticed the look that passed across his face and wondered at it, but she didn't want to pry.

He looked back at his plate 'Mary you say. Nice name.'

'Wait a minute, Jack! Are you the Jack that kicked a .... '

'Yes.'

She threw her head back and laughed and Jack never wanted her to stop. As he listened and watched his heart righted itself in his chest and he was free. Free to love again, the universe was good. Oh, it was good, Jack knew he'd go back and wrestle a hundred creeks for this moment. Would kick a hundred bloody bulls wherever he had to kick em.

He handed her his plate thanking her for the food. He said he felt much better and with an excitement in his gut he'd never known before, he quietly passed out. He smiled as he did so, yes, the bulls had come for him, had come to take him home. They had taken him to heaven. And he had met a Goddess, and her name was Mary. Jack told himself he probably dreamed it.

❖

It had been five days now and the searchers had travelled the length of the creek. They had found the rover and the state of the vehicle caused them much concern for Jack. Wayne knew Jack wasn't coming home alive, but he had to find his body.

Tom and Fred and Ernie and Jimmy had caught up with them and joined in the search. They knew how much Bill had thought of Jack and their hearts grieved with him. Tom knew they had to push on, had to keep searching until they knew. Had to bring the man, the legend that was Jack, home.

Bob and two of his men from the neighbouring stations were helping with the search. Some of the other neighbours downstream were searching their property just in case the water had taken him that far. Eddy had found nothing as the storm and running waters had swept the land clean.

The planes had found no sign and no smoke. Hopes were fading fast for Jack.

Jack got out of bed on the fifth day and looked about him. He looked at the half-built hut and asked Mary if she had built it by herself. She smiled indulgently at Jack and said softly that it was a fair assumption.

Jack laughed and told her he would come back weekends and help her to finish it. Said it was the least he could do and told her some of the structure needed doing again. 'Though to your credit it did withstand that bloody storm.' Jack smiled at her 'and thanks to you, so did I.'

She stepped closer to him, he could feel her, smell her. His heart quickened even more. She took his arm in her hand and smiled at him as she said gently, 'you must go home soon Jack.'

Jack turned quickly towards her, alarm on his face, 'no.'

'People will be worried about you. Stay another day or two and then you should go. Let them know you are alright.'

Jack nodded now and taking her hand from his arm he pulled her gently into them. As his arms went round her, she leaned against him. It seemed like the most natural thing in the world when he dropped his head and kissed her lightly on the lips. They smiled shyly at each other.

'I love you woman' he murmured in her ear. Her arms tightened around him. He could tell she was shy and didn't push her for anymore though he was aroused. And that was a hell of a thing to considering how long it had been since.......

Still holding her to him he said now 'we have just finished building a house which we call a long hut. There are five of us going to live there just now but there will be more. We leased about five thousand acres bordering town. We intend to catch bulls and keep them there for a while.'

'Feral bulls?'

'Yep.' He waited as he watched the mischievous smile spread across her face. How he loved her.

'Because you are so good at it, Jack? I think I understand how you do it.'

'Do you woman. And you are going to share this knowledge with me?'

'You offer them your face as bait and then...... POW!'

Jack threw his head back and laughed. When he had quieted down, he said softly 'I don't want to go.'

She lay her head on his chest, 'I don't want you to go. But you need to Jack. Don't forget me.' She tweaked his nose and he fell deeper.

Jack laughed and shaking his head 'not likely my darling, not likely, I could try for a hundred years.' He held her at arm's length and looked into her eyes, 'I intend to marry you someday girl.'

He stood watching her face closely and saw only pleasure on it. 'I'll be back Mary; we will build you a home.' He looked across at her land rover, it was a good vehicle, and her tent was comfortable. He thought she was lucky, and he said this now. As an afterthought he said, 'do you ever feel afraid here by yourself Mary?'

She shook her head and whistled. Two of the biggest cattle dogs he had ever seen ran out of the scrub to her. 'They are normally very placid Jack, until I yelp and then they will tear down anything that moves.' She got him to pat them, 'now they will remember you but if you walk in of a nighttime call their names. This is Bluey, very original I know, and this is Ginger.' She pointed to a rifle leaning against the tent, 'and I have my security guard.'

'How am I going to leave you Mary. I love it here and thank you again for coming to my rescue. It was worth the long hard swim.' He looked into her face 'do you have family about Mary?'

'No, there was just me and dad. He had a property just out of Brisbane, so I sold it when he died and came here. One day I will run a few cows and a few chooks. I love it to Jack, and you are welcome anytime. But you must go now my love, people will be worried about you. By now they are searching for your body.' She smiled softly, 'Go and put Alby's mind at rest Jack, you called out his name a couple of times, so I know he's important. But come and meet the rest of the boys. In the morning Jack, I will give you directions. I will come with you most of the way. It will take at least two days to get near where you are going.'

Jack was sceptical, these bullocks of hers were amongst the biggest he'd seen. 'This is Caeser' she said, 'he stopped to lick you that night.' The big bull walked over to him and nuzzled his shirt just as a horse would. He was introduced to the rest of them, there were four in all. 'Caeser likes you' she said, and Jack patted the big docile animal. 'Get up on him Jack' she said.

'Oh Christ,' said Jack.

Alby's mind was in turmoil and his heart ached something cruel. He knew the search would be called off soon, but he would roam these damned creeks and waterways, the hills, and canyons, he would search high and low until he found him. Until he found his best mate Jack. He would take Jack home one way or another.

There were two others who had made up their minds to do the same thing.

Alby looked at them now and knew it. First, he looked at Bill then he looked at Tom.

Wayne knew it as he looked at the big man, he worried for him, he'd hardly spoken. Wayne sighed, he could see and feel the sadness and knew it would go on for years. He decided he'd help Alby and go on helping him until he was done. He'd supply the big man with anything he needed.

Wayne also knew that soon; they'd have to start searching the tree roots in the creeks for Jack's body. How did he tell the big man that? He hung his head in absolute misery.

The search crew sat around the fire; it was early evening on a bright sunny day, and they had just finished their tea. There wasn't a lot of talk going on as each man dealt with the sorrow in his own heart. They knew the day was fast approaching when somebody would say the words. 'Jack isn't coming back' they would say, or 'Jack is dead.'

They heard a bull below not too far away and wondered at it. They heard it again soon after and it appeared to be getting closer. After the bull that took out the camp and Russel, Wayne wasn't taking any chances. He picked up his rifle and so did Ernie.

They heard it again and what appeared to be a different bull answering. None of them knew what to make of it. They were camped on the side of a gulley up on the side of a hill on a flat sheltered piece of ground. They kept their eyes trained on where the sound was coming from down in the heavily vegetated area along the gully floor. Water gathered there and so it was thick with all kinds of trees and bushes and wildlife. Waterfowl hung out in there by the hundreds.

This dense vegetation down on the gully floor began to sway about and out poked a giant bulls head, then the shoulders. The two men lifted their rifles to their shoulders and Tom grabbed his, unable to guess what was going on. They strained their eyes in the gathering gloom.

Then as Jack appeared on the back of the huge animal, no one knew if they had been out in the elements too long and were seeing things. Maybe the grief, maybe one of them visitations. Just then the man lifted his arm and waved, and Alby took off at a run. 'It's Jack' he bellowed. He came to an abrupt halt as another bull poked its head through the tangle.

The men watched unable to believe what they saw. On the back of the other bull was a vision. The most beautiful vision they had ever seen. Suddenly it all made sense to Wayne. 'It's Mary' he breathed, 'I heard about her and her bulls, some people think she is a mythical, creature some say she's crazy. Well myth or no she is bringing Jack home. Thank God for her I say.'

A cheer went up in the camp and Caeser stopped, he backed up a couple of paces and Jack jumped down. He gently encouraged the young bull to walk on. The massive bull wouldn't budge so the men were treated to the sight of Jack offering him a bottle of milk to move.

Tom laughed; he had never thought he'd see such a thing. He did realise he was in on and witnessing the making of a legend. Tom felt it, felt an excitement in his gut, and the woman was a vision. And Jack he suspected was the reluctant hero.

Fred walked closer; his interest piqued. He wouldn't have got on that bull for quids. And the woman was absolutely relaxed, and she was a looker. Bill could hardly see for the tears. The men surged forward to meet the strange procession. Ernie stood shaking his head at the sight, but he didn't put his rifle down and neither had Wayne. The massive bull followed Jack and the bottle of milk up the side of the gully. It was a most strange sight and Ernie had been through Devils Canyon.

Jack stood looking at Alby. 'Told you I'd be back in a few days Alby.' He said casually and grinned as the big man rushed at him. He held Alby for some time and then Alby stepped back.

Alby was stunned not only because Jack was alive and well and just jumped from a bull. But Jack, he could see was happy, had found peace. His eyes went to the beautiful woman behind him, and he smiled in wonder as she smiled back at him.

Fred walked up and shook Jacks hand 'didn't wanna be found hay Jack? Funny that, mate.'

Bill and Wayne and the rest of the blokes crowded him and some of them had tears in their eyes. Jack went to Mary and lifted her down from Samson. He introduced them all Mary, Caeser, Samson, Bluey and Ginger. Ernie stepped up to the woman and, taking her hand in his, 'I think we have you to thank for getting Jack home.' He shook hands with her, and the others followed suit.

When they were sitting at the fire with a mug of coffee Jack told them he didn't remember much about the last week or so. Mary nodded and told them that he had been out cold when she found him, and he hadn't woken for two days. 'Took another day to get his memory back. He had a dislocated shoulder' she went on and she had put it back in to place while he was asleep.

'You didn't tell me that' he said.

She smiled, 'we had a lot to talk about and little time' she said.

'Your land borders Mable Downs for about thirty- or forty-miles Mary, doesn't it?' Wayne asked.

She nodded, 'From memory it's thirty-seven miles wide and it's a hundred long. Someday I will get around to getting some cows and some chooks. I have planted fruit trees and I usually plant the seasons vegetables.'

'Where abouts do you live' asked Bill?

'Just about five miles from the boundary and about ten miles along to the west. It's a nice little spot and there's good ground for a garden.'

'She is building a house Wayne' put in Jack, 'I have offered to help her build it.'

'Shit yeah' said Wayne 'we all wanna be in on that. You saved Jack here. We'll come weekends for a while until it's done. That is if its acceptable to you Mary.'

Mary smiled and nodded, 'if it's not too much thanks Wayne.'

The talk went on into the night, it had a surreal quality about it. None of these blokes had expected to see Jack alive again yet here he was sitting beside a myth. And he'd ridden in on a bullock, a very big bullock. It was good to have him back. Some at the fire thought that Jack may not have wanted to be found right away and not a man there could blame him.

Dan learned of Jacks return the following day. He spoke to Hilda, and she told him what she could. 'He will be home day after tomorrow' she said 'you can call him then if you like Dan.'

'And he is fine you say?'

'Yes. The story I have is that he rode into camp on a bull. I'm not sure how that came about Dan. One of our neighbours is a woman called Mary and she found him and brought him back on some bull called Caeser. I don't know much but Wayne wanted you to know he's back and he's fine, though he did get washed away in a flash flood.'

Dan didn't know what to make of it, he was looking forward to speaking with Jack. He turned to Mary, 'he has returned Mary, rode into camp on a bull called Caeser with a woman called Mary.' Dan looked puzzled now, 'we will know more day after tomorrow. That is when they are expected home. They were all out looking for him Mary, even Tom and his crew came to the search. I am glad he has such good and caring friends up there. Maybe...... just maybe I will take you up there to meet them my love.'

He turned now and looked at the rest of his people, the people of the Murrumbidgee who lived in a long hut. He loved them all and counted himself among the very lucky.

Dan had gotten a feeling about another woman though, a woman who lived many miles away in a strange land, way to the north, also called Mary. Once again Dan dared to hope. For Jack, poor bloody Jack, for years his heart had ached for Jack.

Yes, he couldn't wait to speak to Jack, he made up his mind he would phone on Thursday at seven o'clock on the dot. He sat at the table his peace returning to him. Jack was alright, Jack was home and in the bosom of his new family. Dan put his hands to his face and gave a great sob.

Mary slipped her arm about his shoulders and sat on his lap. 'Jack is back dear, thank God. And now you can stop your pacing, we all can.'

Dan smiled at her as he slipped his arms around her. He hoped fervently in his heart that he'd never again have to feel guilty at the pleasure of it. He hoped in his heart that Jack had found love. He didn't know why but he felt happy for him. Yes, and indeed their Jack may be a legend yet in that far off land to the north, a land of strange beauty where everything seems larger than life.

The next morning Jack had kissed the woman Mary goodbye promising he would see her again soon. The men lined up to thank her for returning Jack to them. 'Don't be a stranger' Wayne had said 'come by anytime and stay a few days or as long as you like. Hilda would be only too happy to have some female company for a change. And if there is anything I can do for you lass, anything at all, let me know. We will be over in a couple weeks to start on your house. We begin our muster soon and our camp will be quite close to your boundary.'

Tom and Fred said goodbye and promised they'd never forget her. Tom said earnestly, 'in the event that we don't meet again, I will raise my daughter on stories of you. Don't worry I'll get them from Jack.' Tom smiled and shook hands with the woman he'd realised was shy.

Mary, helped by Jack, got up on Caeser and one of the dogs got up behind her.

The other dog Ginger jumped up on Samson and that was how they disappeared into the vegetation on the gully floor. Jack marvelled at the ease with which she sat the big bull, there was no saddle and it wasn't easy to stay on them when they broke into a run. And they could run for miles, covering long distances quickly, and they loved it. And you only had a lead rope to turn them or stop them with. They responded mainly to shouts.

Jack thought his heart would break, but he knew she had to go. Alby stood beside him and waved to the beautiful woman who had returned Jack to them. In Alby's mind she had returned him from the dead. He said softly now, 'I would like to help with her house Jack, and I would also like to contribute to the cost of materials. I for one would like to think of her as safe in a nice place to live. You are pretty keen on her aren't you, Jack? Can't say as I blame you. Look at her ride that great big bloody bull into the forest. She is a myth Jack, a real live myth.' He watched and waved with Jack even after the woman was gone from view. Alby said softly as if to himself, 'and we thought we were shit hot catching them and tying them to a tree hay. What's it like to actually ride one of those monster's buddy?'

'It's a bit bloody rough, hard to stay on and fairly bloody scary.' He turned to Alby with a smile 'Give me a horse any day Alby.' Jack shook his head and went on 'but you know, they did find me. The bulls, they found me and stopped dead and refused to run over me. Mary got down to see what was up in the fading light and there I was covered in mud. The same colour as the ground.'

Alby stood motionless, listening to the fantastic story. 'Who would have thought Jack?'

'Yeah, apparently it was Caeser who spotted me. I thought they were going to kill me and then I passed out and don't remember any more.'

By this time the others were listening to Jacks story. Ernie scratched his head, 'so one bull tries to kill you, and another saves your life. Funny old-world Jack. Of course, nobody will be all that surprised when this story surfaces. Who's gunna be surprised to hear that the man who kicks their balls is now controlling them hay?' There was loud laughter.

Tom had stood quietly listening to this story and suddenly spoke, 'you know Jack, from what Mary says, she found you about on the edge of her property line. You must have been washed down the creek about thirty miles. From where you got bogged to the spot where Mary found you is roughly between twenty-five and thirty miles. How the hell are you still alive? Not just alive but alive and well and not a scratch on you really.' Tom looked at Ernie who was digesting this piece of news along with the others.

Wayne stood looking at Jack along with everyone else. They all stood in silence gazing at Jack. Jack began to fidget.

'Well, the Gods smiled down on you, old son,' said Fred. 'And they sent you a Goddess riding on bulls to save you.' He turned back to the gully floor, 'lucky bastard.'

Jack looked non plussed himself, he hadn't put it all together either. He knew it was true, knew he'd ended up about thirty miles farther down the creek. And he knew it was water that hit him though it felt like a ton of bricks. He said now, 'it didn't seem that long. I thought about five minutes was all I'd been in the water.'

'Yeah' said Wayne, 'you couldn't have been taken that far in five minutes. Must have been a bit longer than that. Bloody amazing how you survived. I'm bloody glad you did though buddy.' Wayne patted him on the shoulder, 'where were we gunna find another driver like you?' He put his hand on Jack's shoulder, 'bloody good to have you back mate.'

Bill said softly now, 'you survived thirty miles of swirling raging flash flood. Bloody legendary mate.'

Jack smiled and looked down 'it's just water.'

Ernie gave a hic of a laugh and shaking his head said softly, 'just water he says.' Turning away he said, 'alright if you're a fish maybe.'

Amid laughter and good-natured banter, the men swung up in their saddles. It was still a long way home.

They got to within a few miles of where Jack parted company with the land rover they had cut across country and crossed the creek farther down. After they made camp, they sat talking around the fire, the hum of their voices and the odd laughter joined by the cricket's song was a reassuring thing. They were all exhausted and it showed. They all packed the camp up ready for the morning.

'Well, I'm gunna hit the hay' said Wayne, 'we should get home tomorrow. I'd like to get to the truck in the morning.'

Jack climbed into his swag his mind was at peace and his heart beat nice and easy. For the first time in his life Jack was truly happy. He did sense however that Wayne was not, and this concerned him. Why he thought again for the umpteenth time, why couldn't they all be happy and why did it have to be Wayne? The man bloody deserved to be happy he told himself, he was a good and solid man and a good and solid friend.

Alby, Jack knew had found peace and Bill seemed much happier. Now that Tom had been over and told the man that they would be practically neighbours soon, he had brightened considerably. And this time they came over they had brought him letters from the girls and a photo of the baby.

Mike had taken the place of Russel though they would never forget the young ringer. They'd had that written on his head stone 'Russel the Young Ringer. Top End, Top Bloke'. Mike was every bit as keen as Russel had been and his eagerness to get amongst things worried Jack.

Jack sighed and turned over; it was good to be alive. he smiled softly as he pulled his blanket up to his shoulders. As always, the bush caressed his face with her gentle perfumed breezes and holding him gently, sang him to sleep.

The following morning Jack climbed out of his swag and said good morning to Wayne. Jack had been surprised to hear that Jim had joined the search and had gone down stream to search with the station people next door. 'So, what's he doing now' Jack asked Wayne when they got a moment? The others were waking and getting out of bed.

'Well, he says he got hired on the railways over in Darwin in the stockyards. He's driving trains now, says it's a bit easier and he likes it. Yeah, he heard about you on the news and volunteered Jack. He went off with a team from search and rescue searching the creeks for you.' Wayne shook his head now, 'maybe you knocked some sense into him Jack. Least ways that's what he reckons.'

'Did you know he approached me out the back of the pub that time Wayne, remember we ran into him in the pub? He shook my hand and said no hard feelings that morning we left.' Jack smiled, 'I thought he was after having another fight with me. Funny bloke.' Jack looked down at his saddle, 'you don't know what to make of him.'

'Yeah, he just seemed to take a dislike to you, didn't he? Those blokes were about to start searching the creeks and tree roots for your body Jack. We had to try and keep Alby away from that. He maintained you were alright and then when we got a look at your land rover… well, it didn't look good Jack. Even Alby's faith faltered.'

Wayne swallowed and was silent for a bit, 'I couldn't believe my eyes when you wandered in large as life. I thought if we found you alive, you'd be beaten up pretty bad.' He grinned and clapped Jack on the shoulder, 'not in a million years was I thinking maybe Jack will ride in on a bullock any minute.' Wayne laughed 'We thought maybe the heat and the stress had got to us.'

The two men laughed. Jack said, 'Don't know how well I'd have fared if it hadn't been for Mary though Wayne.'

Wayne smiled, 'I sense there's possibly a little something between the two of you. Over and above the gratitude you would naturally feel for her. And by hell she 's a looker Jack and she's strong and independent and bloody smart. She's the whole package, and I'm happy for you mate. I'd heard about her but never met her before.'

Alby walked up, unable to stay away from Jack any longer, and threw his arm around his best mate. Jack smiled at him, 'you knew I'd be back Alby. Didn't you?'

'Yeah, I kept saying "you just wait and see you blokes, he'll be back. Jack will ride up any time now on a big bastard of a bull".' The three men laughed; it was good to be back together. Jack turned and looked at Bill, he got up and came over. The rest followed soon after.

When they reached a spot a few miles downstream of where Jack was taken, he had a flash. A memory of that fateful day flashed in his mind. He remembered the struggle Mary had had to get him into the cart.

He searched his mind; she had unhitched one of the bulls and used it to pull him up on the cart in a sort of sling. She had sat cleaning his face and talking to him. Jack remembered that she had given him a drink of water. He'd thought if she was an angel he didn't want to live.

A smile played around in his mind as he remembered. Yes, she had traced a line along his scar with her finger a few times. 'What has happened to you' she had whispered. Jack mostly couldn't even get his eyes to open though he wanted to.

Jack had moaned, his shoulder hurt like hell. She moved it and he let out a yell. He remembered her feeling around and moving it. It hurt and he wished she'd leave it alone. But Jack was so exhausted he couldn't have stopped her if he'd tried. But something told his tired mind that she was trying to help him and that she needed to do it.

The woman picked up his arm and stretched it out. She pulled hard on it and Jack screamed. 'Please' he had screamed at her. Then he felt a click and all the pain was gone. Now as she moved his arm about it didn't hurt. But it now ached, a dull throbbing ache. 'Thank you' he had whispered to which she had replied 'you are very welcome' and then she was gone.

The woman had sung to him in a sweet voice he remembered. Then he felt her leave him and the cart started to move underneath him. He passed out.

Jack also remembered a flash of a woman taking his shirt off. He had protested and she had laughed. When she reached for his belt, he had closed his eyes in embarrassment. Then he had disgraced himself.

Jack remembered she had got him to pee in a bottle and he had almost died. But all the time she did these things she laughed and talked to him and even in his half consciousness he had been comforted.

Jack didn't remember any more until she had got him down off the cart. She did it in much the same fashion because he felt himself suspended in that sling again. He remembered her talking to a child. He smiled now, it was probably Caeser she had spoken to. She babied that bull, giving him milk to comfort him.

Then he had woken up in the tent but had passed out before he saw anyone. And the day she had come into the tent and smiled at him........ Well, he would remember that day until the day he died. How he loved her. And best of all he was sure she loved him back.

Chapter 19

Now Jack was home with Hilda fussing over him. She had told him that Dan would ring tonight. Jack was tired and thought he would get to bed as soon as he'd spoken to Dan.

Tom, Fred, Jimmy, and Ernie sat talking with everyone. They were happy how things had turned out and they'd be telling the story of Jack the ball kicker, yes siree. The man whose body they searched for, who rode into camp on a bull large as life after surviving thirty miles in a flash flood. And they would tell it for months to come. Maybe even years.

Jack told them how grateful he was to them and said he'd never met finer people. He'd looked at Bill here and said how lucky he was to have friends like them. 'And so am I' he'd said with a grateful smile.

'We had to come Jack' said Tom and left it at that.

The men sat around the table and talked quietly. Tom, Fred Jimmy, and Ernie were to leave in the morning they had a job to do. It was always sad to see them go. Bill realised that they would be two doors down, about five hundred miles away when they moved to their station. He was happy about that.

He intended to do a couple of drives with them in the coming years. He told Tom this and Tom grinned. 'I will hold you to that Bill, after your bull catching season is finished hay.' A mischievous smile appeared on Tom's face. 'And who knows if we are running a bit short of time, we could always take a short cut.'

'Oh, now fuck you, Tom' said Bill emphatically. Jimmy and Ernie agreed loudly. Jack sensed a good story there, but they weren't talking. Fred looked on in stoney silence, his expression unreadable. Yes, a very good story thought Jack but not for now.

Ernie leaned over and patted Bill's shoulder. 'Be bloody nice to work with you again Bill, you left a void in our little team when you left, and we all felt it. Yeah, it'll be nice Bill, don't forget.'

Bill looked at Ernie now, 'How did you get on with that woman you were keen on Ernie?'

'Aww Gawd' moaned Ernie and they all laughed. Ernie scratched his head, 'although that night in the truck was bloody nice……. she ' Ernie was howled down.

'We had to hose that bloody thing out dad.' Tom smiled affectionately at Ernie.

Jack laughed even though he didn't fully get it. Everyone else was laughing and it felt good. Damn good.

At seven o'clock, Wayne was waiting in the office for Dan's call when Jack walked in the door. 'How are you going there, Jack? I suppose if you can survive that torrent of water for thirty miles, you can survive Hilda's loving care for a few days hay. By the way Jack, Mary has been on the radio, she made it home just fine. She says she got home early this morning. Thought you'd want to know Jack.'

Wayne flicked his eyes up at Jack and noted the darker hue of his face and the hint of a smile that played around his mouth. Wayne was pleased, anything to keep the man from running off back to Victoria and the banks of the Murrumbidgee.

'Thanks' said Jack. 'That's a relief, don't know why I worried so much, she is a most capable woman.'

'So is she taking away some of your heart problems Jack. Just between you and me?'

'Hell yeah' smiled Jack. He sat forward now, 'did you end up hearing from Rhonda?'

'No, not yet Jack, I think it's a distinct possibility that I won't.'

The phone rang and Wayne stood up nodding at the phone for Jack to answer it. He put his hand on Jack's shoulder and said, 'I'll leave you to it mate' and walked out.

Jack put the phone to his ear, a voice said 'hello'. It wasn't Dan it was Mary.

Jack couldn't speak for a moment, he hadn't the pain shoot through him that she normally caused in him. It was strange.

'Hello Mary' he said as cheerfully as he could, 'it's good to hear your voice.'

'Hello Jack, are you alright? We were all so worried and they told us that a woman brought you home. Thank goodness Jack.'

'I'm okay Mary thanks. I was knocked out and the lady who found me wasn't sure where I came from and because of the boggy conditions of the roads she just took me home with her. But I'm fine now Mary.'

'We heard you were in the water for a long while and it's a miracle you survived.'

'Yeah well, Mary I'm fine.' Jack couldn't fathom how he now suddenly felt none of the heartache that usually went with a conversation with Mary.

'Dan only told me the other night about your poor face Jack. Just, please come home Jack.'

'No Mary, I love it up here. I belong here now Mary, but I will come for a visit soon, okay? I'm sorry for how I just left without saying goodbye Mary. It was cowardly and I hope you'll forgive me.'

'I understand Jack, you are forgiven. Always. Well Dan is walking around in circles so I will go. I will talk to you again soon but for now you need to get your rest and please take care Jack. I'm glad you are happy, so very glad. Any way goodbye love until next time.'

'Goodbye Mary and thanks.'

There was a moments silence and then 'Hello Jack' it was Dan's voice. 'Are you okay mate?'

'Yes, Dan I am fine. It's good to hear your voice though.'

'So, you are a legend now Jack. They tell me it will spread for the length and breadth of the country you, riding into camp on a bull. A man who by all accounts should be dead.' Jack heard a sigh and knew the man was tired out.

'Yeah, sorry I had everyone worried. I was out to it for a few days and then we had to make it home.'

'Thank God that lady found you. She must be quite a woman Jack, lucky for you.'

Jack knew that Dan was fishing, and he smiled. 'Yes, Dan I was lucky alright. I think I may be going across there to see her, you know to say thanks and that.'

'Really Jack!'

'Yeah, mate really. I'd had my eyes open for at least five minutes before I fell in love with her.'

'Oh, thank the Gods Jack. And you are happy now and not...... well you know Jack?'

'Yes, I know Dan. While we are having this most awkward conversation, I have always been happy for you and Mary. I just wasn't happy for myself and I'm sorry old man.'

'Jesus Jack, you have nothing to apologise for. Now I don't have to feel so bloody..... well guilty Jack. I love you mate; you are my family. It broke my heart that you had to leave. God, it did!'

'I love you to old man, I never forgot what I owed you and Mary.'

'And her name is Mary to Jack?'

'Yes, it is. She was on her way home and one of her bulls found me and refused to walk over the top of me, so she got down to have a look and there I was. Covered in mud, my clothes in tatters, I had the backside out of my pants. Yet she told me I was the most handsome man she had ever seen. Of course, when she saw the scar, she figured what it was and who I was. She got a good laugh out of that Dan.' The two men laughed. 'Then she informs me I will be getting up on one of her monstrous bulls if I wanted to get home.'

The two men laughed. 'It's a bit like old times Jack, talking to you so easy.'

Jack and Dan talked for the best part of an hour, no barriers between them anymore, and then Jack went off to get into bed. He had a new girl to dance with in the space he had once reserved for Mary of the shanty. He had left the Murrumbidgee behind.

The mustering got underway a week after Jacks return. The camp was much the same as the bull catching camps and Jack loved every minute of it. He found he even enjoyed his time in the saddle. That was after he'd got over his soreness. And he loved to be back out in the bush amongst the cattle and even the dust and the flies.

And Jack knew in his heart he would never again be satisfied with the gentler slopes of green on the Murrumbidgee. He had no affinity with growing anything anymore, it held no excitement for him. Up here he was free, and he loved it. He was as wild as the bush he inhabited now. And now he loved a woman here, now he was home.

Wayne had thrown building tools in the land rover, and they would spend their Sundays at least on Mary's house. They had some of it rebuilt, and two rooms finished within the month. Everyone gave up their day off to go and help. They all knew they owed a debt of gratitude to this woman, and they admired her and her abilities. Not one of them wanted her sleeping way out here in a tent. They worked hard and did their best.

They had made the kitchen and another room which would serve as a bedroom for the time being. But the house was sturdy and strong, and she could lock it.

Jack and the men had even made a small room off the kitchen for the dogs to sleep in. Mary was overjoyed.

The men all arrived on Saturday afternoon after work and stayed until Monday morning. Mary was overwhelmed as on the second weekend they arrived in the truck with building materials. On the truck were flyscreens to put at her windows. They would make shutters so she could lock up securely. And at Jack's insistence, insulation.

'Jack' she gasped, 'you spent all this money on me.'

'No' said Jack 'all these blokes put money in a hat. We all want our little hero to be warm and dry and safe at night Mary.'

'I don't know how to thank you.'

He and Mary had gone for a walk and seeing as they were alone, he took her in his arms. When Jack kissed the woman, he felt a need so powerful it took him by surprise. Letting her go he stepped back and gazed at her. She was beautiful. He smiled at her 'I am going to ask you to marry me, Mary. Soon as I get a ring.

As soon as this blasted mustering is over. I want to be married to you before the next wet.'

Mary fell into his arms and kissed him, smiling she said, 'me to.' Jack had never heard two sweeter words. He wished he'd brought a blanket then thought it may be better that he hadn't.

Back at the building site Mike was helping Wayne, 'Where do you think they went' asked Mike?

'Oh, for Christs sake' said Wayne with a grin. 'Somewhere we're not all gawking at them.'

'Oh Okay.'

Alby smiled at the boy. He hadn't seen Sandy for a while, and he missed her.

He'd had a letter from her a couple of weeks ago. He'd been trying unsuccessfully, to find the words to ask her to come and live with him in the long hut. He mentioned this to Wayne now.

'Yeah well, it's a good thing you asked me son as I am a lazy bloody coward and I know the easy way to do just about anything. So, write her a letter, simple. The beauty about writing a letter is, if you get it wrong you just scrap it and start again. Now if you were talking face to face with her you may have fucked everything up, again and again see. So badly, until you fucked it right into the ground.'

Alby stared wide eyed at Wayne for a few moments and then smiled weakly at him. 'You wanna know something really funny Wayne? That bloody dribble actually makes fuckin sense.'

Alby walked off shaking his head while Wayne had a chuckle. Unbeknownst to anyone he was one coward who could even manage to stuff things up in a letter. A letter he had thought was very nice.

Well bugger the women he thought picking up his hammer, he was just no good with them. He sighed and climbed the ladder to get the roof on. If he could just find a woman like Mary, he'd be set. She was easy to talk to. Of course, she wouldn't have to be as good looking as her.

Ater a month the house was finished to lock up standard and the men had to go. They had finished these two paddocks and had to move camp over a hundred miles away. They could move away now at ease in the knowledge that their hero Mary had the ability to lock her house at night and be safe.'

Mary thanked them and cried as they left. 'It is a beautiful little house' she told them, 'And I love it.'

Wayne smiled at her and said softly, 'now remember girl, don't be a stranger. Come and see us over at the station as often as you can. I know Hilda wants to meet you and she said she would love to sit and talk with another woman for a change.'

Bill stepped forward and said 'Hilda is my girlfriend and she told me to tell you that she wants a visit from you. And I hope you have many happy hours in this little house. And know that it will stand most storms. You will be safe, and we will sleep peacefully knowing that.'

'I can't thank you enough. I will come over as soon as I can. It is sad to see you all go.'

The men walked away to the rover to let the two people say their goodbyes.

Jack told Mary he would come over every weekend. She said, 'thank you Jack, thank you so much.' and kissed him long and deep. 'I hope you will come back for a visit as long as the weather holds.'

'Yeah well, I'll walk if I have to.'

'Well, if it rains you could catch the next flash...' Jack pulled her into his arms and laughed. He kissed her with all his might.

During their last few days in that camp, Wayne found a couple of half-grown cows. They were clean skins and he cut them from the herd. He told Eddy to load them on the truck to be taken across to Marys. 'And Jack, you can take them over to her and see if she even wants them. Just remind her that if she doesn't want to breed them, they are good eating.' Wayne said as an afterthought 'and you Jack will do the butchering. We owe her Jack.'

Jack thanked Wayne and the big man smiled. 'Well tell her we'll bring over a few chooks and a rooster soon as we get some time. And we'll do some more work on her house as soon as we get a bit of a let up here. We'll build her a veranda to Jack.'

Jack and Eddy got the cows into the truck and Jack left for Mary's. He hadn't expected to see her again so soon and it was a treat.

Mary was more than happy with the two cows. 'Next season' said Jack, they'll be ready to breed Mary. Are all these bulls of yours related Mary?'

Mary shook her head 'I don't think so Jack.'

'Well, you will need to make sure only one of them mates with them at a time and then remember which one. And Wayne says we will bring you some chooks and a rooster when we come to finish your house. We will bring you meat each time we butcher.'

Chapter 20

Jack was as good as his word and saw Mary almost every weekend. He'd got a double bed and mattress sent out on the cart and now he was on his way to her place to surprise her with it. He'd got a dresser with a mirror, pillows, sheets, and a rug as well. The house was finished, they had put a veranda and bedroom on so Mary had a living room. But she still slept in her swag on the floor.

He arrived there on Friday night; the mustering was done so he had the whole weekend. It was dark and Jack left the furniture till morning. The weekend before he had gone into town with the blokes, and he'd missed her. He'd slept at the long hut as there was some work they needed to do. But this weekend he was off to see his lady love. Yes indeed.

Mary had his dinner ready as always. Jack sat opposite her and managed to finish his dinner. She chatted away about how good it was to be able to get inside and lock the door at night. How safe she felt. How much she loved the house. She finished her dinner; she had a healthy appetite.

'You didn't like it did you Jack' she smiled across at him?

'Yes, Mary it was delicious as always.' He got up and came round the table and turned her chair to face him. Jack knelt down before her and produced the little box. Mary's hands flew to her face, and she went red.

Jack found his voice, 'Mary my Goddess, will you be my wife? Hay? Will you marry me, Mary?'

After a moment she slipped down and knelt in front of him, his head swam as her arms went round him. 'Oh yes Jack, yes. A thousand times yes.' Jack slipped the ring on her finger; it was a tight fit. 'We'll get it made to fit,' he murmured kissing her hand gently.

'I love it Jack, it is the most beautiful thing I've ever had. I shall never take it off darling I promise. I love you so.'

'Oh, I love you to Mary.'

Jack cleared his throat and went red. He had gotten aroused and went to turn away. 'Oh, don't be embarrassed Jack. For one thing I have seen what the bulls do and for another I undressed you the night I found you.'

'Oh Jesus Mary.'

'Well, I wasn't going to put you to bed in my swag with muddy clobber on. I had to sleep in there as well.' She smiled mischievously 'you are nice Jack ' her eyes flicked down to his fly, 'you know.…… nice.' She watched his red face deepen and giggled. 'Did you bring your swag Jack?'

'Yes.' Jack let out a breath he hadn't realised he'd been holding. His face burnt white hot.

'Leave it in the car hay?'

'Oh Jesus Mary. Oh, Mary I have a very powerful need of you woman.' Jack stood up and as she undressed him, he gazed in wonder at her. It hit him when she got to his socks that she had said yes. She was going to marry him. Him! Jack! And he was about to make love to her. He'd have to focus on the job at hand he told himself. It wasn't that he'd got rusty, he never knew anything in the first place.

It had been a long time since that disastrous night in Melbourne with a strange woman. He began to undress her and the sight of her took his breath away.

How he loved her, this woman this wonderful, wild, beautiful woman. And she was his.

And that night Jack got to hold and love a real woman in that space and make love to her. She was eager and he was shy, but they scaled the heights of passion. And Jack couldn't have dragged his focus away if he'd tried.

Mary was farther surprised when, afterwards, he got up and pulled her to her feet. He danced with her that night, both naked, as he sang softly, 'don't sit under the apple tree with anyone else but me.….. '

It was halfway through May and Jack had gotten home from Marys place the day before. A smile played around his lips as he thought of the look on her face when he'd taken her out to the Ute to see his surprise. And when he thought of their loving, he had a desire to get in his Ute and head back there. Bugger the fences and bugger the bores.

She had clapped her hands and jumped about when she had spotted the furniture. 'Oh Jack, for me? I have never had anything so lovely Jack. Can we bring it in and see, please? Oh, Jack thank you.' She had kissed him, and he had responded in the usual way. He held her tight and kissed her with a passion equal to hers.

Inside the bed and dresser looked nice and Mary made the bed. 'Are you staying tonight, Jack? Please?' Jack had smiled and nodded and helped her to mess up her nicely made bed.

He almost jumped now at Waynes outburst. 'Oh, for the love of God man' he said loudly to Jack, 'what gives? You don't half look like the cat that got the bloody cream, now spill it. The double bed did the trick did it?'

Jack was shocked and stared at Wayne as if he'd suddenly grown another head. He sat forward closing his mouth.

'Yeah, come on Jack, how is Mary' said Bill?

Jack got to his feet, 'well for your information I have asked the said lady to marry me, and she has accepted. So there, now I'm off to write a letter home.' He stopped halfway to the door 'that is, I am going to write a letter to Balranald.'

The men were on their feet and clambering around him. They didn't understand it exactly, but this news made them very happy. Jack their hero was gunna get married and he was happy. And this probably meant he would stay.

Alby engaged Jack in a bear hug that made him realise what the man had gone through with a bull pinning him to the rover. Then the big man ruffled his hair and kissed him on the cheek and let him go.

'Jesus Alby' said Wayne. He shook hands with Jack, shrugged and gave the man a hug. 'Congratulations Jack you sly old dog.'

Bill stood his ground when it was his turn, he was going to give a speech. Words failed him of course and he shook Jacks hand. A tear slid down Bill's cheek, his mouth opened and shut, and nothing came out.

Jack smiled at the man, 'it's alright Bill, I know, and thank you.'

When he found his voice, Bill said quietly, 'I thought we'd lost you Jack.'

'Nay, never Bill, you and I will be mates forever.' When it was all over Jack went to his room to write to Dan.

Wayne sat in his office later and wondered at his life. Why Rhonda had not replied to his letters. He tried to concentrate on the ordering he had to do and the bills he had to pay.

Wayne dropped his pen on the desk. Alby had let it slip about these flashbacks and he knew they both were troubled by them. Waynes own flashbacks were few and far between now.

Alby lay awake thinking about Sandy. He knew he'd be in the shit if she left him.

He hoped she and he would marry one day. Alby also hoped that she'd understand about his flash backs and nightmares.

He thought it was good that they were all going to be together and have a network of help. But Alby worried now about the women they were bringing into it with them.

As Bill got farther along in his sobriety, he wondered the same thing. He wondered if he should break it off with Hilda. He had asked Wayne about it and Wayne had told him to ask her about it.

'Hilda isn't a shallow woman Bill' he'd said. 'Talk to her.'

Jack sat at his desk and tried to still his mind and bring it back to Dan and Mary and the Murrumbidgee. He sat down, picked up his pen and filled it with ink.

He wrote:

13/5/1953

Dear Dan,

I hope this letter finds you well as it leaves me. I'm sorry that I caused you to worry, sometimes I think I have been nothing but a worry to you Dan.

I cannot explain it old man, but I was washed for nearly thirty miles in a flash flood, caught in a torrent of water, and I fought it all the way. I thought I would die and when I came to, and a bull was sniffing me, and I heard the voice of an angel I thought it was so. But all I had was a dislocated shoulder which my Mary put back into place for me.

Yes Dan, I do love her, and she loves me. I bought her a ring and asked her to marry me, so we are now engaged. Me and some of the boys went across there during the muster and built her house so she can get in and lock it up. I feel much better about that, she is so isolated see.

I can reach her house in a car in less than half a day but during the wet it sometimes takes two days. Alby is engaged and very happy. I was lucky the day I ran into him. I have been very lucky Dan; I have been blessed with the best damn family a man could ever hope for. And you Dan.

Tom and Ernie, and Fred and Jimmy have gone home. It was good of them to come and help search for me. The station people on all sides were out searching. It was a very humbling experience.

Only a few months to bull season now Dan, and I am looking forward to it. Hopefully this time I will keep my face out of the way. I am hoping that you and Mary can forgive me, I couldn't help loving her Dan. But now I know I was meant to come up here and meet this most beautiful, wild, and lovely woman of mine. I am a very happy man; she is a joy. You will like her Dan.

Anyway, I must go now, early start tomorrow. Give my love to all Dan and thanks for being there for me. Until we talk again, I remain.

Yours faithfully,
Jack

Jack folded the letter carefully, slowly, thoughtfully and put it in the envelope he had ready. It still hurt, still broke his heart that he was so far from home. He wondered just then if he would ever get over it. If he'd ever stop missing his loved ones on the banks of the Murrumbidgee River in that green rolling land so far to the South.

He sighed and got into bed, he had a date with his Mary, and he'd dance with her and sing to her. He'd kiss her and hold her……. And in the wee hours he'd smile, roll over and take her in his arms again. Yes, by Christ, he didn't have to let her go and it felt good.

But what Jack woke up to in the middle of the night was a flash back. Alby had him and was talking softly to him. 'It's alright mate I'm here I've got you. We're gunna be alright Jack. Come on mate let it go hay.' Alby held him to him as you'd hold a child and was stroking his hair.

Jack came out of it, 'I had a nightmare Alby, you know……?'

'Yeah, I know Jack. It's been a while though mate must be six seven eight months hay?'

'Was it very bad Alby?'

'No mate they are never bad. You just yell and sometimes you cry. We all do the same even Bill and Wayne. What is it, Jack?'

'Jesus Alby! How can I marry that girl? I can't put her through this Alby, not her. What'll I do Alby? How can I give her up?'

'What I think you should do is go to Mary and tell her about these. Let her make the decision. She loves you to Jack so she has a right to choose.'

'But if I get like this and you aren't there Alby.' Jack's voice held despair at the thought.

212

Alby sat back letting go of Jack. 'And remember this Jack, if we all live together in the long hut I will be there. Just down the corridor. Why do you think we all want to do this. We all want to stick together because it's the best way to go forward and because we need each other right. We'll all be there for each other. I've told Sandy this and Bill's told Hilda and they are fine with it. Now you must tell Mary.' Alby put his hand on Jack's shoulder now, 'I know that woman loves you, Jack. If you like I can be there when you tell her. Or Bill or Wayne. Or all of us. Just do it Jack, don't lose your chance at real happiness. You told me to go for it.'

Jack nodded, 'you are right Alby. I'll talk to her next time I go over there.'

Alby sat with Jack for a few moments and Jack said, 'you go on to bed Alby, I'm alright.'

'Alright if you're sure Jack. I'm just in there, mate.'

'Thanks Alby. As always that's nice to know mate.'

The following week Jack got to Mary's place at breakfast time. He sat at the table across from Mary and told her of his flashbacks. Told her how he'd had one a couple of nights ago and how Alby had got him through it and told him to come talk to her. Jack told her about the long hut and the others who went through the same thing being nearby to help.

Mary sat opposite him and stared at him. Jack began to fidget; a bad feeling had found its way into his stomach. Mary dropped her eyes and looked at the table. He shuffled his feet.

Jack reached across the table and took her hand in his. 'Mary, can you tell me what you are thinking darling. Please talk to me, no matter how bad it is.'

'I don't want to talk right now Jack.' She pulled her hand back.

Jack felt his innards turn to water; he wouldn't be able to stand it. He sat looking at her for some time. He knew what he had to do but how the hell could he do it?

He rose slowly to his feet he was numb. 'Alright Mary, I will leave you to think on it.' He stood there, willing his feet to walk to the door.

He stood a bit longer waiting for her to forgive him and tell him she loved him anyway and always would. It didn't happen.

You should have known, he told himself harshly in his head, you should have known you were not bloody good enough. Jack felt the old familiar sickening feeling of self-loathing. He turned his head and looked at the door, he'd thought he was finished with his self-loathing yet here he was. And there was the door.

Jack dug deep and found the strength to walk to the door and close it behind him. He walked slowly across the yard to the Ute. This hurt worse than anything ever had, he opened the door and got in. He sat thinking, maybe he was giving up too easily. Maybe he should go back in there and try to talk to her. Something about the look on her face told him no.

He shook his head and put his hand down to the key. He took it in his fingers and turned it, the motor sprang into life. How could he stand it? He couldn't and he knew it, he had lost her without even trying. All because he was too damaged. It was him; she couldn't accept him and his bloody flashbacks.

Jack drove back to the station. As he went through the last creek about five miles from the homestead, he pulled off the road and stopped the car. Jack got out of the car and took up his rifle. He couldn't stand it and he knew it. He just wanted out now, wanted some peace. Jack walked off down the creek for a ways and sat under a huge gum tree. He had a pounding in his ears.

It had come to this. All the pain and suffering and fear he'd ever known had brought him to this. Through no damn fault of his own this time. Jack knew he'd done his best this time and it wasn't good enough. He put the rifle barrel under his chin and reached his thumb down to the trigger. Jack closed his eyes.

A hand went round his and held it gently. 'Don't mate. Just give me five minutes and if you still have a mind to, I will help you.' Wayne held his breath as Jack hesitated for a moment and took his thumb slowly from the trigger.

When Jack looked up at Wayne the pain and confusion in his eyes hurt the big station manager more than anything ever had. Ever could.

'What's going on little mate? Talk to me Jack.'

It was all Jack could do to shake his head. He sat still, Wayne thought he already looked dead. Already looked lifeless. A sob escaped Wayne, and he sat trying desperately to pull himself together. He knew the desolation behind that look. But Jack had let him take the rifle. God help me he thought over and over.

So, I can help him. Wayne had sat here himself, on a lonely creek bank somewhere a rifle at his own head.

'I have to tell you this Jack. Mary got on the radio and said "Jack left here to go home. Find him".' Wayne watched as a look of hope dawned on the bloke and then died again soon after. He went on, 'that's all I got. So, I came looking for you. What happened mate?'

'No go away mate, you can't fix this. I'm tired Wayne, just so tired. I'd like a bit of peace for Christ's sake. I made a mistake Wayne.'

Jack sat staring at the ground for a while. He looked up at Wayne and shook his head. 'Can't take no more.'

'Come on son, get in the car with me and we'll go on over and see Mary hay? This can all be sorted I know it.'

Jack shook his head, 'no Wayne. No, I will never forgive her. And I will never allow myself to love again. Go home Wayne and take the goddamn rifle with you. I'll stay here for a while. Go on Wayne.'

'Nope.'

'I've got my swag and that in the car, I think I'll stay here for a bit hay. You go on home mate I'll be alright.'

'Good.'

Wayne went and put the rifle in his car and got Jacks gear and, after a quick look for any other firearms, took it down to him. He then went and sat down the creek a little.

Around a half an hour passed, and Jack began to cry. He sobbed uncontrollably in Waynes arms. And when it was passed, he felt a little easier. 'And this, Wayne is what I really fought that fuckin creek for. This is what I fought a bloody war for, so's I could end my life alone on a bloody creek bank.'

Jack stopped sobbing and spoke haltingly of his conversation with Mary. Wayne sat back from Jack and studied him. 'Doesn't sound like Mary does it, Jack? Well, it doesn't.'

Jack sat thinking about what Wayne had said. 'No mate she doesn't want me. She found out I'm damaged and she....'

'Bull shit Jack. Something is wrong but this isn't it. If she just didn't care about you, why did she call me on the radio?'

'Go home Wayne for the love of Christ.' Jack flicked his eyes at Wayne. 'Just leave me be mate.' Wayne saw the melancholy had struck him full force.

Wayne sat looking at Jack and knew he had to resolve this, one way or another. 'No, I'm going over to Mary's to find out what's wrong. You fuck off home if you want or you can get in the car with me.'

'Well, I'm doing neither, I'm staying right here.'

'I'll be right back lad.'

Wayne got back well after dark. Jack had lit a fire and sat on his swag. Wayne walked over to him. 'Don't bloody bother Wayne.'

'Listen Jack, I had a long talk with Mary. She's pretty upset mate. I kept on until she told me, she is scared Jack. She thinks...... well she thinks she's in the family way.'

Jack sat forward, 'in the family what?'

'Way Jack. The family way.'

'And what is that, pray?'

'She's having a baby Jack. Yours. She was afraid to tell you.' Jack was on his feet now. 'Shit!'

'Now Jack...'

'I've gotta get back there Wayne.'

'Yes, you do son, yes you do.' Wayne stood up now and took Jacks arm in his hand, 'listen Jack. You went in there and you told her about your little problem and then told her she would be moving into a house with a stack of others also with the same problem. Scary shit mate! Jack, it might be better if you go and find out what you can do, fine out what she wants, what she needs. Women get a little delicate in this condition.' Wayne shrugged, 'so they tell me.'

Jack stared at Wayne in shock, 'are you sure Wayne? A baby? Me and Mary?'

'Go on son go to her, and you probably should set a date. Listen Jack, you might have to go and live with her. Take a couple of months if you like, and see. I can find all sorts of jobs for you over there, mate so you can still work. Go on now and for Christ's sake be gentle.' Wayne didn't let go Jacks arm, 'I told her something about what you go through to and she…… well she understands. She has her place there to consider to Jack. But having a baby is scaring her, and 'Wayne stopped talking and smiled as he heard a car coming across the creek. Sure, enough it turned and came over to them and he wasn't at all surprised when Mary got out.

'Heard you were camping out love' she said to Jack. 'Can I join you?'

'Oh woman.' Jack murmured but he didn't move, he couldn't he'd gone stiff. Wayne smiled at him and told him he was going home. Said he hadn't brought his camping gear. He smiled at Mary as he passed her. Yeah, he thought now women like Mary didn't throw you away because you were a bit of a challenge. She'd been scared. 'See you Monday son' Wayne called back as he walked back to his car and got in it. Not like some.

Mary put her arms gently around Jack, 'forgive me Jack.'

'Oh Mary…… Oh Mary.' He looked into her lovely face 'is it true my love?' Mary smiled as his arms went around her 'it is…… daddy.'

'Oh Jesus, woman. I am the happiest man alive Mary. Oh God woman, don't ever be scared of me. I adore you, Mary. I wouldn't mind if we had triplets or even six or seven. Just love me Mary…… just love me. As long as you love me.' He kissed her softly, 'we will live wherever you want to Mary. Wherever you want.'

Jack climbed into the swag with Mary that night and gave thanks for Wayne, a solid man, and a solid friend. Jack thought the joy he felt that night was more than he deserved.

It was mail day again and Wayne had given up on any letter from his great love Rhonda. Yep, Wayne knew all about disappointments. Of course, he blamed himself mostly, he should never have told her how he felt. What an idiot to talk that way to someone you haven't seen for twenty odd bloody years. Wayne heaved a sigh.

He sat at his desk at the window, he was stacking papers and unstacking them. He didn't know what was wrong with him today. He was restless and couldn't keep his mind on anything.

It still sent shivers down his spine how close he had come to losing Jack. But all was well there now, Jack was living over there with Mary. They were trying to work out where Mary would live when Jack and the rest of them were out bull catching, Mary had her own place to consider. But at least they were all talking. Wayne knew that Mary would follow Jack, but Jack needed to know it.

Wayne watched the truck pull up and was a little surprised when both doors opened. He saw Hilda walk out the mess door and stop. Wayne didn't realise he was holding his breath. Not another fucking visitor he thought. He asked himself what was wrong with him?

Waynes eyes narrowed as a woman's shoe and a very shapely leg came slowly through the passenger side door. Very shapely indeed. Wayne found himself rising slowly to his feet.

Wayne began to feel a bit like a peeping Tom as the other leg appeared also very shapely. But this thought was replaced with another and then another and Wayne was shocked at himself. Wayne told himself he shouldn't be doing this but dragging his eyes away was a small priority right now. He wanted the rest of it.

Bert practically ran around the truck, he put his arms up to the woman. Berty never did that. Waynes's mouth hung open.

A very lovely woman put her arms on his shoulders and jumped down out of the truck. She was dressed in a nice blue and white dress with a belt at the waist and a straw hat on her head. Waynes's mouth fell opened even wider as he began to realise who his visitor was.

'Rhonda' he breathed and sat down heavily in his chair. She was laughing at something Bert had said and she turned to look at the house and then back to Hilda. She walked to Hilda and the two shook hands. Hilda was smiling and now she indicated the house with her hand. Wayne ducked and got down on the floor. 'Fuck.'

Alby was spending some time at the long hut; he had the place to himself for the weekend, so he'd asked Sandy to come and stay there with him. He sat with Sandy at a cafe to eat fish and chips for dinner. He had asked her to spend the weekend with him, but he had other questions. A little more pressing.

Looking across the table at her he knew he had to find the balls to ask her to come and live with him. He'd told Jack he already had, what a lot of fine talk he'd fed Jack. He hated that he'd lied to Jack so he would make it right today.

'Out with it.'

'What?'

'Whatever it is that's got stuck in your craw Alby.'

'No, I'm alright there's nothing stuck…… Oh yeah. Well…….' He put his hand out and picked up Sandy's hand. It was all greasy from the chips, he put it down.

'Well?'

'Yeah, okay Sandy give a man a bit of a go here.' Alby picked up his drink and, spilling most of it down his shirt he swallowed a great mouthful that almost choked him and left him trying to get his breath. He opened and closed his mouth a few times, his gut was in a knot. Finally, he got his breath.

Sandy sat smiling at him, it occurred to Alby that she was enjoying this but who would be that cruel? He shuffled his feet. 'Well Sandy we are engaged now.' He croaked.

Sand looked exasperated 'Alby I hadn't forgotten.'

'Sandy can you be quiet girl.' Alby got his hanky out and wiped the sweat from his brow. 'Well do you think we should move in together Sandy? Here…… move in here.' Alby looked up and waved his hand around, 'well not here exactly, out at the long hut.'

Sandy laughed; Alby was offended. 'Is this because you told Jack that you were all going to move in to… '

'Righto Sandy, I'm glad you've had your fun. Now finish your fish n chips I've gotta bloody go. Do you want me to drop you home Sandy or would you rather walk?'

Alby got up and went to pay for the meals. He stood at the counter for a moment then came back to the table. 'Well?'

'I'll walk Alby.'

'Right. No, come on get in the bloody car.' Sandy sat there. 'Do you want me to throw you over my shoulder girl. I'll bloody do it.'

Sandy started to laugh; she couldn't stop. Alby pulled her to her feet and upset the table a little. A man came over to ask if she was alright and Alby drew him a look. 'Oh, just fuck off mate.' He turned back to Sandy, 'now look what you've done.'

Sandy turned to the man and said she was fine. Out in the car Alby turned to go to Sandy's house. 'Can't we go and have a look at the place Alby? I'd like to see it.'

Alby brought the car to a stop, 'Why Sandy? So, you can get a laugh out of that to.' Sandy went to say something, but Alby interrupted. 'Just shut up Sandy. You think it's all a bloody joke well let me tell you it isn't. Me and Jack and Bill and Wayne we get flash backs of the war. We wake up screaming and then we start crying and we thrash around trying to find a safe place. In our heads bombs are going off and bullets are whistling round our ears and death is all around and you can smell it and taste it. Having some one there who understands is a big bloody deal, Sandy.'

Alby sat looking straight ahead for a moment he was shaking visibly. Sandy spoke, 'Alby I'm sorry.'

Alby turned slowly to her, 'it's okay Sandy, you are just a kid. I was right, this between us won't ever work. I should never have expected so much from you. I love you girl and that is why I have to let you go.'

'No Alby, give me a chance please. I......I love you so much Alby. I just didn't realise what you go through. Give me a go Alby.'

Alby scratched his head, 'you will find somebody your own age Sandy. Some one who is not so damaged. It's not your fault it's not my fault it's that bloody war.'

Alby put the car in gear and carried on to her house. He would turn his back on this great love, on his weekend and on his happy life. And for why? A bloody war between maniacs. Maniacs who couldn't care less about the human carnage they'd caused. And they'd do it again and again feeling as if they have every right to cause such horror. The horrors of war! And he thought for a few beautiful months that he could know happiness. What a fool! And Sue? Well, he'd already turned his back on her, hadn't he?

He pulled up outside Sandy's house and waited for her to get out. 'Do you love me Alby?'

He dragged his eyes round to look at her, 'yes Sandy I do. But please go.'

'You want me to make it easy for you to dump me Alby? Well, I won't. I love you too so how about that? I have learned my lesson here Alby, now I know.'

He kept his eyes to the front 'it's not about lessons S......'

'Then what is it about? If you want me to get out and go, then you turn your head around and kiss me goodbye.'

'Shit Sandy.'

'Alby, I can't bear this. Don't leave me Alby please don't.'

'What if one night I'm having an episode and you get hurt?'

'Oh, Alby I'll take that chance. A thousand times I'll take that chance.' She put her hand on his and felt it tremble. 'We can get single beds Alby, just as long as we are together.'

Alby made a mistake here; he began to think about it. Began to believe they could do it, that they would be fine. It was dark now. Alby made another mistake, he turned his head and looked into her face, into her eyes. The way he saw it they were stuck. He was stuck, he couldn't resist her. 'You'd do that Sandy?'

Sandy leaned across and kissed his neck and whispered his name. 'No don't Sandy. Oh, Jesus girl.' He turned and took her in his arms.

Their weekend at the long hut together was a happy time the happiest in Alby's life. As they lay in bed together Alby asked her if, she was sure. She pulled him into her arms, and he lay his head on her breast. 'Yes, Alby I want only you. No one else will do Alby.'

'Then let's get married hay. Just you and me, we go and get married at the courthouse.'

And that is what they did. Alby got a single bed and put it in the room for him. They had only Wayne, Jack, Mary, Bill, and Hilda there. Sandy saw the sense in having these people around for support now.

When Wayne got himself up off the floor he sat at his desk. He knew Hilda would bring his visitor over to him. He sat and waited, for fifteen minutes he waited. He was behind his desk where he could look a little superior when Rhonda walked in. He ran his fingers through his hair and checked his shirt was clean.

Rhonda didn't show. So, he supposed he'd have to go and see what's what, he would be conspicuous in his absence. The mail cart had gone, he rose slowly out of his chair. He looked out onto the yard and there was no sign of the two women. 'Bloody Hilda' he breathed.

He sauntered casually across the yard to the mess, his belly in a knot. Wayne told himself to expect that the woman would have changed, he had by Christ, she wouldn't be the looker she once was. He could hear the two women talking and he heard Hilda laugh. That's encouraging he thought and reached out towards the door.

Wayne swung it open and stopped dead in his tracks. Jesus, he couldn't make it out. To him she was better than ever. She smiled at him, and Hilda went off to the kitchen.

Wayne walked in and Rhonda thought the same about him. He was still gorgeous and now he looked older and wiser and more worldly though a little thicker around the middle.

Something popped into Wayens mind now as he walked towards her. She stood up and held her arms out to him. As he stepped into them, he murmured 'why have you come woman?'

She kissed him on the cheek and stood back looking at him. 'Because you wanted me to Wayne. Right?'

He pulled her into his arms and kissed her as he had once done. Breathless he said 'of course I did. I never wanted you to go, never wanted anyone but you.'

They held each other for some time and then Wayne sat her at the table. He looked into her eyes, and he was heart sorry to see some pain there. 'Has it been bad Ron?'

She smiled; he'd always called her that. She nodded and left it at that, her eyes imploring him to do the same. He nodded and smiled. Hilda brought them a cup of tea and some lunch.

Wayne asked her now 'are you staying woman or is this a visit?'

'That depends on you Wayne.'

Wayne wasn't sure why that statement irked him so much. 'No, it doesn't. All these years I have waited for you to walk back into my life. No, it's up to you now woman just as it was when you decided to leave.'

Wayne smiled across the table at her. He could see her awkwardness and shrugged. 'Let's just say it's a visit then Ron, I don't want to get all heavy with you. Don't want to scare you off again.' He smiled and thought, what the hell is wrong with me?

Rhonda sat staring at him, 'I was a foolish girl, Wayne. Are you going to forgive me?'

The question stumped Wayne. He nodded and looked into her eyes. When they had finished their lunch Wayne said he'd show her to her room.

'Wayne, Bertie is coming back in a couple of days, I can go back with him.'

Wayne nodded his head vigorously; his temper was rising though he fought against it now. The words that left his mouth were 'if that's what you want Rhonda. Not gunna give me a go? Well come on we'll get you a room. I didn't know you were coming so I haven't got anything ready for you.'

Rhonda grabbed the suitcase and wrestled it out of his grip with surprising strength. 'Hilda stays over there some where Wayne that'll do. I have put you out and I am sorry.'

Wayne felt an anger he knew was not reasonable but damn it all who did she think she was? She walked out and then thinks she can walk back in. But you wanted her back in you dope a tiny voice tried to tell him. And then she comes all this way gets out of the truck and goes off with Hilda. Left him sitting there.

He stood looking down at her, she was still his Goddess but Jesus, she'd hurt him. She saw it now, saw all his pain. Pain, she knew she'd caused. She put her hand on his arm 'I only have a couple of days Wayne I don't want to fight with you. I came because I have always loved you. I wondered if you still loved me, but I can see that you don't. Let's just be friends Wayne.'

The phone rang in the office, and he looked at it. He looked back at Rhonda, a beautiful creature he had nothing in common with now. 'Alright Ron, we'll aim for that hay. I forgive you but there's actually nothing to forgive.' He looked at the office. The phone stopped ringing and then started again.

'You go Wayne I'll just wait around until you are done.'

'No come on woman, I'll see you to your room.' Wayne took the case back and led the way. He gave her a room with a double bed and a French window.

Rhonda took her hat off and looked around the room. 'It's lovely Wayne, thank you so much. Go and answer your phone now dear.'

Wayne picked up the phone with heavy heart and a sick belly, he'd blown it. 'Hello, Wayne here.'

'Hello Wayne, this is pat at the hospital here. One of your men has been brought in in a serious way.'

'Who?'

'All we have so far is Bill. We have to send him to Brisbane.'

'Shit what happened?'

'He has suffered a heart attack and will need surgery. He has a massive burn as well.'

'Oh God no! May I speak to him?'

'No, I'm sorry he is in a coma. The doctor thought it best.'

'What can I do?'

'There's nothing you can do. Jack brought him in, said they were using some welding gear and when Bill keeled over, he somehow got burnt. He will be going just as soon as we have him ready. You won't make it in time to see him, he's leaving in about ten minutes or so. I'm sorry Mr. Strawbridge to dump this on you.'

'Is Jack there?'

'Yes, he's sitting with Bill talking to him, no one knows if they can hear so it does more good than harm we think. Can I give him a message?'

'Tell him to ring me when he can. And thanks for your help.'

Wayne knew Rhonda had walked in on him and he also knew he was in shock. He sat in his chair his face though sweating was as white as a sheet. He didn't care he just dropped his head in his hands and let the tears fall down his face.

Hilda walked in just then 'I wondered if you were going to answer the phone, Wayne. Alright I'll leave you to it.' She walked a little closer 'what is it, Wayne?'

Wayne sat shaking his head at her, how after Russel, was he supposed to tell her about this? He turned to Rhonda and said softly 'can we have a minute please Ron?'

'Of course,' Rhonda said and left the office and went out in the garden.

Wayne stood looking at Hilda, she noted the pale colour and the tear stains. Her hands went to her face 'Bill! Oh, Wayne is it, Bill?'

Wayne nodded and held his arms out to her as she walked into them, he held her gently and they sobbed together. He held her at arm's length 'he had a heart attack Hilda. He has been sent to Brisbane.'

'What'll we do Wayne?'

'Wait Hilda, all we can do is wait. Jack is with him.'

'Good.' Hilda looked up at Wayne now, 'should you let Tom know?" 'Of course, Hilda.'

When Wayne said goodbye to Rhonda his only feeling was regret. He felt disappointed and he was sorry that he had hurt her. He didn't think she deserved that.

But Wayne had bigger things on his mind. Bill wasn't responding!

On the Monday Hilda had gotten herself a ticket to fly to Brisbane, she would leave on the Wednesday. The doctors were not hopeful.

Wayne talked to Jack, he and Bill had been in at the long hut doing copper pipes and such. Alby had been with them but then he'd left to do some fencing. Wayne had come back to the homestead to get some work done here.

Jack sat with Wayne now and started to speak. 'He clutched his chest and keeled over. The welder burnt him before he could let go of it. I picked him up and raced him into town. Bill lost consciousness on the way. Shit Wayne. How is Hilda?'

'She'd not so good mate, not good. I think she wants to go and be with him. What sort of a chance do they give him Jack?'

Jack shook his head. He raised sad eyes to Wayne 'not much mate, not much at all.'

Chapter 21

Bill didn't pull through. He fought for his life for almost a week and gave up. Wayne had his body flown back to town. The company of people and Toms people grieved for weeks.

When Wayne had talked to Tom and Hilda it was decided to bring Bill back to be buried on Tom's station. It was a sad time for everyone. Hilda went into hospital herself she was so overcome with grief she had become ill. Tom went to see her in hospital and Fred went with him.

'Yes Tom, you bury him on your station' she'd said. 'Surrounded by good mates. But I must be able to see him when I need to.'

'Of course, Hilda,' said Tom. 'We'll bury him on the banks of the Katherine River not too far from town. Hilda if you want, we can build you a little place down there near him.'

When the funeral was over, and the Mable Downs crew had been returned home for a couple of months, Hilda spoke to Wayne about it. She hated bothering him with this he had lost his Rhonda. 'We are a fine pair' she said now.

'Hilda if that's what you want you go but I would like you to stay.' He got up from his chair and his arms went around her 'say you'll stay woman. Please.'

'Well, I suppose I could Wayne, but the money....'

'Oh, Gawd woman' Wayne smiled for the first time in weeks. He sat back in his chair, 'how much Hilda?'

Suddenly Hilda saw her future here. 'Wayne, I must consider Tom's offer. When you leave the station, I don't want to stay. I have some money put by; I would probably go to Katherine to live. Buy a little flat and get a little job.'

Wayne stood up and frowned at her, 'You have a little flat and a little job here. You will still come to the long hut and cook for us. It will be hard at first woman I know but we'll be together. Yeah, we're a fine pair Hilly but I bloody need you woman. Don't leave me Hilda.'

'Wayne......'

He walked towards her it was all so clear to him now, 'you should stay with me Hilda. I honestly can't say how long I've been in love with you, from day one probably. But I am a big fool as you know Hilly. Do you hear me Hilda, I love you woman. Say something Hilda.'

Hilda stared at the man standing before her. She lifted her hand to her face. 'I want to take it real slow Wayne.'

'Slow as you like woman you are calling the shots.'

'This is not a ploy to get out of paying me forty pounds a week, is it?'

'Forty pounds Hilda! Who gets that sort of money? Jesus Mary and Joseph woman.' Hilda turned around. Wayne followed her and taking her hand he turned her to face him. 'Alright then but don't tell the blokes for Christ's sake. Does this earn me a kiss woman?'

She looked up at him and wondered why she hadn't seen it before. He suited her, suited her just fine. She smiled at him, and he slipped his arms around her. When he kissed her, his heart righted itself in his chest. 'Oh Hilda...... Oh God Hilda.'

Mary came to stay at the long hut with Jack and she went home every weekend to check on her place though it was still a three-hour drive. When bull catching season came around Hilda did the cooking and Mary helped her. Bill was sorely missed but they all got on with life.

It was Alby who came home early one day and caught Hilda and Wayne. He laughed and said 'bloody good mate. Oh, you to Hilda.'

He grinned at them and their embarrassment and said, 'I couldn't be happier.'

Alby and Sandy had never used the single bed and Sandy said one day that they would have more room in there without it. But Alby flatly refused to get rid of it. When she asked him why he needed to keep it, he'd said 'just because Sandy. Why do you always oppose me? Always gotta know best.'

'We could fit a cot in there.'

'Shit!'

'Yeah, shit Alby.'

'Well get a basket and sit it on the bed Sandy.'

Mary had her baby early the following year after bull catching, she had a boy and Jack experienced more joy than he thought he could stand. How he loved his Goddess. They married before Christmas, Jack said they ought to be married when the baby came.

They all lived in the long hut by then and Hilda and Wayne shared a room. The first time Wayne made love to Hilda he knew he was home, and he had never dreamed he could be so happy. He no longer dreamed of the past. He knew Hilda had taken to mothering Mike and when she had asked to bring him there Wayne was in a dilemma.

'Look what happened last time when I brought Russel into the bull catching.'

'Isn't there anything you do that's safe Wayne?'

He couldn't tell her no. She had him over a barrel and Mike moved in soon after. Wayne was amazed at the family they had in the long hut. They had gotten a contract with two more stations and were able to make a very good living at the bull catching. In the first year all their debts were paid off. Alby got a new car; they were expecting a baby soon. Hilda loved it and spent a lot of time looking after babies.

Hilda spent many happy evenings in there outdoor living area, and she served the men their breakfast there every morning. How she loved it, how she loved Wayne. He took her breath away sometimes when she looked at him. Her love for him was deep, almost as deep as his for her she knew.

Eddy left the station and came into the bull catching with them, the rest of the year he went home. Tom came the next year in January for a visit with his wife Emily and Janet and Fred. They stayed for a week and said they would be back soon. Fred told them to be at his and Janets wedding on the first of March.

They all went to that wedding, and everyone enjoyed themselves immensely. All of Tom's men were there and Jack got to know Herbert. He found the bloke had a shady past and had come out from England. But Jack liked him, he had changed his ways and by all accounts was a hard worker.

The reception was held in the Mataranka pub and Jack and Wayne were introduced to a man called Bradley Ellis and his wife Lilly. He told Wayne he had at one time owned Mable Downs.

When the night was ended Jack and Mary got into a swag. Their swag had been modified to include a baby and Alby was busy modifying theirs. Jack pulled Mary into his arms, 'my favourite part of the day this.' He kissed her and sang softly 'don't sit under the apple tree with anyone else but me...'

'Oh Jack' she whispered a little breathless, 'how I love you.'

Jack smiled, 'you know Mary, I think we should go visit Dan and Mary soon.'

THE END

About the author

Rosanna Mary Seaton 2022

Born Rosanna Mary Seaton in Pemberton WA in 1954 to parents Maida and Arthur Seaton. The daughter of a rabbit trapper (returned war vet) she grew up travelling all over Australia. By school age she had lived in all states of Australia except Tasmania.

Raised and trained by her ex-commando father in hunting and bushcraft Mary could track an animal for miles and shoot it on the run for her dinner by ten years of age. When other girls were learning to cook sew dance and school, she was out with her father learning to trap, track, shoot kill butcher and survival in the harshest of conditions. Mary always says it helped her to focus and deal with life's trials.

She was educated to high school standard doing correspondence (school of the air). Along with her sister Judith Seaton, she was taught by their mother Maida. At age fourteen she was sent to boarding school in Broken Hill and left school at end of year twelve. She was also a rabbit shooter and that was how she earned her pocket money, often coming in gun shooter.

Growing up in the great Australian outback her parents based themselves out of Tibooburra and this she adopted as her hometown. For many years Mary's teacher was her mother Maida and it was from her that Mary developed an interest in writing art and learned to play piano and piano accordion. She also learned violin and guitar from family members.

She left school in 1971. Mary married in South Australia and all four of her children were born in that state.

Rosanna went on to become a truck driver until she could no longer do it and then became a security guard and worked out on the Olympic Dam mine in South Australia. She started writing seriously in her late forties, often making up stories during her long twelve-hour nightshifts. She also worked for Correctional Services. Her other jobs include working for education department, barmaid and factory-work. Whatever pays the mortgage was her motto.

She now resides in Port Pirie SA and works for Red Cross. Mary also is a keen gardener and loves walking the chihuahua. Children have grown up and left home but live nearby.

What a fleeting thing is peace, so quick to come so quick to leave again
Such a tangible thing without shape or form, yet so very much it's needed.

If God had found a cure for sadness and looked to place some gladness there.
The peace to chase away the darkness, deep in the heart may it be seeded.

Be tended, cared for, nurtured there, in no uncertainty it slows the pain. And
may it be when God looks down, He sees Jack no longer wears a frown He
smiles, laughs, and lives for the joy, But Jack he knows what's brought him
here. Down through the ages he ne'er forgets; his lot has been his cross to bear.

And God knows that's a job well done, exacting more from what's begun.

GOD BLESS
(May you never give up)

www.ingramcontent.com/pod-product-compliance
Lightning Source LLC
Chambersburg PA
CBHW021620120626
46545CB00001B/318